Lecture Notes in Economics and Mathematical Systems

Managing Editors: M. Beckmann and W. Krelle

326

Christine Sauer

Alternative Theories of Output, Unemployment, and Inflation in Germany: 1960–1985

Springer-Verlag

New York Berlin Heidelberg London Paris Tokyo

Managing Editors

Prof. Dr. M. Beckmann
Brown University
Providence, RI 02912, USA

Prof. Dr. W. Krelle
Institut für Gesellschafts- und Wirtschaftswissenschaften
der Universität Bonn
Adenauerallee 24–42, D-5300 Bonn, FRG

Author

Christine Sauer
Assistant Professor of Economics
University of New Mexico
Albuquerque, NM 87131, USA

ISBN 3-540-50908-9 Springer-Verlag Berlin Heidelberg New York
ISBN 0-387-50908-9 Springer-Verlag New York Berlin Heidelberg

Printing and binding: Druckhaus Beltz, Hemsbach/Bergstr.
2847/3140-543210

To Gisela and Hermann Sauer.

PREFACE

by
Jerome L. Stein

Disenchantment with Keynesian economics developed during the post-1968 period when the rate of growth of output declined, the rate of unemployment rose, and the rate of inflation increased in the U.S. and in other countries. This paradox, called stagflation, was inconsistent with the tenet of Keynesian economics that cyclical movements in prices and output relative to their respective trends are positively correlated. A search occurred for a more satisfactory theory of macroeconomics which could explain the paradox of stagflation and the observed economic phenomena.

The New Classical Economics (NCE) developed as the total rejection of Keynesian economics. The Keynesians claimed that their demand management policies contributed to the obsolescence of the business cycle and successfully eliminated the gap between full employment (potential) output and actual output. The NCE argued just the opposite: the unemployment rate or growth rate of real output is insensitive to systematic demand management policies [Lucas; Sargent and Wallace].

Crucial to the NCE analysis is the MUTH RATIONAL EXPECTATIONS (MRE) hypothesis, which states that the subjective (or market) anticipation of a variable is equal to the objective expectation based upon the true model. This is a very controversial hypothesis. It implies that forecast errors made by the market are random variables with zero expectations, because the market is alleged to be using all publicly available information efficiently. Its proponents take the MRE hypothesis as a postulate akin to expected utility maximization. Others, such as Alan Blinder, argue that: "...the weight of evidence - both from directly observed expectations and from indirect statistical tests of rationality (usually in conjunction with some other hypothesis) - is overwhelmingly against the RE [rational expectations] hypothesis." The MRE hypothesis underlying the NCE has logical beauty, since anticipations are endogenous. This makes it an extremely attractive research strategy. One must show that its beauty and simplicity are grounded in micro-economic theory and also that it is consistent with the evidence.

The disagreements in macroeconomics do not concern the steady state, but rather the dynamics between steady states, where the unemployment rate or growth rate of output deviates from its respective "equilibrium rate." If there is an excess unemployment (relative to the equilibrium rate), can its convergence to the equilibrium value be accelerated by monetary policy? What will be the resulting effects upon the trajectory of the inflation rate?

The polarization of the profession into the Keynesian, Monetarist, and NCE camps produced a landscape where Milton Friedman seemed like a moderate relative to the NCE. The theories underlying each school of thought used different variables and communication between them was most limited. The econometric testing of hypotheses was done without <u>simultaneously</u> comparing the three different points of view in terms of the same set of data. It was no surprise that one group was unimpressed with another group's econometrics. There was no consensus among economists as to which theory could best be used to evaluate policy.

A school of thought is defined in terms of its empirical propositions or unique conclusions, rather than by the techniques of analysis used by particular proponents. One does not have to use the demand for money equation to be a Monetarist; and one does not have to use the Hicksian IS-LM model with rigid prices to be a Keynesian. Dr. Sauer defines each school of thought precisely within a broad model. The reader can call the model specifications K, M, and NCE if he wishes. What Dr. Sauer calls the Monetarist view is close to Friedman's, but very different from the NCE view. She is concerned with the scientific testing of alternative sets of hypotheses which have different policy implications.

Dr. Christine Sauer's study is a model of objectivity and technical skill. She uses a general dynamic model which is capable of implying either Keynesian, Monetarist, or New Classical results, depending upon the parameter specifications. On the basis of this model, she analyzes the experience of Germany from 1960-85 to determine which specifications are consistent, and which specifications are inconsistent with the evidence. This broad period includes both a subperiod of fixed exchange rates and another with floating exchange rates.

At about the same time that Dr. Sauer was conducting her research, Dr. Roberto Domenech was doing similar research on the Argentine economy. His conclusions were similar to those that I had obtained for the U.S.: the Monetarist specification was always consistent with the data, whereas the Keynesian and NCE specifications were rejected. The only difference between the U.S. and Argentine results was that the speed of response of inflation to money growth was four times as fast in Argentina as in the U.S. Insofar as the real GNP or growth equation is concerned, I was somewhat surprised that the NCE/MRE hypothesis was rejected by the Argentine data. Apparently, even in that high inflation economy, the MRE hypothesis was not valid.

Dr. Sauer's study of Germany has been guided by scientific objectivity rather than by a prior commitment to a particular point of view. Her skilled econometric analysis led Professor Wilhelm Krelle to write: "...the interesting results are acceptable even for those who will be disappointed by them." Her main conclusions are as follows. (1) Concerning the determinants of real GNP, or the unemployment rate, the NCE view is always inconsistent with the evidence from Germany. The Monetarist specification of the output or unemployment equation, which can also be accepted by Keynesians, is consistent with the evidence. Hence, the same results are obtained for the U.S., Germany, and Argentina. (2) The Keynesian explanation of inflation is more consistent with the data than are the Monetarist and NCE specifications. This is different from the U.S. and Argentine results.

Dr. Sauer's book should be studied and critically evaluated by those interested in macroeconomic theory and policy. There are many unanswered questions, which should generate further research. My main questions are: Why are the results different for Germany and the U.S.? What are the results for other EC economies? How can they be explained? The next stage of the analysis should be a deeper probing into the structural equations to account for the differences in the results. I trust that serious economists will derive as much benefit from reading this book as I have.

Providence, Rhode Island
December 1988

ACKNOWLEDGEMENTS

This monograph is a revised and extended version of my Ph.D. dissertation, submitted to and accepted by Brown University. I am indebted to my mentors, editors, colleagues, friends, and family whose comments and continued support facilitated the process of revising and expanding the original work.

My advisor, Jerome Stein, inspired the choice of topic with his challenging contributions to the debate among macroeconomists. His continued interest in my research is gratefully acknowledged.

The correspondence with Professor Wilhelm Krelle has challenged me to clarify several theoretical and empirical issues. This study has benefited greatly from his stimulating comments, and those of an anonymous referee. Of course, any errors are my responsibility.

My colleague at UNM, Alok Bohara, scrutinized my writing and made many editorial suggestions which I gladly followed. My thanks also go to Joachim Scheide at the Institut für Weltwirtschaft in Kiel who helped me with the compilation of a substantial data base. His own work on the German economy has been an inspiration for my research, and his comments were always useful.

Last, but not least, the Economics Department at UNM provided the technical support to prepare a publishable manuscript.

Albuquerque, New Mexico
December 1988

TABLE OF CONTENTS

LIST OF TABLES IN THE TEXT

LIST OF FIGURES

CHAPTER I

INTRODUCTION

The unsettled state of macroeconomics is evidenced by the ongoing controversy in the literature about the determinants of *short-term* fluctuations in unemployment, real output, and inflation. Much of the debate has focused on the disagreement among Monetarists and Keynesians concerning, for example, the extent of fiscal policy induced "crowding out" and the role of money in the aggregate economy. The "rational expectations revolution" gave birth to a third school of macroeconomic thought - New Classical Economics - whose implications for the (in)effectiveness of systematic (anticipated) monetary and fiscal policy actions contradict both Monetarist and Keynesian views.

Many studies have been concerned with the specification and estimation of a *single* theory, presenting theoretical arguments and empirical results in support of the chosen theory. However, these studies have failed to settle the macroeconomic dispute, because opposing views are not contrasted explicitly or tested with the same data set. As a result, the debate between Monetarists, Keynesians, and New Classical economists about the dynamics between steady states remains alive.

Recently, a number of authors have presented evidence which compares the explanatory power of competing macroeconomic theories for the United States economy. Stein (1982b) develops a general macrodynamic model which implies the opposing views of unemployment, output, and inflation as special cases. The controversy between Monetarists, Keynesians, and New Classical economists is thus reduced to direct tests of alternative statistical hypotheses in nested regression equations. Mishkin (1982a,b,1983) proposes an approach for testing New Classical against Non-Classical (i.e., Keynesian) rational expectations theories.[1] Rea (1983) discriminates between Monetarist, Keynesian, and natural rate models of the Phillips curve. Finally, Turnovsky and Wohar (1984) and Benderly and Zwick (1985) compare Monetarist and Keynesian theories of unemployment and inflation.

These contributions have advanced the macroeconomic debate by focusing on the *substantial* disagreements while ignoring differences in the techniques of analysis favored by a particular school of thought. To this date, however, the unsettled state of macroeconomics cannot be considered settled in light of the conflicting empirical evidence presented for the U.S. economy. Stein (1982b) reports that the Monetarist propositions are strongly supported by the data for 1958-79, while the Keynesian and New Classical explanations must be rejected. Adopting Stein's approach, Desai and Blake (1982) argue that the opposite results can be obtained from the same data set when alternative empirical methods are employed. Furthermore, in a comment about Stein (1979), McKenna and Zannoni (1984) report that the Keynesian explanation of inflation is superior to the Monetarist version using U.S. data for the 1958-79 period. Mishkin (1982a,b,1983) finds that unanticipated and anticipated policy variables both matter for the 1954-76 period, thereby rejecting the New Classical hypothesis. Although their models, methods, and sample periods differ, Rea (1983) and Turnovsky and Wohar (1984) find that no single model can explain the U.S. experience over longer periods of time.[2] The earlier sample periods in both studies support the Keynesian view, whereas the U.S. experience since the 1960's is better explained by Monetarist models. Finally, Benderly and Zwick (1985) report that both Monetarist and Keynesian variables affect the U.S. rate of inflation between 1955 and 1982. These conflicting results highlight the need for further research in the area.

Few empirical studies using direct tests of competing macroeconomic theories have been conducted for the U.S. economy, and almost none deal with other industrialized economies. Some laudable exceptions exist. Parkin (1984) studies the

---

[1] Non-Classical theories incorporate the rational expectations assumption, but allow for the short-term stickiness of wages and prices, implying that anticipated as well as unanticipated variables have real effects. See, for example, Fischer (1977).

[2] Rea's (1983) sample period extends from 1895-1979. Turnovsky and Wohar (1984) consider the 1923-82 period.

Japanese business cycle from 1967-82 to discriminate between Keynesian and Classical theories. He finds that the Keynesian explanation is inconsistent with quarterly data, whereas the Classical view cannot be rejected. Scheide (1984), comparing Keynesian and New Classical models of the German economy, rejects the Keynesian specification on the basis of structural instability over the 1960-80 sample period. Darrat (1985) investigates the relative importance of anticipated and unanticipated money growth for German real output from 1960-83 and finds strong evidence in support of the New Classical proposition of policy ineffectiveness.

The current state of affairs clearly warrants further theoretical and empirical work. As an important contribution to the ongoing macroeconomic debate, we propose to analyze the aggregate German economy between 1960 and 1985. There are several reasons why the German economy is of interest in the present context.

First, to our knowledge, no studies using direct tests of all three competing schools of thought - Monetarist, Keynesian, and New Classical Economics - have been rigorously conducted for the German case to this date. Compared to the United States, long considered the prototype of a closed economy, the German case presents the additional challenge of modeling an open economy. The field of open economy macroeconomics is characterized by controversies of its own, regarding, for instance, the channels of transmission for foreign impulses and the mechanisms of balance of payments adjustment and exchange rate determination. Germany is commonly perceived to be a large open economy because of its share in world trade and the role of its currency, the Deutsche Mark, as one of the world's reserve currencies. Yet, earlier studies of Germany's macroeconomic behavior report conflicting evidence about the importance of external variables in driving the German business cycle.[3] Our re-examination of the relevant time series data indicates to what extent the openness of the German economy is essential for the macrodynamics of unemployment, real output, and inflation.

Second, the performance of the German economy over the 1960-85 sample period[4] is

---

[3] A critical survey of the literature is presented in chapter III.

[4] Our sample period excludes the so-called "Golden Fifties" for two reasons. First, Germany's economic performance in the 1950's was largely dominated by special

characterized by distinct periods of economic "success" and "failure." After a decade
of uninterrupted brisk growth throughout the 1950's, the economic miracle - the
"Wirtschaftswunder" - slowed its pace during the 1960's, albeit maintaining the aura
of postwar success and stability. In the early 1970's, along with other industrial
nations, the former miracle turned into a stagflation-ridden economy which continues
to experience sluggish real output growth accompanied by moderate inflation and
record unemployment rates in the aftermath of the 1981-82 world recession. Also, the
German economy reacted quite differently to the two oil price shocks of 1973-74 and
1978-79. In an attempt to resolve the macroeconomic controversy and the dispute about
the monetary/fiscal policy mix, it is important to investigate the driving forces
behind Germany's macroeconomic performance.

Third, the international monetary system changed fundamentally when the Bretton
Woods system of fixed exchange rates finally collapsed in March 1973. Since then, the
Deutsche Mark has been allowed to "float" vis-a-vis the U.S. Dollar, except during
periods when the German Bundesbank intervened directly in foreign exchange markets,
attempting - often unsuccessfully - to sterilize speculative capital flows. Among
most European currencies, a system of relatively fixed exchange rates continues to
exist, initially under the "snake-in-the-tunnel" arrangements (1972-79), and, since
1979, under the European Monetary System (EMS). Theoretically, the exchange rate
regime has important implications for the degree of economic interdependence, the
endogeneity or exogeneity of the domestic money supply, the efficacy of domestic
monetary and fiscal policies, and the financing of balance of payments imbalances.
Tests of alternative macroeconomic theories for the two exchange rate systems can
also be interpreted as evidence for or against the hypothesis of a monetary regime
break in 1973.

The structural model in chapter V focuses on the key features of the German
economy in order to discriminate between opposing interpretations of the German

post World War II conditions such as the huge influx of refugees from Eastern Europe,
the Marshall Plan aid, and the Korea Boom. Second, political factors delayed the full
economic and statistical integration of two regions - the Saarland and West Berlin -
into today's Federal Republic until the late 1950's. The time series data thus
exhibit inconsistencies and structural breaks prior to 1960.

experience between 1960 and 1985. Although many new elements are introduced into the discussion, this study is rooted in previous work on the German and the U.S. economies.

The next chapter reviews the performance of the German economy over the 1960-85 sample period and discusses its institutional features. Major domestic and international economic events are identified, and we propose "stylized facts" about the relationships of macroeconomic variables.

Chapter III presents a survey and critique of the empirical literature dealing with the German economy either exclusively or in the context of cross-country comparisons.

Chapter IV introduces a synthesis view of the open economy, highlighting the dichotomy with respect to the behavior of key macroeconomic variables under fixed and flexible exchange rates. We proceed to assess the empirical validity of these and alternative maintained hypotheses about the relationships among macrovariables for the German case. Most importantly, our empirical method (bivariate and multivariate Granger causality tests) does not impose any a priori restrictions concerning the exogeneity or endogeneity of the included variables. The causality test results indicate that a structural model of the German economy should incorporate the small country assumption, allow for the sterilization of exogenous international reserve flows under fixed exchange rates, and include both trade and capital flows as transmission channels for foreign influences. Furthermore, the DM/$ exchange rate can be ignored as a determinant of aggregate spending, and the money supply has different effects on output and inflation under the two exchange rate regimes.

Taking these findings about the dynamic structure and the causal relationships among German macrovariables into account, a full structural model is specified in chapter V. After summarizing the key propositions of each school of thought, we derive regression equations for unemployment, output, and inflation under Monetarist, Keynesian, and New Classical parameter specifications. The opposing statistical hypotheses are tested against each other in nested regression equations to determine the "correct" model of the German economy. While the evidence suggests that no single model can explain the German experience over the 1960-85 sample period, the NCE hypotheses are clearly inconsistent with the data. The Monetarist specification of the unemployment or output equation, which can also be accepted by Keynesians, is favored by the data. The results for the inflation equation overwhelmingly support the Keynesian model while the Monetarist and New Classical propositions must be rejected. These findings are robust for different specifications of the nested regression equations, even though the estimated equations are not structurally stable across the two exchange rate regimes.

CHAPTER II

THE GERMAN ECONOMY: 1960 - 1985

1. INSTITUTIONAL ARRANGEMENTS

The emergence of the German economy as a bastion of economic stability and its success in dealing with major economic shocks since the 1960's can largely be attributed to the consensus among all groups involved in the economic decision making process. Historical, political, and psychological factors - the experience of two hyperinflations and the vast destruction of World War II - explain the overriding concern with economic stability and security which is reflected in many of the formal and informal institutional arrangements in Germany today.

The objectives of overall economic policy - price stability, full employment, steady and appropriate growth, and external balance - are formulated in the 1967 *Act to Promote Economic Stability and Growth* ("Stabilitätsgesetz"). At the center of the consensus stands the autonomous central bank, the Deutsche Bundesbank, which maintains strong ties with all sectors of the economy.

Created by the *Deutsche Bundesbank Act* in 1957, the central bank is prohibited from monetizing the medium and long-term "deficit spending" of the federal government. Its primary task is that of guardian of the currency, the Deutsche Mark. Nevertheless, the Bank has generally been concerned with the country's overall economic conditions when formulating its monetary policy goals. It is Bundesbank philosophy that the success of its policies depends crucially upon credibility, public understanding of its goals and instruments, and public cooperation. Its policy instruments include open market operations, changes in discount rates and reserve requirements, and foreign exchange operations.[1]

Open market operations played a limited role until the 1970's, but have been used more frequently since then, particularly, in the fine-tuning of commercial bank liquidity. The Bundesbank's most important and most often used tools for liquidity control are interest rate policy and reserve requirements. Short-term money market rates respond to changes in the discount and lombard rates at which commercial banks borrow from the central bank.[2] These rates have been changed over sixty times from 1948 to 1985. Similarly, between 1948 and 1981, required reserve ratios were altered about eighty times. At times, the Bundesbank has imposed higher reserve ratios on non-resident deposit liabilities attempting to control the speculative inflow of foreign funds. Direct exchange controls are largely avoided because of their association with the financial practices of the Third Reich. Instead, the Bank favors swap operations in its attempts to influence international capital flows and fine-tune the domestic money market.[3]

Since December 1974, the Bundesbank has been announcing target ranges for monetary growth in an effort to reduce economic uncertainty and control inflationary expectations associated with shocks such as the 1973-74 oil price hike. Until 1988, the Bank's target has been the Central Bank Money Stock (CBM), which consists of coins and currency in circulation and required reserves on domestic liabilities, evaluated at constant January 1974 reserve ratios. Among the advantages of the Central Bank Money Stock are its closeness to high-powered money, its low volatility compared to monetary aggregates such as M1 or M2, and its relatively close relationship with nominal GNP. Target ranges for the rate of monetary growth are announced each January, prior to the first round of yearly wage negotiations (which

---

[1]See Deutsche Bundesbank (1982) for a detailed discussion of the central bank's functions and monetary policy instruments.

[2]Under the discount rate, commercial banks can rediscount short-term commercial bills until their rediscount quota is exhausted. Additional borrowing without a formal quota is possible at the lombard rate, which is usually set one percentage point above the discount rate. For all practical purposes, however, the lombard facility is limited to 30% of the rediscount quota.

[3]A swap transaction involves the purchase (sale) of foreign exchange on the spot market and its simultaneous sale (purchase) on the forward market. The swap rate is the difference between spot and forward rates.

typically determines all subsequent settlements) and the annual meeting of the foreign ministers from the European Community (EC) in Brussels.

By comparison with the central bank, the government's role is more limited. Until the 1966-67 recession, fiscal demand management policies were hardly used or needed for economic stabilization purposes. Fiscal policies were largely motivated by supply side considerations, such as the tax reforms (reducing average tax rates and correcting for the distortions created by Allied policies from 1945-49) and the public investment programs (reconstruction of housing and infrastructure) in the 1950's.

Prompted by Germany's first major recession since 1949, the "Stabilitätsgesetz" (*Growth Act*) of 1967 spells out a list of countercyclical fiscal measures designed to eliminate the business cycle. "Deficit spending" is condoned for stabilization purposes, arguing that the resulting short-term national debt can be retired in the subsequent expansion of the economy through increased tax revenues. The events of the 1970's, combined with the activist policy prescriptions of the *Growth Act*, contributed to an unprecedented expansion of the public sector. The share of total government outlays in potential GNP rose to 44.8% in the 1970's from 36.2% in the previous decade. In the 1980's, however, Keynesian demand management and fiscal fine-tuning are largely out of favor with policy makers while structural policy and the reduction of public sector budget deficits are in vogue. Figure 2.1 illustrates the changes in German fiscal policy since 1960.

The federal government's industrial policy consists of tax relief measures and research and development grants. Incentives are generally favored over direct assistance to stimulate technological innovation and improve the country's international competitiveness. Exceptions are the subsidies to basic industries such as coal, steel, shipbuilding, and the railway system. At the state and local levels, the government provides loan guarantees to businesses.

Germany's commercial banks play a crucial and direct role in business sector decisions. First, business investment depends heavily on loaned capital due to a relatively small domestic stock market. In 1984, for instance, business fixed

Figure 2.1

Total Government Revenue and Outlays

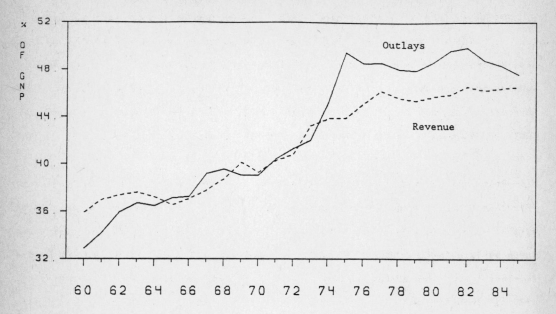

Total Government Budget Deficit

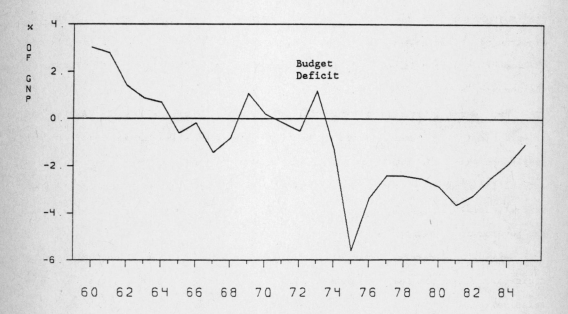

investment amounted to DM 137.58 billion, of which DM 6.28 billion (or 4.5%) were equity-financed. Second, Germany's export sector is dominated by small and medium-sized firms which depend on the export assistance provided by commercial banks to settle their international transactions. As a result, a system of "house-banking" has developed under which most firms deal exclusively with "their" bank. Third, commercial banks exert a direct influence on corporate decision-making through their ownership of businesses, their representation on corporate supervisory boards, and their control of corporate stock through proxy votes.[4]

The banking sector is dominated by three large universal banks - Deutsche Bank, Dresdner Bank, and Commerzbank - which engage in commercial and investment banking activities. Together, they control approximately 10% of the banking business volume. However, their role in the industrial sector is far greater, because they sit on 70 supervisory boards among the top 100 corporations and vote approximately 35% of the shares in annual meetings.

The investment decisions of the business sector are influenced by two exogenous factors. First, production costs are relatively high because of the costs of imported raw materials and energy (Germany imports over 65% of her fuel), the costs of meeting strict environmental standards, and direct and indirect labor costs.[5] In addition, German producers today face strong labor protection and anti-plant closing laws. These labor market conditions have induced industries such as steel, automobiles, and textiles to "rationalize," that is, to use more capital-intensive production methods.

The second factor is the well-documented export dependency of German producers. Over 30% of real GNP is exported, and almost every recovery of the German economy has been export-led.[6] Faced with growing competition from non-Western economies in export

---

[4] Commercial banks vote approximately 63% of the shares in the annual meetings of the 74 largest corporations. On average, two bankers sit on the supervisory boards of 80% of the top 400 companies. See Joint Economic Committee of the Congress of the United States (1981, p. 119).

[5] The costs of meeting environmental standards have been estimated to account for ca. 6% of total capital outlays. Per hour labor costs, which include health, pension, and social security benefits, as well as vacation time, are among the highest in OECD countries (based on current exchange rates). See Joint Economic Committee of the Congress of the United States (1981, p. 120).

[6] See table 2.3 and figure 2.7 for detailed evidence.

markets and shrinking domestic markets for domestic goods, Germany's industrial sector is under pressure to innovate, "rationalize," and develop sophisticated production methods for its highly skilled labor force.

The general consensus about economic stability has had a particularly strong impact on the relationship between labor and entrepreneurs. Approximately 30% of Germany's labor force is organized in sixteen unions. A climate of relative labor peace, evidenced by a general unwillingness to strike, a moderation of wage demands,[7] and the toleration of sectoral shifts in the job mix, has been achieved through the cooperation of the "social partners." In return, German workers are among the highest paid in the industrial world, receive generous fringe benefits, and enjoy a high degree of job security.

Foreign ("guest") workers, typically unskilled and often non-unionized, have often been the first to carry the burden of unemployment in recessionary periods. Figure 2.2 shows that the fluctuations in the employment of foreign workers are much more pronounced than those in total employment. Until 1973, many "Gastarbeiter" were actively recruited in Turkey, Yugoslavia, Greece, Spain, and Portugal to assure an adequate labor supply, especially for the tertiary sector. However, employment of nonresidents declined from a peak of 2.5 million in 1973 to 1.6 million in 1985, while overall employment fell only slightly from 22.9 to 22.2 million during the same time period. Legislation introduced in the 1970's extended the labor protection laws to foreign workers and ended the practice of sending "unwanted" guest workers back to their home countries during recessions.

The extent of operational and organizational cooperation between the "social partners" is prescribed by the 1952 *Law of Codetermination* ("Mitbestimmungsgesetz") and its much-debated 1976 extension. Between 1967 and 1976, an informal forum of government officials, bankers, industrialists, and labor representatives met on a regular basis to monitor economic conditions, discuss policy options, and coordinate the respective goals of the participants. However, the employers' legal challenge of

---

[7]Exceptions are the double-digit wage increases after major strikes in 1974. At issue in the 1985 strike of the metal workers was a shortening of the average work week and of the overall work life.

Figure 2.2

Employment Fluctuations:
Total versus Foreign Wage Employment

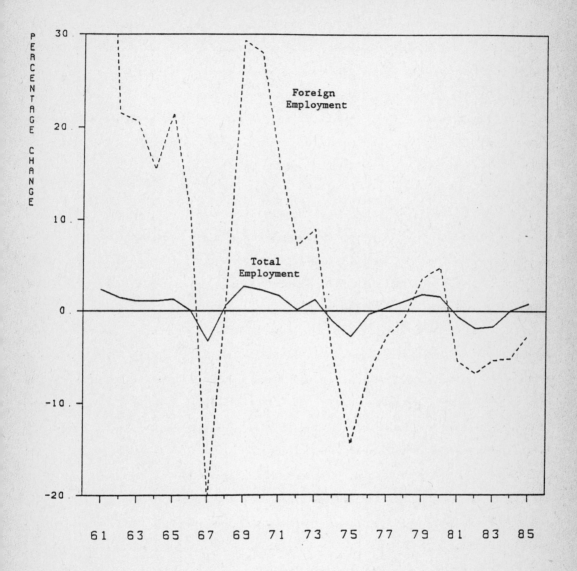

the 1976 extension of codetermination statutes, although ultimately rejected by the Supreme Court, alienated the "social partners" and led to the breakdown of their informal policy coordination meetings.

Based on this brief review of the institutional setup of the German economy, let us now explore the last three decades of economic policy making "German style" and the economic performance of Europe's "engine of growth."

2. TWENTY-FIVE YEARS OF ECONOMIC POLICY MAKING

The transition of the German economy from the maturing "Wirtschaftswunder" - the economic miracle - of the 1960's to the "Wirtschaftsfrage" - the economic riddle - of the 1980's has been accompanied by fundamental changes in the domestic and worldwide economic environment since the 1960's.

Increased international trade and capital flows have raised the degree of economic interdependence substantially, as documented most recently by the severity of the 1981-82 world recession. Since the breakdown of the Bretton Woods system of fixed exchange rates in March 1973, wide and largely unpredictable exchange rate fluctuations have increased the uncertainty in international goods and capital markets. In addition, the world economy suffered two supply shocks in 1973-74 and 1978-79, when OPEC raised oil prices significantly. As a consequence, most oil-importing countries experienced sustained periods of stagflation.

The dominance of the U.S. economy declined during the 1970's as the Dollar depreciated against most other currencies. Germany and Japan, countries with sustained trade surpluses, appreciating currencies, and relatively low inflation rates, gained reserve currency status. Yet, after overcoming the deep 1981-82 recession, the U.S. economy again functions as the world's "engine of growth." Most Western European economies struggle to catch up and maintain their shares in export markets, which are increasingly penetrated by newly-industrializing non-Western competitors such as South Korea, Taiwan, HongKong, and Singapore (also known as the "Asian Tigers"). At the same time, the stability of the international monetary system continues to be threatened by the Third World debt crisis, especially that of the Latin American countries.

These changes in international conditions certainly shaped the theory and practice of economic policy-making in Germany over the last three decades. To be sure, "extreme" economic policy experiments such as Reaganomics in the U.S. or Britain's Thatcherism are unthinkable in Germany. Policy makers have generally favored the "golden middle road" approach, while incorporating some policy recommendations of academic circles.

The German success story of the 1950's has been attributed, to some extent, to Germany's postwar economic system. The "Soziale Marktwirtschaft" (social market economy) - brain-child of the first postwar Economics Minister, Ludwig Erhard - is committed to free markets and free competition, along with an autonomous central bank and limited government intervention, while promoting social welfare. Correspondingly, economic policy in the 1960's was guided by the motto: "As little government as possible, as much government as necessary." Fiscal policy amounted to anti-trust policy, incomes and social policy, and a combination of investment subsidies and public investment programs to promote capital formation.

Monetary policy was designed to guarantee the stability of the currency, while providing the credit and liquidity necessary for continued economic growth. Central bankers rejected the notion of an exploitable tradeoff between inflation and unemployment early on, arguing that the degree of money illusion was relatively low. Confined by the fixed exchange rate system of the 1960's and early 1970's, the Bundesbank frequently faced a conflict between internal and external goals.[8] Giving priority to domestic price stability, the central bank would pursue a restrictive course to quell inflationary tendencies spilling over from the reserve currency country. The resulting increase in Germany's current account surplus and subsequent

---

[8]Emminger (1976) discusses Bundesbank policy between 1948-75, emphazising the internal versus external balance dilemma.

speculative capital inflows would lead to an accumulation of foreign exchange reserves which could not be restricted or sterilized successfully. The goal of domestic price stability in an inflationary world would ultimately prove to be self-defeating. Often, the Bank would follow an ambiguous monetary policy in the short run, restricting domestic liquidity by raising the required reserve ratio while maintaining low interest rates to discourage further capital flows. In the end, though, it would sacrifice the goal of domestic price stability and switch to a policy consistent with external balance. The revaluations of the Deutsche Mark in 1961 and 1969, considered only as ultima ratio and denied until the last minute, would usually come too late and do too little.[9]

The 1966-67 recession convinced policy makers to pursue activist stabilization policies in an attempt to fine-tune the economy ("Globalsteuerung der Wirtschaft") and eliminate the business cycle. The resulting "Stabilitätsgesetz" - the 1967 *Act to Promote Stability and Economic Growth* - was, however, a Keynesian revolution German style. Thirty years late, it recognizes the inherent instability of the market economy and advocates the use of "market-consistent" Keynesian demand management policies, accompanied by a strong autonomous monetary policy, to simultaneously promote the four goals of economic policy: the "magic quadrangle" of price stability, full employment, steady and appropriate growth, and external balance. While the *Growth Act* only reiterates the role and instruments of monetary policy previously defined in the 1957 *Bundesbank Act*, it lists the conditions under which to use specific countercyclical fiscal measures. The measures include temporary changes in income tax rates, investment tax credits, and spending freezes.

The 1970's witnessed an unprecedented expansion of the public sector. Overall government outlays as a percentage of potential nominal GNP rose from 32.8% in 1960 to a peak of 47.5% in 1981.[10] However, it is not clear that this development is entirely due to the increased use of countercyclical policies since it coincided with a general expansion of public sector services under the newly elected coalition

---

[9]The Deutsche Mark was revalued by 5% against the U.S. Dollar in March 1961 and, again, by 9.3% in October 1969 after a brief period of floating exchange rates.

[10]In 1985, the government share had fallen to 45.3%. See table 2.1.

Figure 2.3

The Cyclical Behavior of Total Government Outlays

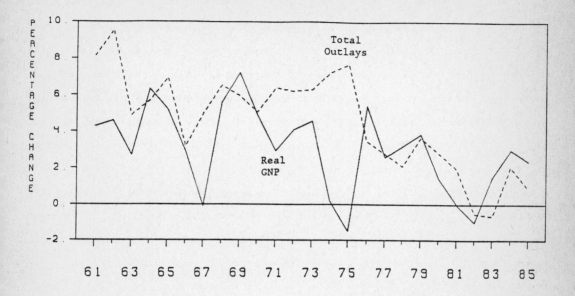

The Cyclical Behavior of Total Government Spending

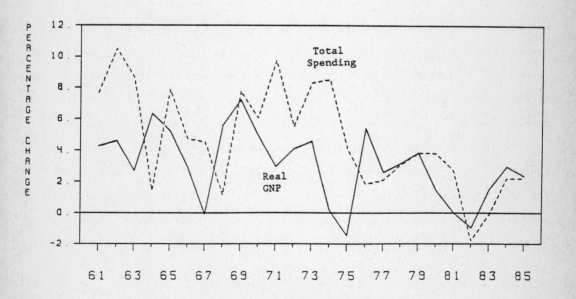

government of Social Democrats and Liberals. Furthermore, as illustrated in figure 2.3, the countercyclical measures taken by the federal government did not always succeed in offsetting the procyclical nature of state and local government spending. For example, the combined fiscal stimulus was procyclical from 1970 to 1973.

The first oil crisis of 1973-74 gave priority to monetary policy and domestic price stability. During the final weeks of the Bretton Woods system, the Bundesbank accumulated massive amounts of U.S. Dollars - an unprecedented $2.7 billion purchase in a single day on March 1, 1973 - which made domestic monetary control all but impossible. With the collapse of the fixed exchange rate regime on March 19, the Bank was freed of its commitment to maintain a fixed parity and could pursue a "new monetary policy" geared toward fighting inflationary pressures. Acknowledging that "moral suasion" alone had done little to moderate wage and price increases immediately after the oil crisis,[11] the Bank started announcing target ranges for monetary growth in December 1974. The newly gained monetary independence was, however, constrained by the commitment to fixed exchange rates under the European Monetary System (EMS) and the frequent official intervention in foreign exchange markets intended to stabilize excessive exchange rate volatility.

During the 1970's, the rest of the world looked enviously upon German policy makers who seemed to have mastered the art of economic crisis management, thereby creating "Modell Deutschland" - an "island of stability and wealth," by foreign standards, in an "ocean of international crises." However, "Modell Deutschland" fell victim to the second oil price shock of 1978-79, the ill-fated attempt to take over as the "locomotive" for the world economy in 1978, and the 1981-82 world recession.

Faced with greater international interdependence and instability, increasing competition in traditional export markets, and structural unemployment, the German fiscal authorities rediscovered structural policy after demand management policies proved insufficient to deal with the economic problems of the 1980's. Some elements of supply side economics, such as tax incentives for certain industries and regions

---

[11]While "moral suasion" by the Bundesbank could not moderate the double-digit wage settlements in 1973-74, it nevertheless convinced the business sector not to pass on higher production costs to consumers and to accept a temporary cut in profit

and personal and corporate income tax cuts, have been adopted along with the reduction of government budget deficits. Monetary policy continues to focus on price stability, with occasional episodes of foreign exchange market intervention attempting to reduce exchange rate fluctuations.

Despite these gradual shifts in the use of policy instruments, German economic policy throughout the last twenty-five years has always been devised and implemented with a global rather than a national perspective. It will be of interest to see whether this fact is reflected in the macroeconomic behavior of the German economy.

3. THE PERFORMANCE OF THE GERMAN ECONOMY: 1960-1985

Germany's macroeconomic performance over the last three decades is highlighted by figure 2.4. Between 1960 and 1985, the economy experienced six business cycles with a duration of two to five years from peak to peak (1962-64, 1964-69, 1969-73, 1973-76, 1976-79, 1979-84). The trend, computed as a five year moving average, indicates that the average growth rate of real GNP declined steadily except during the fifth cycle (1976-79). The recessionary periods include three so-called "growth recessions" (1963, 1971, 1977) when economic growth slowed significantly, but did not turn negative. Recessions with negative growth rates of real GNP occurred in 1966-67, 1974-75, and 1981-82. In each episode, a sharp decline in the rate of monetary expansion (by more than four percentage points) preceded the contraction.[12] As a result, nominal and real interest rates increased markedly (except during the 1966-67 recession) and depressed real investment spending, which contributed to the severity of the economic downturn. According to Giersch (1977, p. 22), the postwar business cycles exhibit a specific pattern: every "maxi-boom" was followed by a

_____

margins.

[12] Batten and Hafer (1982) find a similar relationship between money growth and the "growth recessions" in 1963, 1971, and 1977.

Figure 2.4

Characteristics of the German Business Cycle

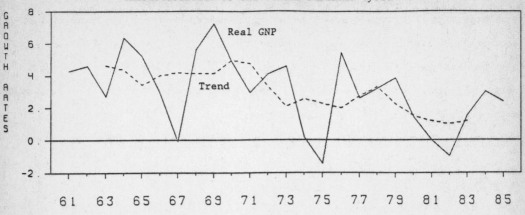

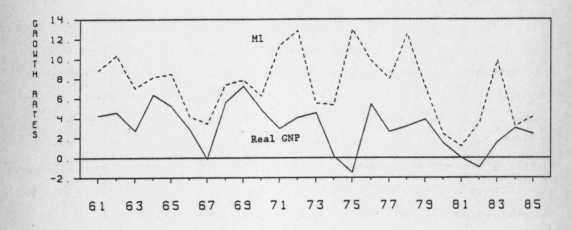

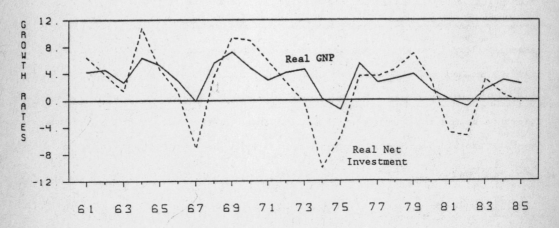

"mini-recession" which, in turn, was followed by a "mini-boom;" each "maxi-recession" was preceded by a "mini-boom."

Tables 2.1 and 2.2 present evidence that the 1960's ("The Stable Sixties"), 1970's ("The Decade of Crises"), and 1980's ("The Uncertain Eighties") differ substantially with respect to the behavior of key macroeconomic variables. The reported figures are averages of annual data, with standard deviations in parantheses to measure the variablility of the macroeconomic indicators for the different subperiods. In addition, figures 2.5 and 2.6 show the relationships of selected variables.

High growth rates of real output, negligible unemployment rates, moderate wage and price inflation characterize the 1960's. Money growth and inflation generally covaried, while inflation and unemployment were negatively related in accordance with the Phillips curve. The 1966-67 recession was short-lived, but contributed to the lower growth of real investment during the 1966-70 period. The "Stabilitätsgesetz" of 1967 [introduced Keynesian demand management policies which were used extensively during the early 1970's. Nevertheless, real output growth fell drastically during this period causing unemployment to increase fourfold by the end of the decade]13 The Phillips curve tradeoff did not hold for this period of stagflation.

Wage and price inflation accelerated markedly during the 1971-75 period, but the 1976-80 rates again match those of the 1960's. The same holds true for the rate of monetary expansion, even though the recession years 1973-74 were characterized by monetary restraint, indicating the Bundesbank's efforts to stem inflationary pressures. Nevertheless, money growth and inflation moved in opposite directions over most of the period. Real investment declined sharply during the 1971-75 period, but recovered later in the decade.

In the 1980's, wage and price inflation slowed down. Real output growth and growth rates of real investment, however, were negative during the 1981-82 recession while unemployment rose to unprecedented levels. Monetary policy was tight through

---

[13]The natural rate of unemployment increased from 1.5% prior to the first oil price shock to 4% by the late 1970's due to slower productivity growth and increased female labor force participation.

Table 2.1

The Business Cycle and the Role of the Government:
1960 - 1985

Period	1961-65	1966-70	1971-75	1976-80	1981-85	1961-72	1973-85
Unemployment	.83	1.20	2.13	4.24	8.20	1.00	5.45
Rate	(.21)	(.63)	(1.61)	(.37)	(1.62)	(.43)	(2.61)
Growth of Total	.48	-.16	-.65	.40	-.61	.16	-.35
Employment	(.49)	(1.87)	(1.48)	(.91)	(1.03)	(1.22)	(1.26)
Real GNP	4.64	4.12	2.08	3.32	1.19	4.24	1.99
Growth	(1.33)	(2.81)	(2.61)	(1.48)	(1.65)	(1.94)	(2.11)
Growth of Real	5.41	3.19	-1.47	4.27	-1.35	4.29	-.10
Net Investment	(3.51)	(6.79)	(6.73)	(1.65)	(3.69)	(4.76)	(4.97)
Growth of Real	7.21	4.85	7.24	2.97	1.04	6.30	3.15
Gvt. Spending	(3.42)	(2.44)	(2.33)	(.94)	(1.94)	(2.98)	(2.84)
Gvt. Spending	14.58	15.72	18.30	19.71	20.20	15.39	19.77
as % of RGNP	(.83)	(.30)	(1.52)	(.20)	(.31)	(1.06)	(.71)
Gvt. Outlays	35.57	38.83	43.69	48.35	48.84	37.65	47.88
as % of GNP	(1.67)	(.90)	(3.67)	(.32)	(.92)	(2.44)	(2.11)
Gvt. Revenue	34.48	35.94	39.55	42.45	42.37	35.55	42.02
as % of GNP	(.67)	(1.09)	(1.63)	(.43)	(.16)	(1.44)	(.80)
Budget Deficit	-10.53	1.84	16.01	38.50	37.43	-3.51	34.72
(1980 Bio. DM)	(10.42)	(9.71)	(32.54)	(5.32)	(14.92)	(11.13)	(20.86)
Budget Deficit	-1.38	.22	1.28	2.74	2.50	-.50	2.45
as % of RGNP	(1.37)	(.96)	(2.58)	(.41)	(1.04)	(1.35)	(1.58)

Note: All figures are computed as five-year averages of annual data, with standard deviations in parantheses. Where available, data for 1960 are included for the 1961-65 and 1961-72 subperiods. *Total employment* includes self-employed workers. The *real gross national product* (RGNP) is expressed in 1980 billions of DM. *Government spending* refers to the purchases of goods and services by federal, state, and local governments (inclusive of the social security system). In addition to purchases of goods and services, *government outlays* include government transfer payments, interest payments on the national debt, and gross investments. *Government revenue* is defined here as the sum of tax revenues and social security contributions, ignoring other transfer receipts. Data sources are given at the end of the book.

Table 2.2

Inflation, Money Growth, and Interest Rates:
1960 - 1985

Period	1961-65	1966-70	1971-75	1976-80	1981-85	1961-72	1973-85
Productivity Growth	4.22 (1.51)	4.23 (1.16)	2.68 (1.37)	2.87 (2.09)	1.81 (.86)	4.07 (1.28)	2.32 (1.51)
Money Wage Inflation	7.21 (1.31)	6.71 (3.29)	10.71 (1.91)	5.85 (.77)	3.77 (1.03)	7.66 (2.84)	6.10 (2.82)
Price Inflation (GNP-Deflator)	3.66 (.69)	3.63 (2.31)	6.35 (.99)	4.02 (.47)	3.07 (1.08)	4.11 (1.90)	4.18 (1.46)
Price Inflation (Consumer Prices)	2.96 (.67)	40 (.98)	5.94 (.77)	3.96 (.95)	3.81 (1.75)	3.10 (1.25)	4.47 (1.62)
Import Price Inflation	1.01 (2.15)	.83 (1.58)	6.90 (7.70)	4.84 (5.07)	4.16 (3.81)	1.07 (1.65)	5.83 (5.70)
Central Bank Money Growth	8.70 (.98)	7.26 (1.79)	9.06 (2.31)	7.69 (1.69)	5.06 (1.12)	8.46 (1.84)	6.72 (1.99)
M1 Money Growth	8.57 (1.22)	5.82 (1.93)	9.60 (3.87)	7.99 (3.75)	4.37 (3.26)	8.01 (2.71)	6.58 (3.83)
Long-Term Interest Rate	6.23 (.33)	7.33 (.63)	9.04 (1.01)	7.36 (1.07)	8.46 (1.39)	6.96 (.87)	8.30 (1.40)
Real Interest Rate (ex post)	2.55 (.87)	3.70 (1.85)	2.69 (1.30)	3.34 (1.01)	5.40 (.85)	2.89 (1.55)	4.12 (1.31)

Note: All figures are computed as five-year averages of annual data, with standard
deviations in parantheses. Where available, data for 1960 are included for the
1961-65 and 1961-72 subperiods. The *central bank money stock* (CBM) includes currency
in circulation and required reserves on domestic liabilities (evaluated at constant
January 1974 reserve ratios). The *real interest rate* is defined as the long-term
nominal rate minus the rate of inflation (measured by the implicit GNP-deflator).
Data sources are given at the end of the book.

Figure 2.5

Indicators for Economic Policy Decisions

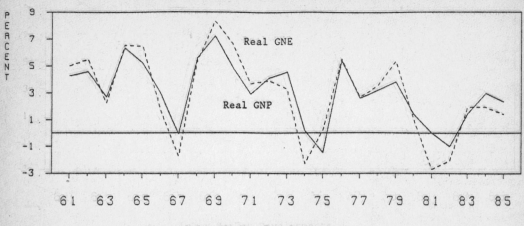

Labor Market Developments

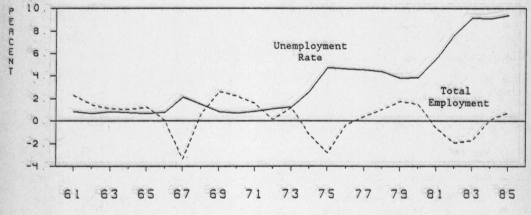

Inflation

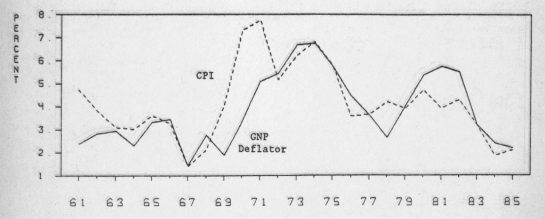

Figure 2.6

Money Growth and Inflation

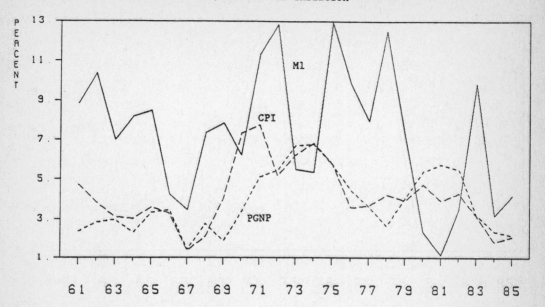

The Tradeoff between Unemployment and Inflation

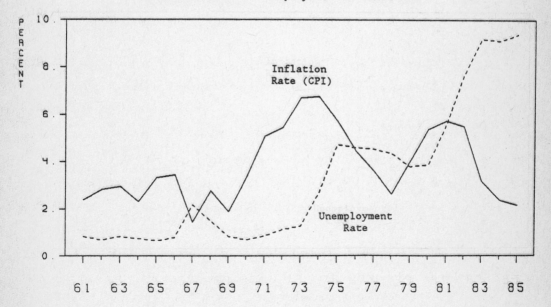

1982 in an effort to control capital flows to high interest rate countries such as the U.S. and Great Britain.

Table 2.3 and figure 2.7 consider the role of external factors for the German economy. German and U.S. inflation rates have generally covaried, but less so since the late 1970's. Import prices, which fluctuated substantially over the entire sample period (primarily reflecting oil price changes and exchange rate fluctuations), hardly affected domestic inflation (measured by the GNP deflator) at all, but covaried slightly more with the deflator of domestic absorption. This seems to indicate that the Bundesbank more or less successfully neutralized the impact of imported inflation on the domestic price level.

Exports and imports as a percentage of real GNP have steadily increased from about 16% in the early 1960's to over 30% in 1985. By comparison, the share of exports to the U.S. has increased slightly from 7.5% in the early 1960's to 8.3% in the 1980's. The share of imports from the U.S. has steadily declined to 7.3% from 13.9% over the sample period. Almost half of Germany's merchandise trade is conducted with other members of the European Community (EC).

Germany's merchandise trade balance and the balance on goods and services have never been in deficit. Current account deficits occurred in 1962, 1965, and 1979-81. The appreciation of the Deutsche Mark (DM) against the U.S. Dollar and other European currencies apparently did not affect Germany's international competitiveness. The highest rates of appreciation occured in 1973-74, when Germany ran a current account surplus in the first year after the oil price shock. By contrast, the DM-depreciation between 1980-83 might have improved Germany's competitiveness in export markets, which are increasingly threatened by non-Western competitors.

The inflation differential between Germany and the U.S. has been negative for all three decades, with the exception of the 1961-65 period. From 1960-80, the Deutsche Mark appreciated against the U.S. Dollar in accordance with the relative purchasing power parity (PPP) condition. However, the 1981-85 DM-depreciation cannot be accounted for by the hypothesis of relative purchasing power parity. In addition, the values of the inflation differential and exchange rate changes do not even match

Table 2.3

Balance of Payments and Exchange Rate Data: 1960 - 1985

Period	1961-65	1966-70	1971-75	1976-80	1981-85	1961-72	1973-85
Balance on Goods/Services	5.22 (2.67)	15.26 (4.84)	27.08 (11.44)	20.86 (16.37)	42.46 (21.04)	10.80 (6.34)	32.25 (18.63)
Current Acct. Balance	.28 (3.87)	6.61 (4.72)	10.89 (9.77)	-.43 (18.99)	13.49 (18.32)	3.09 (4.77)	8.79 (17.45)
Capital Acct. Balance	-.48 (2.55)	-4.43 (12.82)	-.52 (17.67)	3.10 (3.99)	-18.56 (21.42)	-.17 (9.35)	-7.90 (17.90)
Exports as % of RGNP	16.74 (.43)	20.60 (1.45)	24.65 (1.90)	27.39 (.62)	32.37 (1.52)	19.18 (2.63)	28.94 (3.10)
Imports as % of RGNP	15.74 (1.18)	19.09 (1.92)	23.93 (.37)	26.87 (1.38)	28.75 (.56)	18.24 (3.18)	26.96 (2.03)
Exports: % to EC	45.36%	48.74%	49.11%	49.77%	49.93%	48.10%	49.68%
Exports: % to US	7.46%	9.48%	7.92%	6.22%	8.29%	8.85%	7.51%
Imports: % from EC	42.86%	49.39%	52.93%	50.31%	50.16%	48.65%	50.46%
Imports: % from US	13.94%	11.33%	8.39%	7.34%	7.26%	11.66%	7.38%
Exchange Rate Index (weighted)	82.75 (1.41)	86.91 (4.71)	108.59 (9.67)	139.38 (9.51)	147.75 (4.74)	86.78 (6.30)	137.03 (14.45)
Exchange Rate (DM/$)	4.02 (.07)	3.91 (.15)	2.88 (.44)	2.10 (.31)	2.61 (.29)	3.87 (.27)	2.40 (.35)
Rate of Depreciation	-.86 (1.63)	-1.82 (3.18)	-7.87 (5.87)	-6.06 (6.76)	9.65 (7.34)	-2.24 (3.16)	-.61 (10.77)
Inflation Differential	1.91 (1.07)	-.74 (1.72)	-.54 (2.23)	-3.35 (.86)	-2.19 (1.82)	.73 (1.82)	-2.55 (1.51)
Interest Differential	2.15 (.23)	1.65 (.89)	1.94 (.80)	-1.59 (1.14)	-3.82 (.60)	1.95 (.59)	-1.66 (2.39)
Real Interest Differential	.22 (1.22)	2.38 (1.81)	2.48 (1.86)	1.76 (.99)	-1.63 (2.13)	1.20 (1.73)	.89 (2.62)

Note: *Balance of payments* data are expressed in billions of current DM. The trade-weighted *exchange rate index* (end of 1972=100) measures the performance of the DM against the currencies of 14 industrialized countries. An increase in the index indicates a DM-appreciation. The *rate of depreciation* is the percentage change in the nominal DM/$ exchange rate. A negative rate indicates a DM-appreciation against the U.S. Dollar. *Inflation* and *interest rate differentials* are computed as German minus U.S. rates. Inflation rates are computed from implicit GNP-deflators, and the interest rates are long-term rates. See table 2.1 for more notes.

Figure 2.7

Foreign Trade

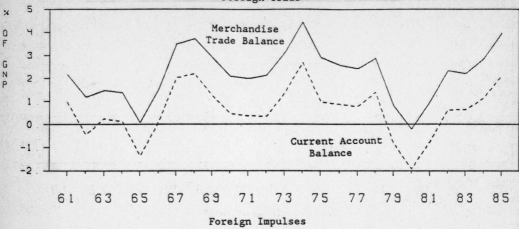

Foreign Impulses

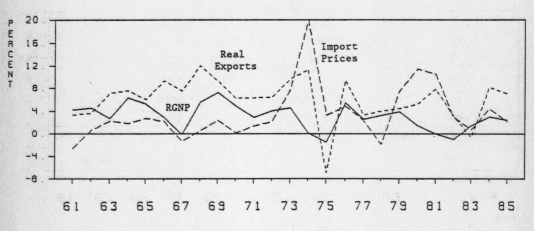

German and U.S. Inflation

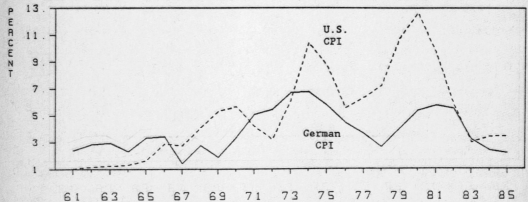

in the long run. Thus, the evidence in support of relative purchasing power parity is weak at best.

The nominal interest differential between the two countries was positive over the 1960-75 period and has been negative since then. If actual exchange rate changes are an unbiased predictor of expected changes and no risk premium exists, uncovered interest rate parity (UIP) holds. During the 1960-75 period, the Deutsche Mark thus should have been depreciating when it actually *appreciated*. The 1976-85 period lends weak support to uncovered interest rate parity. The Deutsche Mark either appreciated at declining rates (1976-80) or depreciated (1981-85) while the German-U.S. interest differential was negative.

The real interest differential, on the other hand, has been approximately consistent with uncovered interest rate parity. For both exchange rate periods, the differential between German and U.S. rates has been positive (except for the 1981-85 period). Considering the average values over the two subperiods, the size of the real interest differential corresponds roughly to the rate of depreciation of the DM/$ exchange rate, thus lending some support to uncovered interest rate parity.

The next chapter contains a survey and critique of the existing empirical literature which examines some of the stylized facts about the German macroeconomy presented here.

CHAPTER III

SURVEY AND CRITIQUE OF THE LITERATURE:

EMPIRICAL STUDIES OF THE GERMAN MACROECONOMY

1. INTRODUCTION

A complete literature survey for our study would encompass numerous theoretical
and empirical contributions covering a wide spectrum of issues in "traditional" as
well as open economy macroeconomics. Given the abundance of material available to the
researcher and, hence, the need to be selective, this review highlights the findings
of previous empirical studies which deal with the German macroeconomy either
exclusively or in the context of cross-country comparisons. When of interest, studies
of other open economies are also mentioned.

The papers surveyed here are selected from the viewpoint of the problem at hand.
Our ultimate goal is the testing of competing macroeconomic hypotheses about the
short-term determinants of unemployment, real output, and inflation in Germany. The
opposing views, which imply different statistical hypotheses about the values of
parameter estimates, can all be derived as special cases from a single structural
model. The small-scale nature of our model allows for analytical tractability and
minimizes the possibility that specification errors in sectors of marginal interest
affect the tests of alternative aggregative theories. Accordingly, this literature
review considers only small-scale models of the German macroeconomy with up to ten
structural equations.[1]

---

[1] The only exception is Minford's (1980) twenty-equation structural model of the
U.K. economy.

Large-scale forecasting models, which consist of several disaggregated submodels for different sectors of the economy and, in some cases, numbering more than one thousand equations, are excluded from our discussion since they are designed primarily for the purpose of forecasting and policy simulation. Since 1959, almost one hundred large-scale forecasting models have been developed for the German economy, among them several versions of the Bundesbank model, the Bonn/Krelle model, and the joint model of the economic research institutes. The reader is referred to Uebe (1981) for a survey and classification. A historical overview is presented by Jäger and Ocker (1978). Heilemann (1981) analyzes the predictive performance of three major econometric models.

To provide a fairly structured survey of the smaller aggregate models of the German economy, the empirical studies are grouped according to the type of model specified. The following categories are distinguished: (1) impulse-theoretic models in the tradition of the St.Louis spending equation and the St.Louis monetarist model, (2) Monetarist, Keynesian, and rational expectations models (including examples of work on other open economies), (3) studies of the Phillips curve relationships, and (4) causality studies. Within these categories, differences in sample periods and the treatment of expectations often produce results which can only be judged on their own merit. Furthermore, a comparative evaluation of the results is difficult since open economy modifications, if considered at all, are not implemented uniformly.

In the following sections, we summarize the theoretical approach and the major findings from each paper. A comparative critical evaluation of all papers is presented in the final section of this chapter, where we also outline the nature of our contributions with respect to each criticism raised.

2. IMPULSE-THEORETIC MODELS

Fundamental to the impulse-theoretic approach is the assumption that systematic monetary, fiscal, financial, and foreign impulses operating on the economy dominate aggregate fluctuations. These impulses are generally assumed to be transmitted through a relative-price/stock-flow mechanism describing the interaction of output and asset markets in response to these impulses. Most studies considered here try to determine the relative impact of different impulses upon the German economy within the framework of a small aggregate demand and supply model in the tradition of the St.Louis one-equation model. The St.Louis spending equation, first developed by Andersen and Jordan (1968), incorporates the monetarist view that the rate of monetary expansion is the major determinant of total nominal spending, which in turn affects real output, employment, and prices. Several authors have been concerned with the specification and estimation of a German St.Louis spending equation.

Läufer (1975,1977) presents a comprehensive analysis, taking into account the criticism advanced against the original version of the St.Louis spending equation and its empirical implementation. In addition to monetary and fiscal policy variables, Läufer's spending equation includes exports as an indicator of foreign impulses.[2] After converting all variables to growth rates to eliminate the nonlinear trend present in quarterly GNP and money stock data, Läufer uses Almon-lags with coefficients restricted to lie on a fourth-degree polynomial without endpoint restrictions. To avoid misspecification, a minimum standard error criterion is applied in searching for the optimal lag length.

Estimation of the St.Louis spending equation with quarterly seasonally adjusted data (1960.1-70.4) leads to the rejection of the original Andersen and Jordan

---

[2] The impact of fiscal policy is measured by the "initial stimulus concept" which only considers budget movements due to discretionary policy changes. Discretionary monetary policy is captured by changes in the extended monetary base, which accounts for changes in reserve requirements, but eliminates non-discretionary movements of the money multiplier.

findings for the German case. Over a period of approximately ten quarterly lags, monetary and fiscal policy have equally strong effects. However, fiscal policy is more rapid and more reliable as a policy instrument. Use of a broader money definition changes these results somewhat in favor of monetary policy. Fiscal policy still affects total spending contemporaneously with a highly significant positive coefficient. Monetary policy works only over three lagged quarters.

Dewald and Marchon (1978) fail to replicate the Anderson and Jordan (1968) findings for six industrial countries - Canada, France, Germany, Italy, Britain, and the U.S. - using the exact St.Louis specification and sample periods extending to the mid-1970's. Their results indicate that both monetary and fiscal policy influence total spending, except in Germany (where only money matters) and in the U.K. (where only government spending matters). Subsequently, they consider a modified St.Louis spending equation similar to Läufer's (1975,1977) specification. Their modified equation (1) includes exports as an additional explanatory variable, (2) uses growth rates (first differences in logs) and, alternatively, first differences in the levels of variables, (3) searches for the best-fit lag length, and (4) uses third-degree polynomials without endpoint constraints.

The results for Germany (using non-logs) show a highly significant, but reduced money multiplier, an insignificant spending multiplier, and a significant export multiplier, thus supporting the Anderson and Jordan findings. In addition, the best-fit lag length is relatively short for all three variables. The effect of fiscal policy is sensitive to the choice of sample period, money definition, and log versus non-log specification. This also holds for monetary policy to a lesser degree. Under the log-specification, the fit of the equation deteriorates slightly for most countries, and - in the German case - fiscal policy now has a significant contemporaneous effect.

Batten and Hafer (1983) present further evidence on the modified St.Louis equation by applying it to different countries - Canada, France, Germany, Japan, Great Britain, and the U.S. - as well as to the different exchange rate regimes. The authors use sophisticated estimation techniques, unconstrained ordinary least squares (OLS), and determine the appropriate lag lengths via Gram-Schmidt orthogonalization with sequential hypothesis testing. The results for Germany, using seasonally adjusted quarterly data for the 1963.2-82.1 period, confirm the generality of the original St.Louis equation. Money growth significantly and permanently affects nominal income with a relatively short lag. The cumulative impact of fiscal policy changes is insignificantly negative, and export growth has a small significant effect on nominal spending. Moreover, tests of structural stability across the two superiods of fixed and flexible exchange rates confirm the robustness of the estimated income relationship.

Incorporating their earlier work on the St.Louis spending equation into a modified version of the St.Louis monetarist model, Dewald and Marchon (1979) study the determination of inflation, real output, and unemployment in response to demand pressures and import prices in six industrial countries.[3] This modified version of the model includes a price equation consistent with "weakly" rational expectations, where anticipated inflation depends on lagged values of demand pressure, domestic inflation, and import price changes. The spending equation includes exports as an autonomous influence on total spending. The unemployment rate is regressed upon the (estimated) contemporaneous and two lagged values of the percentage gap between potential and actual real output.

Estimation of the model with quarterly data extended to the mid-1970's yields large short-run effects of all three autonomous impulses on aggregate demand, short-run effects of demand pressure on output and unemployment, and positive, but weak price effects - paradoxically a Keynesian finding in a monetarist model. The demand pressure variable has only weak direct effects on anticipated and actual inflation, with the strongest statistically significant effects in Germany, Canada, and the U.S.[4] The elasticity of domestic prices with respect to import price changes is very large in Germany (30-40%), where imports amount to approximately one quarter of total spending. "Okun's Law" reveals that the unemployment rate is sensitive to

---

[3] The original St.Louis model - first developed by Andersen and Carlson (1970) - is recursive in nominal spending and consists of seven equations.

[4] The authors acknowledge that their empirical measure of demand pressure might be biased downward, thus possibly understating the effect of excess demand pressures on prices.

fluctuations in the percentage output gap with similar coefficients for all countries but Italy and France. This result is surprising since Germany and the U.K. experienced much lower unemployment rates over the sample period. However, these comparative results are not conclusive given the incompatibility of unemployment data across countries.

Dewald and Gavin (1981) develop a small aggregate demand and supply model of the German economy to evaluate alternative anti-inflation monetary policies. Assuming that aggregate supply is exogenous and equal to its potential value, their model consists of three equations. (1) Growth in nominal aggregate demand depends on distributed lags of exogenous domestic and foreign monetary and fiscal impulses, measured by growth rates of the domestic money stock (M1), government spending, and exports.[5] (2) The "core" inflation rate is expected to equilibrate the growth rates in nominal aggregate demand and real aggregate supply in the long run. Due to adjustment cost and/or imperfect information, the "core" inflation rate adjusts with a distributed lag; in the short run it also responds to changes in foreign prices (measured by the import price level). By assumption, nominal aggregate demand responds mainly to changes in money growth, implying that "core" inflation is primarily a monetary phenomenon. (3) The short-run inflation rate deviates from the "core" rate by the weighted amount of a demand pressure variable, which represents the difference between (expected) real demand and real supply.

The empirical evidence, based on seasonally adjusted data from 1961.1-78.4, is consistent with the maintained hypotheses. Domestic money growth is the main influence on aggregate demand. The "core" inflation rate depends significantly on the difference between nominal demand and real supply and adjusts fully after eight quarters. Changes in import prices do not have a significant cumulative effect. In the short run, inflation responds significantly to real variables represented by the (expected) demand pressure variable. Tradeoffs between inflation and real output growth exist only in the short run, so that policy makers face a "cruel choice"

---

[5]This equation corresponds to the St.Louis spending equation in Dewald and Marchon (1978,1979).

between a short severe recession with fast reduction of the "core" inflation rate and a longer moderate recession with gradual reduction of the inflation rate.

The models discussed so far are built around modified versions of the St.Louis spending equation where the dependent variable is the change in *nominal* spending. Neumann (1978) considers a small aggregate demand and supply model in which the *components* of nominal income changes - price and real output changes - are the dependent variables. Furthermore, the explicit incorporation of rational expectations allows the distinction between anticipated and unanticipated movements in the impulses.[6] In his dominant-impulse-cum-rational-expectations (DIRE) approach to explain fluctuations of inflation and output growth in Germany from 1956 to 1975, Neumann identifies three relevant impulse forces:[7] (1) foreign monetary and fiscal impulses, (2) the domestic fiscal impulse, and (3) the domestic monetary impulse. Foreign impulses are measured by the growth rate of real exports and inflation of import prices. The three-equation model is based on an expectations-augmented Phillips curve. Excess demand is modeled as a function of unanticipated impulse forces. Consequently, the semi-reduced forms express deviations of actual from anticipated inflation as well as deviations of real output growth from its potential value as functions of unanticipated impulses.

Regression equations are derived by replacing the unobservable expectations with observable variables generated under three alternative expectations hypotheses: the "Dominance Variance Hypothesis," the "Rational Expectations Hypothesis I," and the "Rational Expectations Hypothesis II." However, the "Dominance Variance Hypothesis" avoids the expectations issue altogether since unanticipated variables are simply replaced by actual values. The resulting reduced-form output equation actually constitutes a second-order St.Louis spending equation in real terms. The rational expectations hypotheses "I" and "II" impose adaptive instead of rational

---

[6] The studies by Korteweg (1978) for the Netherlands, Fourcans (1978) for France, Fratianni (1978) for Italy, and Dutton (1978) for the U.S. use the same approach.

[7] A fourth impulse force, the Keynes-Wicksell effect of autonomous changes in the anticipated net yield on real output, is dismissed on a priori grounds. The author finds that real rates of return and the inflation rate are not positively correlated over the sample period.

expectations. Estimation of the observable reduced forms proceeds with annual data for the fixed exchange rate period (1956-73) and the longer period from 1956-75.

The model explains observed fluctuations of inflation and real output growth consistently, supporting the accelerationist hypothesis: unanticipated changes in the impulses have no effect on the inflation rate (which thus depends solely on "rationally" formed inflationary expectations), but they determine fluctuations of real output growth. Furthermore, the evidence supports the monetarist hypothesis that monetary rather than fiscal impulses are the dominant driving force. Anticipated accelerations of real exports affect inflation fluctuations, whereas unanticipated accelerations affect fluctuations in real output growth. The respective effects of monetary impulses are comparatively larger, however. For the fixed exchange rate period, accelerations of the import price level influence the domestic inflation rate, but not real output growth. The evidence for the extended sample period seems to reverse these results. This conclusion is based on an insufficient number of observations.

3. MONETARIST, KEYNESIAN, AND RATIONAL EXPECTATIONS MODELS

Trapp (1976) investigates the role of money in the German economy between 1951 and 1973. Keynesian models of the standard IS-LM type are quickly renounced because the estimated interest rate elasticities of money demand and investment prove unsatisfactory. Trapp consequently conducts a detailed analysis of the relationship between money, prices, and real and nominal GNP within a monetarist framework. His methods include descriptive time series analysis, cross-correlograms, and distributed lag regressions. Changes in the money stock are found to cause changes in domestic absorption and the price level with a four and ten quarter lag, respectively. The monetarist hypothesis is thus confirmed: money has significant short-run effects on output and employment which are later offset by the induced inflation.

In a Keynesian framework, Gschwendtner (1977) studies the effects of business cycles and growth on inflation in Germany over the 1953-74 period. Using a simple mark-up pricing equation, the inflation rate can be expressed as a weighted average of increases in unit labor costs and other production costs.[8] Unit labor costs are closely related to the degree of capacity utilization in the economy. Assuming that other production costs are exogenous and constant, inflation is determined by the capacity utilization coefficient and the growth rate of real output. The empirical evidence confirms the postulated cyclical relationship. A higher degree of capacity utilization raises inflation, but higher real output growth tends to reduce inflation. The fit of the estimated equation is remarkably good given the long sample period, despite significant structural changes in the German economy.

König (1978) develops a small monetarist model to explain inflation and unemployment in Germany from 1962-76. The model consists of four equations: (1) a quantity theoretic money demand function allowing for lagged adjustment of real balances, (2) the "Okun Law" describing the short-term cyclical relationship between the unemployment rate and real output growth, (3) an expectations-augmented Phillips curve, and (4) adaptive inflationary expectations. The model implies the usual monetarist propositions. Inflation depends on contemporaneous and lagged differences between money growth and potential real GNP growth. Changes in money growth have real effects only in the short run - in accordance with the accelerationist hypothesis - while raising inflation permanently.

Regression equations for unemployment, real output growth, and inflation are estimated using 2SLS and 3SLS methods with quarterly data. For the fixed exchange rate period (1962-70), the monetarist model successfully explains inflation and unemployment; neither "Okun's Law" nor the expectations-augmented Phillips curve can be rejected. However, the estimated slope of the Phillips curve is sensitive to the

---

[8]Other production costs - user costs of capital, indirect taxes, the costs of imported raw materials and intermediate goods - change in response to monetary, fiscal, and foreign impulses.

regression technique. Based on 2SLS parameter estimates, the long-run vertical Phillips curve is reached after ten quarters. The 3SLS estimates, on the other hand, show a downward sloping Phillips curve for both the short and the long run.

When data for the flexible exchange rate period are included (1962-76), the model fails. König attributes the failure to a change in the expectations formation after the transition to flexible exchange rates. He argues that this regime break might have been captured by an assumption of rational expectations, but does not substantiate his claim empirically. In general, König's empirical results are difficult to evaluate since he only reports coefficient estimates and t-values.

Leiderman (1980a) derives and tests alternative specifications of output supply in the open economy. Assuming perfect price information, utility maximization, and a classical labor market, real output is an increasing function of the real exchange rate (terms of trade) and a time trend. Alternatively, under imperfect information, unanticipated inflation in domestic and import prices must be added to the list of explanatory variables. Allowing for the lagged adjustment of actual output to its potential level, both models are tested with annual data from 1955-75 for the major industrialized countries: Canada, France, Germany, Italy, Japan, Britain, and the U.S. Rational expectations are imposed to eliminate the unobservable unanticipated inflation rates, which are measured by the residuals from simple AR(1) processes.

The empirical results for the inflationary processes in Germany are not very strong. Domestic inflation follows an AR(1) process, but with a low coefficient of determination. Import price inflation follows an AR(2) process. In both versions of the output equation, the terms of trade coefficient is significantly positive as predicted. In addition, unanticipated import price inflation is significant in the imperfect information version, whereas unanticipated *domestic* inflation is not significant. This lends support to an open economy version of the Lucas supply curve. Tests of zero and cross-equation restrictions in the nested model further substantiate these findings. While the model excludes several variables such as monetary and fiscal policy variables that have a potential influence on real GNP, it explicitely incorporates a transmission mechanism for foreign economic disturbances on the supply side of the economy.

Neumann (1981) formulates a short-run equilibrium model of the goods and money markets to analyze the flexible exchange rate period (1973-80). His model assumes: (1) a Lucas aggregate supply curve which includes unanticipated changes in relative import prices for raw materials and intermediate goods, (2) an endogenous money supply, (3) stochastic versions of the Fisher equation (linking nominal and real interest rates) and relative purchasing power parity, and (4) rational expectations. Inflation depends on potential output, anticipated and unanticipated monetary, fiscal, and foreign impulses. Real output is a function of unanticipated impulses only.[9] To estimate the equations, Neumann approximates the expected variables by two-year distributed lags. Thus, "rational" expectations are invoked in a very narrow sense. The information set of rational economic agents excludes any knowledge about the determination of the impulse variables.

The estimated inflation equation indicates that unanticipated impulses are insignificant. Over 80% of inflation can be explained by potential output growth as well as anticipated impulses from monetary policy, government spending, and relative import prices. Monetary impulses are the dominant force. Real output growth depends significantly on the growth of potential GNP and on unanticipated impulses from monetary policy, government spending, export demand, and relative import prices. The coefficients on unexpected money growth and export demand are relatively large compared those on unanticipated fiscal impulses. Unanticipated changes in import prices affect output negatively, so that the contractionary effect of higher import prices for raw materials and intermediate goods on output supply outweighs the expansionary effect on output demand. Neumann concludes that (unanticipated) monetary policy, which is designed to offset the effects of unanticipated foreign impulses, fails to stabilize real output growth over the sample period, thus making a strong case for credible and publicly announced money growth targets.

Batchelor (1982) uses quantitative measures of inflation and output growth expectations to test the New Classical hypothesis that only unanticipated variables

---

[9] In an earlier paper, Neumann (1978) derives reduced-form equations for *rates of change* in inflation and output growth.

have real effects. The expectations measures are based on monthly tendency survey data for 1965-77 for four European countries - Belgium, France, Germany, and Italy. Analysis of the generated data reveals that expectations are not fully rational. However, they are superior to simple extrapolative and ARIMA predictors, and the systematic expectational errors do not persist for more than a year. In Germany, actual and unanticipated inflation rates are negatively correlated with output growth, which contradicts the New Classical paradigm. The correlations between unemployment and actual and unanticipated inflation strongly support the existence of a short-run Phillips curve. Inflation and output uncertainties are accociated with low current growth and high unemployment. The results vary, however, in their significance and differ across countries. Expectations and uncertainties are found to be highly correlated across countries.

Scheide (1984) analyzes the effects of money growth on the business cycle to determine the relevance of rational expectations models in Germany between 1960 and 1980. An investigation of the cyclical relationship between income, money growth, and the variability of money growth seems to suggest that monetary policy became less effective as the variance of monetary policy increased in the 1970's. The claim that rational expectations models fit the German evidence is substantiated through Granger causality tests and regression analysis. The level and the variability of the money stock Granger-cause real income without feedback.[10] Bidirectional causality exists between the money stock and its variance. Actual and unanticipated money both Granger-cause real income without feedback, with relatively stronger effects of unanticipated money. Expected money is neutral with respect to real income. Assuming that monetary policy follows a simple reaction function, structural stability tests of Keynesian and New Classical regression equations for real output are performed. The evidence further supports the superiority of rational expectations models, because the coefficient estimates from Keynesian models fail the structural stability test.

---

[10] Income is measured by domestic absorption to eliminate exogenous fluctuations in export demand which are an important source of GNP variability in Germany.

Darrat (1985) tests the rational-expectations-natural-rate (RENR) hypothesis with quarterly German data for the 1960-83 period. Great care is taken with the decomposition of actual money growth into its anticipated and unanticipated components. Due to the lack of a theoretical reaction function for the monetary authorities, multivariate Granger causality tests and Theil's residual-variance criterion are applied to a list of potential money growth predictors for which data are easily and cheaply available. The specified forecasting equation includes lagged money growth, two lags of short-term nominal interest rates, two lags of inflation, and three lags of real government budget deficits scaled by potential real output.

The RENR hypothesis is tested by including potential real GNP (approximated by a linear time trend) and lagged values of anticipated and unanticipated money growth in the regression equation for real output. Estimation proceeds after correcting for negligible first-order autocorrelation, and the Theil criterion is used to determine the lag length and the degree of the polynomial. The results strongly support the RENR hypothesis that only unanticipated money growth has significant real effects, a result which is structurally stable across different subperiods. Interestingly, neither foreign variables nor the exchange rate regime have any bearing on the results.

Hansen (1986) introduces fiscal and foreign variables into a rational expectations model to test the New Classical hypotheses about the determination of real output and the price level with German data from 1972-82. Three equations describe the goods market. (1) Real aggregate demand in the open economy consists of consumption, investment, exogenous government spending, and exogenous exports net of (endogenous) imports, which fluctuate with the real exchange rate. (2) An extended version of the Lucas supply curve states that real output deviates from the natural level only in the presence of domestic and/or foreign price shocks. (3) Market clearing is imposed by the goods market equilibrium condition.

The remaining six equations of the structural model are used to express the output equations in terms of predetermined, exogenous, and expected variables only. The (nominal) interest rate adjusts to clear the money market, where money supply is endogenous, although the central bank controls the monetary base under flexible exchange rates. The money demand function includes a real balance effect. Nominal and real interest rates are linked by the Fisher equation; the exchange rate is explained by a stochastic version of purchasing power parity; the real exchange rate is defined as the price-adjusted nominal rate.

The (linearized) reduced-form equations for real output and the price level are subject to structural cross-equation restrictions. Furthermore, the equations are "unobservable" since they include (endogenous) price expectations. Invoking rational expectations, the "observable" reduced forms can be derived. The price level equation includes "permanent" (i.e., anticipated) as well as unanticipated values of the exogenous variables as regressors. Real output, on the other hand, only depends on unanticipated monetary, fiscal, and foreign variables.

The structural and observable reduced-form equations are estimated using the FIML-method to obtain more efficient parameter estimates in the presence of nonlinear cross-equation restrictions. The coefficient estimates for the output equation imply significant multipliers for unanticipated changes in fiscal and foreign variables. Unanticipated changes in the monetary base are insignificant in most cases, a result which contradicts Neumann's (1981) findings. In the unrestricted reduced-form price equation, neither anticipated nor unanticipated exogenous variables are significant. In particular, the price level determination appears to be independent of monetary policy which is consistent with previous findings (e.g., Scheide, 1984).

The crucial assumptions of the New Classical theory, the Lucas supply curve and rational expectations, are tested using likelihood-ratio tests. The test statistic is constructed by estimating the restricted and unrestricted reduced-form models. The structural restrictions from the Lucas supply function must be rejected. The rational expectations hypothesis is accepted when forecasts of exogenous variables are based on univariate autoregressive processes; it must be rejected when the forecasts are based on moving average processes.

4. STRUCTURAL MODELS OF OTHER OPEN ECONOMIES

Aghevli and Rodriguez (1979) examine the effects of monetary changes on inflation, the output gap, and the trade balance in Japan between 1965.1-76.4. Their model is essentially monetarist in that an excess supply of money results in higher prices, higher output, and a deterioration of the trade balance. Furthermore, the short-run adjustment of prices, output, and the trade balance depends on the degree of openness of the economy and on the percentage output gap.

The economy is assumed to be a price taker in world markets for its imports, but can affect the world prices of its exports. The overall inflation rate is thus a weighted average of inflation in home goods (i.e., export and nontraded goods) and in import prices. The reduced-form equation includes inflation of imported goods, real GNP, lagged real balances, and the lagged output gap as explanatory variables. Inflationary expectations are excluded after preliminary tests produce unsatisfactory results. According to the authors, inflationary expectations are captured by the constant term in the equation since actual inflation fluctuated without trend over the sample period, thus implying approximately static expectations. The output gap depends on its own lag, potential real GNP, and lagged real balances. This specification incorporates the classical/monetarist view that output adjusts toward its potential level by a self-correcting process without any Keynesian structural rigidities. The trade balance is a negative function of the excess supply of money and the lagged output gap; the terms of trade effect can be negative or positive.

The system of three equations is recursive and nonlinear in variables, so it can be estimated by ordinary least squares (OLS). After a correction for first-order autocorrelation, the model performs well. All estimated coefficients have the expected sign and are significant at standard significance levels. Nonlinear estimates of the structural speed-of-adjustment parameters indicate that the excess supply of money has pronounced short-run effects on inflation, the output gap, and the trade balance. Also, the output gap tends to close with a lag, and there is a strong Phillips curve relationship between inflation and the output gap.

The model is compelling in its simplicity, and the strong short-run results in support of the monetarist approach are convincing. But three shortcomings must be mentioned. First, international capital flows are ignored. Second, the assumption of an exogenous domestic money supply is justified only if capital flows are largely sterilized. Third, the expectations formation mechanism is treated only superficially.

Laidler and O'Shea (1980) test a small Keynesian model for an open economy under fixed exchange rates with annual (1954-70) British data. The model consists of six equations: (1) a real money demand function, (2) an output equation with excess supply of money, terms of trade, and fiscal policy parameters as explanatory variables, (3) an expectations-augmented Phillips curve, (4) an expectations formation hypothesis which implicitely assumes that economic agents expect monetary authorities to maintain a constant level of foreign exchange reserves in the long run, (5) a balance of payments equation where the level of reserves fluctuates with the excess supply of money and the terms of trade, and, finally, (6) an identity decomposing the domestic money supply into its two components, foreign reserves and domestic credit.

Full-information-maximum-likelihood (FIML) estimation of the model produces coefficient estimates that are of the correct sign and, with one exception, statistically significant. Fiscal policy strongly dominates monetary policy as an influence on real income, but monetary policy determines the balance of payments. The authors argue that misspecification of the money demand function, indicated by a low estimate of the income elasticity of money demand, might bias their results against detecting real effects of monetary policy. The evidence also supports the existence of an expectations-augmented Phillips curve. The parameter estimates are robust across small changes in the model's specification, strengthening the findings about the importance of fiscal over monetary policies. Over the sample period, the estimated equations for inflation, output, and money growth predict the actual behavior of the U.K. economy well. However, extrapolation beyond 1970 indicates a breakdown of the equations which the authors attribute to missing variables such as the world excess supply of money and the world interest rate. Shortcomings of the study include the relatively small number of degrees of freedom due to the use of annual data and the exclusion of additional foreign variables possibly driving the open economy.

Minford (1980) develops and estimates a full structural model of a large open economy under fixed and flexible exchange rates in which expectations are rational, financial markets are efficient, and stock/flow specifications are integrated with the appropriate budget constraints. The twenty-equation model is estimated with U.K. data from 1954-76 (?) using errors-in-variables and substitution methods.

Despite some misspecification problems, the model predicts the behavior of major macrovariables reasonably well. The exchange rate regime has important policy implications. Under fixed exchange rates, only fiscal policy has real effects unless a vicious circle of devaluation/inflation is triggered by an unexpected fiscal expansion. Under flexible exchange rates, both inflation and interest rates increase in response to expansionary monetary and fiscal policies, causing a short-run contraction of the economy. Overall, the behavior of the macroeconomy under flexible exchange rates is dominated by financial market rather than real sector conditions, a predictable response to unpredictable national policies.

Parkin (1984) studies the Japanese business cycle over the 1967-82 period to discriminate between Keynesian and Classical theories of output determination. In the Keynesian model, non-staggered wage contracts set the money wage at which the labor market is expected to clear, whereas actual employment and output depend on labor demand. The reduced-form equation states that cyclical output follows an AR-process with a seasonal order and is Granger-caused by both the money stock and velocity. In the Classical model, money wages adjust to clear the labor market in each period given incomplete information about the contemporaneous aggregate price level. Using rational expectations, the reduced-form equation for output is a nonseasonal AR(1) process with a white noise error term. Parkin proposes two approaches to discriminate between Keynesian and Classical theories.

First, after visually examining the raw time series data for real GDP, he formulates a general time series model incorporating the Keynesian/Classical hypotheses and alternative models of trends and seasonality. Estimation of different specifications of the equation yields mixed results. With seasonally adjusted data, the Classical explanation must be rejected. With seasonally unadjusted data, the results depend on the trend and seasonality specifications, but generally reject the Keynesian explanation.

Second, Parkin formulates seven alternative time series models to decompose output into its trend, seasonal, and business cycle components. The residuals from these regressions are examined in their autocorrelations and causal relationships with the money supply. With seasonally unadjusted data, cyclical output follows a simple AR(1) process and is not Granger-caused by money. This implies that the Keynesian model must be rejected. With seasonally adjusted data, however, the Keynesian model cannot be rejected in most cases. Parkin conjectures that seasonal adjustment procedures cause spurious causality between the money stock and output, so that the use of seasonally adjusted data biases results toward rejecting the Classical model. The main conclusion is that the Japanese data reject the Keynesian explanation of the business cycle whereas the Classical model is consistent with the data.

5. PHILLIPS CURVE STUDIES

Knöbl (1974) seeks to determine the role of price expectations in actual price behavior in Germany for the period from 1965-72. Price survey results are used to derive an explicit time series of inflationary expectations. Testing the generated data for extrapolative versus adaptive expectations hypotheses, the author finds that inflationary expectations depend largely on past information, in particular past inflation and demand pressure (measured by deviations of capacity utilization from trend). Estimates for the actual inflation equation, which relates inflation to cost increases, demand pressure, and expected inflation, indicate that lagged price inflation dominates in the explanation of actual inflation.[11] Thus, anti-inflationary policies must be geared toward breaking rising price expectations to prevent the expectations-augmented Phillips curve from shifting upward.

Risch (1980) contrasts monetary and Keynesian explanations of stagflation (Phillips loops). Models in the Keynesian tradition consist of a mark-up pricing equation and an expectations-augmented Phillips curve. Under adaptive expectations, the acceleration/deceleration of inflation is a function of the level and the rate of change of the unemployment rate. Stagflation occurs in a situation of declining overemployment, that is, increasing unemployment tends to decelerate inflation, but rising price expectations lead to further money wage increases and accelerated inflation. However, the Keynesian approach cannot explain "counter-clockwise" Phillips loops, and it neglects monetary factors in the inflation process. The proposed monetary model assumes that only unanticipated money has real effects since it creates unanticipated inflation. The structural equations describe: (1) the quantity theory of money, (2) a version of "Okun's Law" decomposing nominal GNP growth into its trend and cyclical components, (3) adaptive expectations, (4) a central bank reaction function,[12] and (5) expectations about monetary policy which use information about the structure of the central bank's reaction function, but not the coefficients.

The reduced-form equation expresses changes in the inflation rate as a function of the level, the rate of change, and the acceleration/deceleration of unemployment. The four phases of unemployment-inflation combinations over the course of the business cycle, including "clockwise" and "counter-clockwise" Phillips loops, are explained by this equation. The estimated coefficients, however, cannot be

---

[11]The regression equation includes a dummy variable to account for the break in the PPI series after the introduction of the value-added tax (VAT) in 1968.

[12]The specified reaction function implies stop-and-go monetary policy. During recessions, monetary policy is geared toward reaching full employment. During booms, as inflation accelerates, price stability is the dominant policy goal.

interpreted as tradeoff coefficients like in Keynesian models. Here, they constitute estimates of actual and expected policy reaction parameters.

The empirical evidence for Germany using quarterly data (1960.1-80.2) lends weak support to the model, but the results for the U.S. are much more favorable. The German public seems to assess future monetary policy fairly accurately so that unanticipated inflation is hardly an effective tool of stabilization policy.

Ohr and Lang (1982) examine the relationship between wage and price inflation and unemployment in Germany between 1968 and 1981. The raw data reveal a structural break in these relationships in 1973-74 which coincides with the collapse of the Bretton Woods system of fixed exchange rates and the first oil price shock. Besides the rate of unemployment, the estimated "Phillips curves" consider the impact of imported inflation on domestic price inflation and the impact of price inflation on wage inflation (i.e., the price-wage spiral).

For the period of fixed exchange rates, a significant tradeoff exists only between wage inflation and unemployment. The impact of imported inflation is relatively strong, whereas price inflation hardly affects wage inflation, indicating the presence of money illusion. Under flexible exchange rates, a significantly *positive* relationship between price inflation and unemployment emerges, a finding which contradicts the Phillips curve. Imported inflation is now less important with respect to domestic inflation. But price inflation significantly affects wage inflation with a coefficient close to unity, which indicates that money illusion is absent under flexible exchange rates. The evidence supports the hypothesis of a structural break in the Phillips curve which the authors attribute to the exchange rate regime break. The sample excludes observations for 1974 to eliminate the atypical period of adjustment to extreme external shocks, but direct regime break tests are not conducted. The absence of a pronounced tradeoff under flexible exchange rates is explained with the stimulative effects of price stability. The observed increase in unemployment after 1973 is attributed to the first oil price shock.

Incorporating supply shocks in the 1970's explicitely, Franz (1983) presents a theoretical and empirical analysis of the "non-accelerating inflation rate of unemployment" (NAIRU) in Germany for the 1965.1-81.4 period. Visual inspection of the unemployment-inflation tradeoff suggests that the German Phillips curve is steep with a substantial increase in the natural rate of unemployment from 1.6% prior to 1974 to 4.3% during the late 1970's.

Franz derives the theoretical Phillips curve under the assumption of profit-maximizing firms which follow an optimal pricing strategy. It includes as explanatory variables: (1) adaptive inflationary expectations, which are approximated by lagged actual inflation, (2) the level and the growth rate of unemployment, joint proxies for excess demand pressures in the labor market, (3) the lagged growth rate of productivity and the growth rate of the productivity trend, (4) the growth rates of user costs of capital, indirect taxes, social security contributions, and import prices (including changes in food prices and excluding exchange rate changes), and (5) a dummy variable for the possible upward shift of the NAIRU in 1974.[13]

The evidence supports the existence of a long-run vertical Phillips curve. The significant shift of the NAIRU in 1974 was indirectly caused by supply shocks, leading to a decline in the productivity trend. Lagged inflation, unemployment, and the productivity trend are the major factors contributing to inflation.

In a comment, Gerfin (1983) presents additional results based on time switching regressions. There is strong evidence for several structural breaks and shifts in the slope of the Phillips curve, which the author attributes to a change in the pricing behaviour. In another comment, Gordon (1983) criticizes the econometric specification and methodology used by Franz (1983). Gordon's results indicate that: (1) the natural rate of unemployment increased steadily after 1973, (2) the post-1973 productivity slowdown did not significantly contribute to the rising natural rate, and (3) the slope of the Phillips curve is sensitive to the measure of inflation used.

---

[13]Estimation of this equation is a joint test of (1) the natural rate hypothesis, (2) the price-setting behavior, and (3) the expectations formation

6. CAUSALITY STUDIES

Dyreyes, Starleaf, and Wang (1980) test the causal relationship between money and nominal GNP in Australia, Canada, Germany, Japan, the U.K., and the U.S. Three alternative test procedures are used to determine whether the causal relationships are invariant with respect to the test procedures.[14] Using seasonally adjusted quarterly data from 1960.1-75.4, the results for Germany are puzzling. Independent of the test procedure used, no relationship of any kind, apart from contemporaneous "causality," can be detected between money and nominal income.

Scheide (1982,1984) presents a more thorough and conclusive study of the causal relationships between money, GNP, and prices in Germany. The simple monetarist hypothesis that money affects both income and prices is tested against the Keynesian hypothesis that income causes money, and also against the hypothesis of a central bank reaction function according to which prices influence the course of monetary policy. Granger causality tests are used in connection with Akaike's final prediction error (FPE) criterion to determine the optimal lag length. The quarterly data from 1960.1-80.4 are seasonally unadjusted. There is strong evidence that money is exogenous to income with only weak feedback from income to money.[15] The evidence for the monetarist inflation hypothesis is inconclusive. Import prices are discarded as an additional explanatory variable for the price level. Causality from prices to money is only detected for M1, but the central bank's control variable (MB) is exogenous.

---

mechanism.

[14]The procedures are: (1) Sims's test, (2) a modified version of Sims's test, using a different filter to guarantee serially uncorrelated errors and, thus, unbiased F-test results, and (3) the Haugh-Pierce residual cross-correlation test.

[15]Different measures of money and income are considered: the monetary base (MB), M1, M2, nominal and real GNP, nominal and real domestic absorption. No feedback from income to the central bank's control variable (MB) can be detected. Scheide (1982) argues that the combination of a negative feedback from income to M1 and a positive feedback to M2 reflect agents' liquidity preferences over the course of the business cycle.

Weissenberger and Thomas (1983) examine the causal role of money over the same sample period as Scheide (1982), but they include a long-term interest rate in the equations for money, price, and real income. Their results are inconclusive since the causal relationships vary with the test procedure used. Unlike Dyreyes, Starleaf, and Wang (1980), the three test procedures - Granger's direct test, Sims's test, and the Haugh-Pierce test - yield (albeit conflicting) results supporting the existence of causal relationships between money, prices, and real income.

Using quarterly seasonally adjusted data for the 1965.1-79.4 period, Fitzgerald and Pollio (1983) examine the causal relationships between monetary variables, real economic activity, and prices in six OECD countries: France, Germany, Italy, Japan, Britain, and the U.S. To explore the implications of rational expectations models, the monetary variables (growth rates of M1, M2, and domestic credit) are decomposed into anticipated and unanticipated components.[16] Causality tests are conducted in two parts. First, the Pierce S-statistic from univariate ARIMA models is used to test for the independence of the time series. Strong evidence of systematic relationships between money, real GNP, and prices is found for all countries in the sample, despite less general results for inflation. The strongest results are obtained for domestic credit expansion.

Next, bivariate "state space" models for real GNP growth and inflation are estimated to determine the additional explanatory power of monetary variables. The results appear to contradict the Policy Ineffectiveness Proposition (PIP) of rational expectations models. Anticipated money growth strongly affects real economic activity and inflation. The evidence for unanticipated money growth is generally weaker. However, these results are country specific and/or sensitive to the choice of monetary aggregates. Finally, the causality results are found to be structurally stable over different subperiods, in particular, for the two exchange rate regimes.

---

[16]Optimal forecasts of the monetary policy variables are obtained from so-called "state space" models which automatically allow the estimation of univariate and multivariate ARIMA models. Four economic variables improve the fit of the univariate models significantly: GNP growth, unemployment, and - to a lesser degree - inflation and the current account balance.

Von Hagen (1984) argues that the failure to detect a causal role for money in most previous studies depends on technical and statistical factors. First, the use of GNP data leads to specification errors since it includes public sector production and goods traded on non-competitive markets. The theoretical hypotheses, however, refer to private sector decisions and actions in competitive markets, implying that the appropriate measures of production and prices are the index of industrial production and the producer price index (PPI) for manufactured goods, respectively. Second, temporal aggregation of data has been shown to affect detectable dynamic interdependencies between variables. Therefore, causality tests should always use the lowest frequency of data available.

Taking into account these considerations, the Granger causality tests with seasonally unadjusted monthly data betweem 1970.1-82.12 clearly confirm the causality from money to output and prices. Some evidence for feedback relationships is also detected. By comparing monthly and quarterly causality tests, the temporal aggregation is found to affect the results significantly.

7. A CRITICAL EVALUATION OF PREVIOUS STUDIES OF GERMANY

The studies reviewed here offer many different approaches toward modeling and estimating inflation, output, and unemployment fluctuations in the German economy. As a consequence, the empirical results often vary with the particular theoretical framework, the sample period, the frequency of the data, and/or the estimation technique. The areas of consensus and disagreement among macroeconomists studying the German economy can be identified by evaluating and comparing the results from each of the studies surveyed.

Impulse-theoretic models in the tradition of the St.Louis equation and the St.Louis monetarist model generally support the dominance of monetary over fiscal impulses in their effects on income. The exception is Läufer (1975,1977) who presents evidence to the contrary. Dewald and Marchon (1979) find that all three impulses have large short-run effects. This holds true independent of whether actual or anticipated and unanticipated impulses are considered. All studies unanimously find that foreign impulses, measured by exports, have small and significant effects. The importance of the foreign sector for the German economy is thus documented. In addition, Neumann's (1978,1981) findings support the accelerationist hypothesis that unanticipated impulses only affect real output, but not inflation.

The studies which include the formulation and estimation of an inflation equation yield some conflicting evidence. Dewald and Marchon (1979) discover positive, but weak direct effects of demand pressures on inflation. Dewald and Gavin (1981) report significant effects of excess demand on both the short-run and the "core" inflation rates. Dewald and Marchon (1979) and Neumann (1978,1981) agree on the importance of import price inflation with respect to German inflation in the short run. Consensus exists about the dominance of monetary impulses in the determination of inflation. Only Batten and Hafer (1982) deal with the issue of structural stability across the two exchange rate regimes. Their results indicate the absence of structural instability. To summarize, the impulse-theoretic models seem to favor monetarist approaches to inflation and output fluctuations in Germany.

Structural macromodels in the Monetarist, Keynesian, or New Classical tradition are less unanimous in their implications. None of the studies explicitly formulates a Keynesian model of the German economy.[17] Trapp (1976) examines and quickly refutes a Keynesian framework, and Scheide (1984) tests its validity only indirectly. Thus, monetarist models tend to be favored by the evidence.[18] König's (1976) framework, however, fails to explain the behavior of the German economy under flexible exchange rates.

---

[17]Laidler and O'Shea (1980) examine the U.K. experience under fixed exchange rates within a Keynesian framework. Their findings support the superiority of fiscal policy with respect to real output. However, the model fails during the flexible exchange rate period.

[18]The studies of the Japanese economy by Aghevli and Rodriguez (1979) and Parkin (1984) also favor the monetarist/classical explanation.

Rational expectations models appear to confirm the Policy Ineffectiveness Proposition (PIP) since unanticipated variables are found to have real effects. Several studies [Leiderman (1980a), Batchelor (1982), Scheide (1984)] detect an influence of actual and/or anticipated variables as well. The relative importance of monetary, fiscal, and foreign unanticipated variables cannot be established unambiguously. Neumann (1981) finds that unanticipated money growth and unanticipated foreign variables dominate real output fluctuations in the short run, thus lending support to the monetarist view that (unanticipated) monetary policy dominates (unanticipated) fiscal policy. Hansen (1986) comes to the opposite conclusion that only unanticipated fiscal and foreign variables are significant. Unanticipated money growth is insignificant.

Similarly, the role of (anticipated) money for the determination of inflation differs from study to study. Neumann (1981) reports significant coefficient estimates for anticipated money growth, whereas Scheide (1982,1984) and Hansen (1986) determine that inflation is largely independent of monetary policy.

Scheide (1984) and Darrat (1985) both confirm the structural stability of their estimated equations across the two exchange rate regimes. Hansen (1986), on the other hand, refutes structural stability for the Lucas supply curve on the basis of a generalized test.[19] Leiderman (1980a) stresses the influence of foreign variables on output supply. Batchelor (1982) presents evidence that price expectations, generated from tendency survey data, are only asymptotically rational.

The Phillips curve studies confirm the existence of an expectations-augmented Phillips curve. Risch (1980) rejects a Keynesian explanation of the stagflation phenomenon on theoretical grounds and proposes a monetarist alternative. The empirical evidence for Germany is relatively weak, suggesting that the course of monetary policy is predicted fairly accurately by the public. Ohr and Lang (1982) and Franz (1983) identify structural breaks in the Phillips curve and an increase in the natural rate of unemployment, which they attribute to external shocks in the 1970's.

----

[19] Minford (1980) stresses the role of the exchange rate regime for the U.K. economy. Under fixed exchange rates, only fiscal policy has real effects. Under flexible exchange rates, both monetary and fiscal policy determine real output growth.

Finally, the causality studies present the most contradictory evidence. Two studies - Dyreyes, Starleaf, and Wang (1980) and Weissenberger and Thomas (1983) - using alternative test procedures find either no causality at all or results which vary with the test procedures implemented. Scheide (1982,1984), Fitzgerald and Pollio (1983), and von Hagen (1984) report causality from actual or anticipated money to income with only weak feedback. But they disagree on the causal relationship between money and prices.

No attempt is made to critically evaluate each of the papers surveyed. Some general comments are called for since they pertain to our approach toward modeling the German economy.

First, the majority of the studies do not specify a full structural model from which regression equations can be derived. This is true for St.Louis type analyses, Phillips curve, and causality studies. It has been shown that the St.Louis equation can be derived from a conventional macromodel built around the ex-post GNP identity. The use of growth rates creates identification and interpretation problems, since regression coefficients can no longer be expressed in terms of the structural parameters alone. Causality studies do not replace economic theories and are plagued by the missing variable problem. In addition, "causality" may be a mere indication of lagged relationships between macrovariables, so a "post-hoc-ergo-propter-hoc" argument is to be avoided. We propose a two-step procedure. Initially, the relationships among key variables are investigated on the basis of bivariate and multivariate causality tests. Incorporating the information gathered, we then specify a full macrodynamic model of the German economy.

Second, no study of the German economy uses direct (i.e., nested) tests of competing macroeconomic hypotheses. As a result, the explanatory power of alternative theories cannot be evaluated properly. Our structural model of the German economy is general enough to imply different schools of economic thought as special cases, resulting in different statistical hypotheses about the values of parameter estimates.

Third, most of the studies either ignore or make ad hoc assumptions about the expectations formation mechanism. When rational expectations are invoked by Neumann (1979,1981), he assumes that rational agents form their expectations based on a very limited information set rather than the full structural model of the economy. In chapter V, we allow for different expectations hypotheses and derive the rationally expected variables from a large of set of macrovariables accessible to rational economic agents.

Fourth, several regression equations merely correlate dependent and independent variables contemporaneously without any implications for predictions. Our regression equations include only lagged regressors, so that the estimated equations correspond to predictions of unemployment, real output, and inflation.

Finally, many authors acknowledge the role of external factors in the German economy and attribute observed breaks in the behavior of macrovariables as well as the failure of their models over extended sample periods to the transition from fixed to flexible exchange rates. Yet, with few exceptions, no direct regime break tests are conducted. We present evidence in chapter IV that the distinction between fixed and flexible exchange rates is a valid maintained hypothesis. In addition, the role of foreign factors in influencing the German economy is established by bivariate and multivariate causality tests for both subperiods.

Chapter IV considers the role of the exchange rate regime and its impact on the domestic money supply and other macrovariables. Chapter V presents the general macrodynamic model which implies alternative theories of unemployment, real output, and inflation as special cases.

CHAPTER IV

FIXED VERSUS FLEXIBLE EXCHANGE RATES IN THE OPEN ECONOMY:

THEORY AND REALITY

1. INTRODUCTION

The literature survey of the previous chapter indicates that the openness of the German economy has concerned many researchers. Macromodels are "opened up" to include external factors which affect the domestic economy through different channels. Empirical results, revealing structural breaks in the behavior of macrovariables and their relationships, are attributed to the transition from fixed to more flexible exchange rates in the early 1970's. Yet, few authors subject their open economy modifications to rigorous statistical tests.

This chapter presents an empirical analysis of some key hypotheses about the relationships among macroeconomic variables in an open economy. The results provide useful guidelines for the specification of the dynamic structure and the causal relationships in a full structural model of the German economy in chapter V.

The extensive body of theoretical and empirical literature in open economy macroeconomics points to the complexity of the issues in open economy modeling. In general, the features of the open economy are captured by incorporating transmission mechanisms for foreign impulses which operate on the domestic economy. Two channels account for the openness of the economy. First, international trade flows affect the composition of aggregate spending and the demand for domestic output. The relative price of importables in terms of domestic goods is a major determinant of export and import demand. In addition, trade flows are affected by real factors such as supply shocks and exogenous shifts in foreign demand. Second, international interest rate differentials and exchange rate expectations affect the composition of domestic private portfolios and account for international capital flows.

Different models of the balance of payments or the exchange rate stress different channels of adjustment. For instance, the elasticities and absorption approaches to the balance of payments focus on the effects of relative price and income changes on the trade balance, while ignoring the monetary implications of trade imbalances. The monetary approach, on the other hand, analyzes the overall balance of payments in terms of money market equilibrium. One purpose of the empirical study in this chapter is to determine the relative importance of the different transmission channels for the German economy since 1960. The results allow us to check the validity of the maintained hypotheses used in different open economy macromodels for the German case.

The existence of different exchange rate regimes over the 1960-85 sample period adds another layer of complexity to our analysis. Different exchange rate systems have different theoretical implications for the degree of economic and monetary interdependence, the effectiveness of domestic monetary and fiscal policies (which also depends on the degree of international capital mobility), and the financing of balance of payments imbalances.

This chapter assesses the empirical validity of the theoretical relationships among macrovariables under fixed and flexible exchange rates. In particular, we are interested in: (1) the role of domestic versus foreign factors with respect to the German money supply and the inflation process, (2) the relative importance of different transmission channels for foreign impulses, and (3) the relevant sets of exogenous and endogenous variables.

The distinction between the two exchange rate regimes is relevant for the exchange rate between the Deutsche Mark and the U.S. Dollar. Under the Bretton Woods system of fixed exchange rates, the exchange rates of the major industrial countries remained practically fixed over the period from 1955-67. The following five years saw substantial shifts in the parities, including the revaluation of the Deutsche Mark in

1969. By 1971, the currency crisis had become acute and ultimately led to the suspension of the gold convertibility of the reserve currency, the U.S. Dollar. The *Smithsonian Agreement* of December 1971 realigned the currencies, but could not halt the continuing depreciation of the Dollar.

Since the collapse of the Bretton Woods system in March 1973, the Deutsche Mark has been allowed to "float" vis-a-vis the U.S. Dollar along with most other major currencies. However, the period since 1973 has not been a textbook example of a flexible exchange rate system because the German Bundesbank has intervened frequently in foreign exchange markets attempting to sterilize speculative capital flows. Nevertheless, the post-Bretton-Woods era has been characterized by sharply increased exchange rate volatility against the U.S. Dollar.

A system of relatively fixed exchange rates continues to exist among most European currencies under the European Monetary System (EMS). Until the establishment of the EMS in 1979, most currencies were linked by the "snake-in-the-tunnel" arrangements while jointly floating against the U.S. Dollar. Given her economic and political clout, Germany has usually been the "locomotive" for European economic developments, and the Deutsche Mark has become a reserve and intervention currency for European central banks.

The remainder of the chapter is organized as follows. Section 2 introduces a simple synthesis model of the open economy which combines the various channels of transmission and focuses on its steady state properties. We derive the standard theoretical implications for domestic money growth and inflation under the two exchange rate regimes. The previous empirical evidence in support of the synthesis model has been mixed at best. The lack of support is attributed to limitations of the theoretical model as well as the standard empirical procedure of fitting and evaluating the performance of a model without testing a priori assumptions. Section 3 proposes an alternative approach to study the dynamic structure and relationships among macrovariables under different exchange rate systems. Maintained hypotheses regarding the exogeneity and endogeneity of variables in different open economy models are subjected to bivariate and multivariate Granger causality tests. The results provide useful information for the specification of a full macrodynamic model of the German economy in chapter V.

2. OPEN ECONOMY MACROECONOMICS: A SYNTHESIS VIEW

Open economy macromodels address a multitude of issues based on an even greater number of often highly specialized theoretical frameworks and their empirical counterparts.[1] Yet, most of the theoretical and empirical work can be characterized by a common core of assumptions about the sets of exogenous and endogenous variables. The list of endogenous variables usually includes domestic prices, interest rates, and output for both fixed and flexible exchange rate regimes. Domestic monetary and fiscal policy variables as well as foreign variables (e.g., prices, interest rates, and output) are commonly considered to be exogenous.

Under fixed exchange rates, the balance of payments (i.e., the *foreign* component of the domestic money supply) is an additional endogenous variable, implying that the *domestic* component of the money supply and the exchange rate are exogenous. For the flexible exchange rate economy, the list of endogenous variables includes the exchange rate, whereas the overall domestic money supply is typically treated as exogenous.

This section takes these common core assumptions and derives the theoretical implications for the behavior of domestic macrovariables under the different exchange rate regimes. We introduce a simple general equilibrium model in the Mundell-Fleming tradition, an open economy version of the standard IS-LM framework. The steady state properties of this model are generally agreed upon and represent the consensus view of the small open economy. Controversy arises about the dynamics of adjustment between steady states. Due to different assumptions about (1) the expectation

---

[1]See, for example, Dornbusch (1980) for a taste of model variety.

formation for the domestic price level and/or the exchange rate and (2) the degree of wage and price flexibility, economists disagree about the time required until the economy returns to long-run equilibrium after a disturbance has occurred. The purpose of our analysis is to study the steady state dichotomy between fixed and flexible exchange rates with respect to the domestic money supply and inflation processes.

2.1. The Theoretical Framework

The model presented here has been widely discussed in the literature.[2] It incorporates both international trade and capital flows as transmission mechanisms for foreign impulses. Assuming that the economy is producing at capacity (i.e., there is no "Okun gap") and that expectations about the domestic price level and the exchange rate are static, the synthesis model can be represented by three equilibrium conditions:

$$y = a_0 + a_1(e+p*-p) - a_2r \qquad (4.1)$$

$$r = r* \qquad (4.2)$$

$$m-p = b_1y - b_2r \qquad (4.3)$$

For analytical convenience, all variables enter in logarithmic form. Foreign variables are denoted by the $*$ superscript. The symbols used are: y real capacity output; m money stock; p domestic price index; $p*$ foreign price index; e domestic currency price of foreign exchange; r domestic interest rate; $r*$ foreign interest rate.

Equation (4.1) is the IS-curve describing the goods market equilibrium for the open economy where aggregate demand depends on the real exchange rate $(e+p*-p)$ and the domestic interest rate. The constant a_0 denotes exogenous demand shift

---

[2]See Dornbusch (1980, Part 4) for references. Stein (1982a) studies the realism and empirical relevance of the "Consensus Model."

parameters such as changes in government spending and/or export demand.[3] A real depreciation, or an increase in (e+p*-p), raises aggregate demand since domestic goods become relatively cheaper. The price elasticity $a_1>0$ indicates the degree of substitutability between domestic and foreign goods. Absolute purchasing power parity holds if $a_1 \to \infty$, implying that domestic and foreign goods are perfect substitutes, and there are no transportation costs. Nominal and real interest rate changes coincide under the assumption of static price expectations. The interest rate effect on aggregate demand is reflected by $a_2>0$, which enters the expenditure function with a negative sign. A real balance effect in the expenditure function is ignored to simplify the analysis. Stein (1982a) accounts for this effect by including (m-p) as an additional variable in equation (4.1).

Capital market equilibrium under conditions of perfect capital mobility, perfect asset substitutability, and static exchange rate expectations is described by equation (4.2). Capital inflows (outflows) occur if the domestic interest rate is above (below) the foreign rate. Until capital market equilibrium (CM) is reached, asset prices keep changing, and net capital flows occur. The assumption of perfect asset substitutability can be relaxed to introduce a non-zero risk premium on holdings of foreign assets. If domestic residents require such a risk premium, the domestic interest rate differs from the foreign interest rate even under perfect capital mobility. Nevertheless, capital market equilibrium for the small economy implies that the domestic interest rate is a *function* of the foreign rate.[4]

Equation (4.3) is the LM-curve describing money market equilibrium. Real money demand depends positively on real income and negatively on the domestic interest rate. The income and interest rate elasticities of money demand are given by $b_1>0$ and $b_2>0$, where b_2 enters the function with a negative sign.

The three equilibrium conditions (4.1), (4.2), and (4.3) form a recursive system for both exchange rate regimes. Endogenous variables are the domestic price level,

---

[3]Dornbusch (1980, p. 194) explicitly models spillover effects by including foreign output as an independent exogenous component of aggregate demand for domestic output.

[4]If domestic residents require a risk premium to hold foreign rather than domestic assets, capital market equilibrium implies $r = f(r*)$.

the domestic interest rate, and - depending on the exchange rate regime - the money stock or the exchange rate. Exogenous variables are full-employment output, the foreign price level, the foreign interest rate, and the exchange rate (under fixed exchange rates) or the money stock (under flexible exchange rates). This a priori classification of endogenous and exogenous variables implicitly assumes the absence of sterilization policies under fixed exchange rates and the absence of unsterilized official intervention under flexible rates. Let us consider the implications of the synthesis model for domestic money growth and inflation under the two exchange rate regimes.

2.2. The Fixed Exchange Rate Case

In the absence of sterilization policies, the money stock and the rate of monetary expansion in the open economy are not controlled by the domestic monetary authority. The central bank is obliged to engage in open market purchases (sales) of foreign exchange in order to stabilize the exchange rate, thereby inducing a monetary expansion (contraction) whenever an excess supply of (excess demand for) foreign exchange prevails at the fixed price of foreign exchange. Consequently, the money stock and the rate of monetary expansion are endogenously determined by the country's balance of payments position.

General equilibrium prevails when the goods, capital, and money markets are simultaneously in equilibrium. Joint equilibrium in the capital and money markets is described by equation (4.4) and graphed as LM-CM-curve in figure 4.1 below.

$$m = p + b_1 y - b_2 r* \qquad (4.4)$$

The LM-CM-curve is a 45-degree line in $(m-p)$ space with a non-negative intercept on the m-axis. For levels of p to the right (left) of the LM-CM-curve, there exists an excess demand for (excess supply of) money. Domestic interest rates rise above (fall below) r* and induce a capital inflow (outflow). The resulting excess supply of (excess demand for) foreign exchange by the private sector requires an open market purchase (sale) of foreign exchange by the central bank, which - if unsterilized - leads to an expansion (contraction) of the monetary base and the money stock.

Joint equilibrium in the goods and money markets is described by equation (4.5) and graphed as IS-LM-curve in figure 4.1.

$$m = \frac{b_2}{a_2} \cdot (a_1 + a_2/b_2) \cdot p + \frac{b_2}{a_2} \cdot \left[(1 + a_2 b_1/b_2) \cdot y - a_0 - a_1 (e+p^*) \right] \qquad (4.5)$$

The IS-LM curve is steeper than the LM-CM-curve. It is defined for positive values of m and p only. For levels of m above (below) the IS-LM-curve, an excess demand for (excess supply of) goods exists and exerts upward (downward) pressure on the domestic price level.

Figure 4.1

The Transmission of Foreign Inflation under Fixed Exchange Rates

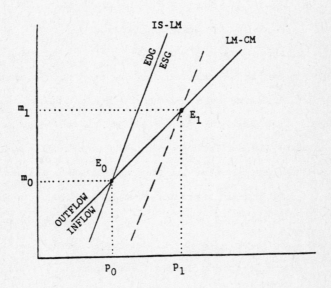

General equilibrium in all three markets occurs at the intersection of the IS-LM and LM-CM-curves at E_0. To guarantee positive equilibrium values for p_0 and m_0, the vertical intercept of the LM-CM-curve must lie above the IS-LM intercept, a necessary condition which is satisfied for $y < [a_0 + a_1(e + p^*) - a_2 r^*]$.

Setting equations (4.4)-(4.5) and solving for p, the equilibrium price level can be written as equation (4.6), where the exchange rate is stabilized at $e = \bar{e}$.

$$p = p^* + \bar{e} - \frac{1}{a_1}\left[(y - a_0) + a_2 r^*\right] \tag{4.6}$$

Consequently, the steady state rate of inflation depends on foreign inflation $\dot{p}^*$, real capacity growth $\dot{y}$, foreign interest rate changes $\dot{r}^*$, and exogenous disturbances ϵ_1. Under fixed exchange rates, $\dot{e} = 0$.

$$\dot{p} = \dot{p}^* - \frac{1}{a_1}\left[\dot{y} + a_2 \dot{r}^*\right] + \epsilon_1 \tag{4.6'}$$

The equilibrium money stock is described by

$$m = p^* + \bar{e} - \frac{1}{a_1}\left[(1 - a_1 b_1)\cdot y - a_0 + (a_2 + a_1 b_2)\cdot r^*\right] \tag{4.7}$$

Accordingly, the steady state rate of money growth is

$$\dot{m} = \dot{p}^* - \frac{1}{a_1}\left[(1 - a_1 b_1)\cdot \dot{y} + (a_2 + a_1 b_2)\cdot \dot{r}^*\right] + \epsilon_2 \tag{4.7'}$$

where ϵ_2 denotes exogenous disturbances.

Equations (4.6) and (4.7) summarize the implications for the determination of the domestic price level under fixed exchange rates:

(1) The domestic price level is not determined by the (endogenous) money stock. For example, an increase in the money stock above its equilibrium value m_0 causes domestic interest rates to fall. The results are an excess demand for goods and incipient capital outflows, the latter leading to an excess demand for foreign exchange. To stabilize the exchange rate, the central bank has to sell foreign exchange. In the absence of sterilization, the monetary base and the money stock contract until equilibrium is restored at E_0 where the money stock has returned to its initial level m_0.

(2) A rise in the foreign price level is transmitted by the following mechanism. A higher p^* causes a real depreciation and substitution of domestic for foreign goods. At the initial equilibrium E_0, there now exists an excess demand for

domestic goods as the IS-LM-curve in figure 4.1 shifts to the right. Upward pressure on domestic prices is exerted and real balances fall, creating an excess demand for money. Domestic interest rates rise, inducing a capital inflow and an excess supply of foreign exchange. To stabilize the exchange rate, the central bank is obliged to purchase foreign exchange. In the absence of sterilization, the monetary base and the money stock expand until equilibrium is re-established at E_1 where both the money stock and the domestic price level have increased proportionally.

2.3. <u>The Flexible Exchange Rate Case</u>

Under flexible exchange rates, the money stock and the rate of monetary expansion are control variables. The central bank does not have to engage in open market purchases or sales of foreign exchange, because the exchange rate is allowed to adjust freely in response to balance of payments disequilibria.

General equilibrium prevails when the goods, capital, and money markets are simultaneously in equilibrium. Joint equilibrium of the capital and money markets is described by equation (4.8) and graphed as LM-CM-curve in figure 4.2a.

$$p = m - b_1 y + b_2 r* \qquad\qquad (4.8)$$

The LM-CM-curve is independent of the exchange rate and is defined for positive values of p only. For levels of p above (below) p_0, an excess demand for (excess supply of) money exists. Domestic interest rates rise above (fall below) $r*$ and induce a capital inflow (outflow). The resulting excess supply of (excess demand for) foreign exchange causes the exchange rate to fall (rise), implying that the domestic currency appreciates (depreciates).

Joint equilibrium of the goods and money markets is described by equation (4.9) or (4.9′) and graphed as IS-LM-curve in figure 4.2a.

$$e - p - p\ast + \frac{1}{a_1}\left[(1+a_2b_1/b_2)\cdot y - a_0 - a_2/b_2(m-p)\right] \tag{4.9}$$

$$e + p\ast - (1+a_2/a_1b_2)\cdot p + \frac{1}{a_1}\left[(1+a_2b_1/b_2)\cdot y - a_0 - (a_2/b_2)\cdot m\right] \tag{4.9'}$$

The IS-LM-curve is steeper than the 45-degree line in (e-p) space, and requires positive values of p and e. For levels of e above (below) the IS-LM-curve, the real exchange rate has risen (fallen) so that domestic goods are relatively cheaper. The resulting excess demand for (excess supply of) domestic goods causes the domestic price level to increase (fall).

Figure 4.2a

The Insulation Property of Flexible Exchange Rates

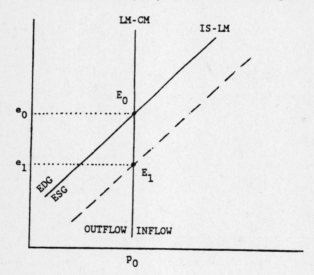

General equilibrium in all three markets occurs at the intersection of the IS-LM and LM-CM-curves at E_0. To assure positive equilibrium values for e_0 and p_0, the horizontal intercept of the LM-CM-curve must lie above the IS-LM intercept. This necessary condition is satisfied for $a_1(m-p\ast)>[a_0-(1-a_1b_1)\cdot y-(a_1b_2+a_2)\cdot r\ast]$.

The equilibrium price level is given by equation (4.8). Substitution of equation (4.9) into (4.8) yields the equilibrium exchange rate.

$$e + p* = m + \frac{1}{a_1}\left[(1-a_1 b_1)\cdot y - a_0 + (a_2+a_1 b_2)\cdot r*\right] \qquad (4.10)$$

The steady state rates of inflation and depreciation are given by

$$\dot{p} = \dot{m} - b_1 \dot{y} + b_2 \dot{r}* \qquad (4.8')$$

$$\dot{e} + \dot{p}* = \dot{m} + \frac{1}{a_1}\left[(1-a_1 b_1)\cdot \dot{y} + (a_2+a_1 b_2)\cdot \dot{r}*\right] + \epsilon_3 \qquad (4.10')$$

where ϵ_3 denotes exogenous demand disturbances.

Equations (4.8) and (4.10) summarize the implications for the determination of the domestic price level under flexible exchange rates:

(1) Changes in the foreign price level have only temporary effects on the domestic price level. A higher p*, for example, induces substitution of domestic for foreign goods and creates an excess demand for domestic goods at the initial equilibrium E_0. The IS-LM-curve in figure 4.2a shifts to the right. Upward pressure on domestic prices is exerted, lowering real balances and creating an excess demand for money. Domestic interest rates rise above r*, inducing a capital inflow, which is associated with an excess supply of foreign exchange. The resulting decline in the exchange rate tends to offset the initial real depreciation. The excess demand pressure in the goods market is reduced and equilibrium is re-established at E_1 where the exchange rate has declined, but the domestic price level is back at its initial level p_0.

(2) The price level is determined by the domestically controlled money stock. A monetary expansion has two effects which are depicted in figure 4.2b. At the initial price level p_0, there now exists an excess supply of money since real balances have increased. Domestic interest rates fall and induce a capital outflow as the LM-CM-curve in figure 4.2b shifts out. The resulting excess demand for foreign exchange causes the exchange rate to rise, implying a domestic currency depreciation. Furthermore, higher real balances and lower domestic interest rates raise aggregate demand. An excess demand for goods exists at the initial equilibrium E_0, and the IS-LM-curve in figure 4.2b shifts down. Consequently, the domestic price level rises. Equilibrium is

re-established at E_2, where the exchange rate and the domestic price level both have increased as a result of the increase in the money stock.

Figure 4.2b

The Effects of a Monetary Expansion
under Flexible Exchange Rates

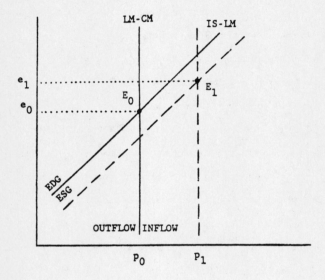

2.4. Summary and Critique of the Synthesis View

The theoretical implications of the consensus model for the determination of the domestic price level and the domestic control over monetary aggregates highlight the dichotomy between the two exchange rate regimes. Under fixed exchange rates, domestic variables such as the rate of money growth and inflation are driven by foreign variables. The domestic money supply expands and contracts in response to balance of payments imbalances. Foreign inflation affects domestic inflation directly. Domestic money growth is neutralized by offsetting capital flows and, thus, cannot influence the domestic inflation rate. A system of flexible exchange rates, on the other hand, guarantees monetary independence. The domestic money supply is under the control of domestic authorities, and domestic inflation depends primarily on the rate of money growth.

Any theory, however, must be subjected to empirical verification. How well does the proposed model capture the empirical realities of the two exchange rate regimes? Stein (1982a) investigates the relationships between domestic variables (inflation, money growth, and output growth) and their U.S. counterparts for the seven largest industrialized countries over the 1960-78 period. His results are strongly inconsistent with the model's implications, leading him to conclude that "...the Consensus Model fails to capture with clarity and simplicity the key elements of a complicated process" (p. 426).

The empirical failure of the synthesis model appears somewhat less spectacular in light of the underlying explicit and implicit assumptions. Most importantly, a priori restrictions on the exogeneity and endogeneity of variables entering the model are imposed. While these a priori assumptions may be plausible and theoretically well founded, alternative maintained hypotheses exist which are equally plausible.

For instance, the small country assumption employed to "close" our open economy macromodel will be violated by the existence of spillover effects from the domestic to the foreign economy under both fixed and flexible exchange rates. The German economy is often considered a large open economy, given its share in world trade and the contribution of its foreign sector to German GNP. In addition, the Deutsche Mark - though not "the" reserve currency - enjoys popularity with international investors and foreign central banks, particularly within the European Monetary System (EMS). Does the commonly perceived openness of the German economy imply that the small country assumption is violated?

Furthermore, in the presence of sterilization policies and/or a significant nontraded goods sector, short-term monetary independence may be possible even under fixed exchange rates.[5] For Germany, conflicting evidence about the active use of sterilization policy by the Bundesbank has been presented. Herring and Marston (1977), Cassese and Lothian (1982), and Obstfeld (1983) show that the Bundesbank engaged in substantial sterilization of foreign exchange flows under both exchange rate regimes. Similar findings are reported by Willms (1971), Argy and Kouri (1974), Artus (1976), Darby and Stockman (1983), and Black (1983). Blejer (1979), on the other hand, finds no evidence of sterilization, whereas Feige and Johannes (1981) detect a bidirectional causal relationship between domestic credit and international reserves.

Finally, the existence of policy reaction functions introduces elements of endogeneity in domestic policy variables even under flexible exchange rates.

Without explicitely testing the validity of the underlying maintained hypotheses, the standard procedure of fitting a proposed model may produce biased and inconsistent coefficient estimates and, thus, unreliable statistical tests. The next section suggests a general approach to test several key hypotheses of open economy macromodels. The results provide useful information about the causal orderings and the dynamic structure of the German economy.

3. OPEN ECONOMY MACROECONOMICS AND REALITY

The standard procedure used in empirical studies is to fit the proposed model and evaluate its performance without explicitely testing the validity of the underlying maintained hypotheses. Such tests, however, are an important exercise. Sims (1980) argues that empirically invalid maintained hypotheses can produce biased and inconsistent coefficient estimates, leading to unreliable statistical tests.

---

[5]Borts and Hanson (1979), for example, bring monetary policy back into the monetary approach to the balance of payments by introducing nontraded goods whose relative prices can be influenced by domestic monetary actions.

Our approach is to conduct bivariate and multivariate Granger causality tests of different maintained hypotheses for the open economy. Leiderman (1980b) uses this procedure to analyze the causal orderings for the Italian economy during the fixed exchange rate period. Cassese and Lothian (1982) propose a similar method to investigate the international transmission of inflation in eight industrial countries between 1958-76. Fitzgerald and Pollio (1983) examine the causal relationships among anticipated and unanticipated monetary variables, real output, and prices in the six largest industrialized economies over the 1965-79 period.

The Granger causality tests have the advantage of providing evidence on some commonly used model-identifying restrictions which may reveal alternative empirical relationships. However, the following limitations of the approach should be pointed out. First, bivariate causality tests can be subject to specification bias to the extent that other important variables (e.g., expectations) have been omitted. Given the importance of expectations particularly in foreign exchange markets, this criticism may weaken our conclusions. Second, causality tests are based on reduced-form equations which may be consistent with a number of structural models. As a result the task of specifying *one* structural model of the German economy may be rendered impossible in light of the observational equivalence problem.

3.1. Theoretical Considerations

Let us contrast the assumptions and implications of the synthesis model presented in section 2 with alternative hypotheses about the relationships among macrovariables in the open economy.

First, foreign variables in the synthesis model are considered to be exogenously determined. Germany, on the other hand, is commonly perceived to be a large open economy. If the small country assumption is indeed violated, causality tests should reveal a feedback relationship between German and foreign variables such as output growth, inflation, money growth, and interest rate changes.

Second, the synthesis model incorporates both international trade and capital flows as channels through which exogenous foreign impulses are transmitted to the domestic economy. The relative importance of these channels of transmission under the two exchange rate regimes can be established empirically by causality tests.

Third, the synthesis view holds that inflation under fixed exchange rates can be explained by the phenomenon of imported inflation, whereas flexible rates guarantee - in principle - the insulation from foreign price disturbances. Thus, the worldwide inflationary experience of the 1970's appears to contradict the insulation property of flexible exchange rates. However, if the worldwide acceleration of inflation can be attributed to the oil price shocks of 1973-74 and 1978-79, German and foreign inflation rates simply covaried because they were both driven by an omitted supply side variable. To model the German inflationary process correctly, we need to establish the relative contributions of domestic and foreign factors for the two exchange rate periods. Special attention is given to the role of import prices in general and oil prices in particular.

Fourth, the synthesis model ignores supply side considerations. Fluctuations in aggregate spending affect real output in the short run, but they only lead to price or exchange rate changes in the long run. The stagflationary experience of the 1970's indicates that actual and potential output supply are also determined by the relative price of imported intermediate goods and raw materials. Causality tests can reveal to what extent supply side shocks influence real variables.

Fifth, the monetary approach to the balance of payments and the exchange rate has important implications for the degree of monetary (in)dependence under the alternative exchange rate regimes. The synthesis model assumes the absence of sterilization policies and a negligible nontraded goods sector. As a result, domestic money growth is not a control variable under fixed exchange rates since ceteris paribus exogenous changes in domestic credit are offset by induced changes in international reserves.[6] The maintained hypothesis is that domestic monetary policy is totally ineffective.[7] However, the direction of causality between domestic and foreign components of the German money supply under fixed exchange rates may be exactly opposite. With active sterilization policy, the central bank neutralizes exogenous changes in foreign reserves with opposite changes in domestic credit to maintain monetary independence at least in the short run. Furthermore, commercial banks may offset exogenous outflows of reserves by increased central bank borrowing to avoid large fluctuations in their credit volume. If a sizeable nontraded goods sector exists, monetary policy can play an active role even without sterilization and/or commercial bank credit policy. Causality tests of the relationship between the domestic credit and international reserves will test the validity of the standard monetary approach. In addition, we will assess the influence of various monetary aggregates on the domestic economy over the two subperiods.

3.2. Methodological Considerations

Since Granger's (1969) original contribution, three asymptotically equivalent tests of causality - the Granger, Sims, and Haugh-Pierce procedures - have been developed.[8] Of these, only the Granger test can be applied to multivariate time series. In addition, Sims's (1972) approach for the bivariate case involves a substantial loss of degrees of freedom, an important consideration given our two subperiods with 48 quarterly observations at most. Sims's procedure is also sensitive

---

[6] Blejer (1979, p. 290) makes this point forcefully by stating that "...the direction of causality postulated by the monetary approach is therefore clearly from domestic credit to foreign reserves." Johnson (1972, pp. 238-240) agrees with this conclusion.

[7] Flexible exchange rates, on the other hand, put the money supply under the control of domestic authorities since central bank holdings of international reserves no longer fluctuate endogenously with the balance of payments.

[8] See Granger (1969), Sims (1972), and Pierce and Haugh (1977).

to prefiltering of the data. Two drawbacks have been mentioned for the Haugh-Pierce test. Geweke (1981) suggests that this test is less powerful than the Granger test, and Sims (1977) argues that it is biased toward accepting the null hypothesis of independence. By selecting the Granger method, we avoid the aforementioned problems and obtain consistent parameter estimates, provided that the residuals in the bivariate and multivariate AR-representations are serially uncorrelated.

The tests are performed using seasonally unadjusted quarterly data. All German and foreign variables are expressed as rates of change and computed as logarithmic first differences. The use of seasonally unadjusted data in causality tests is fairly common.[9] Scheide (1984, pp. 67-68) argues that the use of moving averages in many seasonal adjustment procedures violates the axiom of Granger causality that "...the past and the present may cause the future, but the future cannot cause the past [Granger, 1980, p. 330]." Nevertheless, as long as the method of seasonal adjustment is uniform across all variables, seasonally adjusted data will not produce spurious causality. Our German data base consists of seasonally unadjusted data, and we do not attempt to replicate the Census X-11 method to achieve consistency with adjusted foreign data. For estimation purposes, each equation includes three seasonal dummies and a linear time trend. If the autocorrelation function of the residuals does not exhibit any seasonal patterns, the seasonal dummy specification is justified.

The bivariate tests include four and six lags of the variables. Multivariate tests are based on four lags. These lag structures, though commonly found in the literature, are chosen on an ad hoc basis, and different specifications could affect significance levels arbitrarily. A search procedure to determine the optimal number of lags for each regression, using a minimum standard error or final prediction error criterion, is preferable.[10] However, such a search procedure is impractical due to the limited number of degrees of freedom offered by our relatively short subperiods.

---

[9] See, for example, Leiderman (1980b), Feige and Johannes (1981), Van Hoa (1981), Scheide (1982,1984), Fitzgerald and Pollio (1983), Weissenberger and Thomas (1983), and von Hagen (1984).

[10] The final prediction error criterion was proposed by Akaike (1969) and first applied by Hsiao (1981). Scheide (1982,1984) uses this approach to test the causal relationships between money, prices, and output in Germany.

3.3. Empirical Realities

To conduct the causality tests, we estimate regression equations of the form

$$Y_t = \alpha_0 + \sum_{i=1}^{3} \alpha_i SEAS_i + \alpha_4 t + \sum_{i=1}^{m} \beta_i Y_{t-i} + \sum_{i=1}^{m} \gamma_i X_{t-i} + \epsilon_t$$

where $SEAS_i$ is a seasonal dummy for the i-th quarter, t is a linear time trend, Y is the caused variable, and X is the (block of) causal variable(s). Since no evidence of serial correlation can be detected, estimation by ordinary least squares (OLS) yields consistent parameter estimates and reliable test statistics. The resulting residual autocorrelation functions do not exhibit any seasonal spikes. We test the null hypothesis of no causality from X to Y by restricting the coefficients of the causal variable to zero (i.e., $\gamma_i = 0$). Complete regression results are not reported here. The following tables contain the F-statistics for bivariate and multivariate Granger causality tests for the periods of fixed (1960.1-72.4) and flexible (1973.1-85.4) exchange rates.

Tables 4.1 and 4.2 summarize the evidence about the relationships among domestic and foreign variables which are commonly included in small open economy models. Theoretically, the foreign variables should be represented by "rest of the world" data in the empirical tests, but such data are not readily available. Furthermore, their construction poses the question of adequate weights for the countries included in the composite measure. The "rest of the world" should include a country's major trading partners, implying that bilateral trade shares could be used to derive the appropriate weights. Two problems arise with the constructed data. First, the "rest of the world" data fail to capture the changes in worldwide trade patterns since the 1960's if the weights are computed for a fixed base year. Any results based on such data must be interpreted with caution. Second, if the weighting scheme is revised over time to reflect the changing trade patterns, the constructed time series contains structural breaks which make the interpretation of results more difficult. In light of these technical difficulties, we elect to use U.S. data as a proxy for the "rest of the world" variables. Even though the U.S. is not the most important trading partner for Germany, the importance of the U.S. economy in world markets justifies our choice.

The variables in tables 4.1 and 4.2, all expressed as rates of change, are: Y* U.S. industrial production; P* U.S. consumer price index; PO German price index for imported crude oil; Y German industrial production; P German consumer price index; IR international reserves (the *foreign* component of the German money supply); DC domestic credit (the *domestic* component of the German money supply); G real federal government expenditures; E nominal (DM/$) exchange rate; ER real (inflation-adjusted) exchange rate.[11]

First, consider the evidence pertaining to the small country assumption that foreign variables are independent of domestic variables. According to the bivariate tests in table 4.1, foreign real output is unaffected by German output in both subperiods. Similarly, foreign prices are independent of German prices over the entire sample period. It follows that the small country assumption cannot be rejected when it is interpreted as the absence of causality from domestic variables to their foreign counterparts. The multivariate tests in table 4.2, which consider the causal relationship between blocks of domestic variables and foreign output and prices, weaken this conclusion for the flexible exchange rate period. Foreign output is affected by all blocks of German variables, and foreign prices are caused by one group of variables.

Considering the bivariate relationships between other German variables and U.S. output and prices, several incidents of causality can be detected. No clear pattern

---

[11]Industrial production and the CPI are chosen as measures of economic activity and the aggregate price level for Germany and the U.S. because the Bureau of Economic Analysis (BEA) does not compile seasonally *unadjusted* real GNP and GNP deflator series for the U.S. The series for international reserves, which excludes official holdings of gold, is denominated in U.S. Dollars. Domestic credit is the difference between the monetary base and international reserves converted to domestic currency units at par. The real exchange rate is based on U.S. and German consumer prices.

Table 4.1

Bivariate Relationships among Domestic and
Foreign Variables in Open Economy Models

Causal Variable		Y*	P*	PO	Y	P	IR	DC	G	E	ER
						Caused Variable					
Fixed Exchange Rates (1960.1-1972.4)											
Y*	4 lags	-	-	.95	.73	1.53	1.06	.81	.19	.54	.39
	6 lags	-	-	1.01	.73	.69	.95	.78	.46	1.09	.46
P*	4 lags	-	-	1.15	.71	.65	.86	**2.71**	.64	.90	.39
	6 lags	-	-	1.19	.36	.80	.88	1.58	1.53	1.20	.75
PO	4 lags	.90	.42	-	*2.45*	*2.09*	.97	1.47	.16	.76	1.04
	6 lags	1.55	.18	-	*2.25*	1.38	.96	1.50	.11	1.32	1.28
Y	4 lags	.56	*2.68*	2.55	-	.69	.29	.98	1.61	.48	.47
	6 lags	1.30	1.71	1.42	-	.89	.42	.92	1.18	1.01	.91
P	4 lags	.82	1.68	.58	**2.61**	-	1.08	.65	.84	.19	.91
	6 lags	.63	1.19	.49	*2.19*	-	1.17	.62	.88	.31	.71
IR	4 lags	**2.59**	1.77	.24	.21	.39	-	**2.84**	.71	**5.21**	**4.37**
	6 lags	1.65	1.95	.67	.12	.86	-	1.60	.49	**3.43**	**2.93**
DC	4 lags	**3.09**	1.50	.29	.16	.65	.71	-	.96	**5.52**	**4.31**
	6 lags	*2.01*	1.66	.85	.13	1.07	.54	-	.55	**3.33**	**2.91**
G	4 lags	.96	.36	1.21	1.82	*2.16*	1.39	.43	-	.62	.48
	6 lags	.21	.18	.83	*2.26*	**2.97**	.85	.41	-	.85	1.43
E	4 lags	1.06	1.13	1.17	.16	.63	1.27	1.80	.96	-	-
	6 lags	*2.28*	1.29	1.46	.39	1.29	.90	1.51	.97	-	-
ER	4 lags	1.13	1.70	.82	.44	.91	1.62	1.88	1.41	-	-
	6 lags	*2.38*	1.53	1.18	.53	1.68	1.02	1.86	1.74	-	-
Flexible Exchange Rates (1973.1-1985.4)											
Y*	4 lags	-	-	.83	*2.29*	.07	1.11	**3.30**	1.05	1.28	1.45
	6 lags	-	-	**2.46**	1.86	.06	.84	**2.55**	.65	.98	1.17
P*	4 lags	-	-	.80	.78	**5.41**	1.03	.22	.58	**3.31**	**2.95**
	6 lags	-	-	**2.86**	.64	**4.24**	.98	2.03	.93	*2.21*	**2.42**
PO	4 lags	**7.34**	.70	-	**2.58**	.41	1.30	*2.42*	.33	1.69	1.63
	6 lags	**5.22**	1.22	-	1.87	1.60	1.26	**3.97**	.37	**2.70**	**3.17**
Y	4 lags	1.84	.32	.23	-	**3.86**	.82	.70	1.36	*2.18*	1.61
	6 lags	.70	.59	.76	-	**2.80**	1.11	.98	1.15	2.04	1.83
P	4 lags	**2.34**	1.31	**2.60**	2.42	-	1.32	.27	.27	1.66	1.33
	6 lags	**2.40**	1.27	.33	1.78	-	1.21	.74	.53	1.34	.97
IR	4 lags	1.93	**7.72**	**5.67**	.63	1.04	-	.78	1.02	2.06	*2.45*
	6 lags	**3.80**	**7.29**	**3.36**	.90	1.48	-	2.03	.34	1.27	1.48
DC	4 lags	1.05	1.85	**13.7**	.69	.29	.44	-	.43	2.40	**2.57**
	6 lags	.87	1.97	.89	.89	.91	.66	-	.82	1.38	1.42
G	4 lags	1.72	.28	.45	**8.01**	1.24	.57	.33	-	.39	.46
	6 lags	.44	.20	.41	**4.79**	1.04	.86	.35	-	.50	.47
E	4 lags	2.00	*2.14*	**3.82**	.80	.52	1.08	**3.20**	.27	-	-
	6 lags	**3.42**	*2.16*	**2.75**	.41	.86	1.22	**2.53**	.65	-	-
ER	4 lags	**2.80**	1.97	**3.04**	.70	.56	1.18	**2.89**	.23	-	-
	6 lags	**3.69**	1.85	**2.58**	.43	1.03	1.09	**2.60**	.64	-	-

Note: **Boldface** (5% and 1%) and *italics* (10%) denote significant F-statistics. The variables are defined in the text. Data sources are given at the end of the book.

Table 4.2

Multivariate Relationships among Domestic
and Foreign Variables in Open Economy Models

Causal Block of Variables	Caused Variable								
	Y*	P*	Y	P	IR	DC	G	E	ER
Fixed Exchange Rates (1960.1-1972.4)									
Y*, P*	-	-	.88	1.37	.98	1.63	.60	.54	.45
Y*, PO	-	-	1.72	1.62	1.04	1.29	.17	.56	.63
DC, G	1.76	.84	.99	1.68	1.23	-	-	**2.83**	**2.64**
Y, P, IR	1.16	1.61	-	-	-	*1.84*	.71	1.78	*2.00*
Y, P, E	.82	1.46	-	-	.95	1.44	.80	-	-
Y, P, ER	.71	1.46	-	-	.87	1.17	.82	-	-
Flexible Exchange Rates (1973.1-1985.4)									
Y*, P*	-	-	1.23	**2.76**	1.49	*1.92*	.62	**2.43**	**2.70**
Y*, PO	-	-	**2.67**	.29	1.24	**2.90**	.63	1.09	1.16
DC, G	1.17	1.07	**3.96**	.94	.66	-	-	1.43	1.59
Y, P, IR	**2.96**	**2.80**	-	-	-	.44	1.23	**2.09**	*1.93*
Y, P, E	**2.28**	.81	-	-	.75	1.03	.90	-	-
Y, P, ER	**2.45**	.81	-	-	.74	.90	.85	-	-

Note: **Boldface** (5% and 1%) and *italics* (10%) denote significant F-statistics. The variables are: Y* foreign (U.S.) industrial production; Y German industrial production; P* foreign (U.S.) CPI; P German CPI; PO price index for imported crude oil; IR international reserves; DC domestic credit; G real government spending; E nominal (DM/$) exchange rate; ER real (CPI-based) exchange rate. All variables are expressed as logarithmic first differences. Data sources are given at the end of the book.

evolves for the fixed exchange rate period since the results are sensitive to the lag specification. For the flexible exchange period, however, foreign output is affected consistently by German prices and real exchange rates. German international reserves are significant for the determination of foreign prices, a result which is difficult to rationalize and probably spurious. To summarize, the bivariate and multivariate tests unambiguously support the small country assumption for the fixed exchange rate period. For the flexible exchange rate period, on the other hand, the assumption might be violated.

Since the two subperiods coincide with the pre- and post-oil shock periods, we consider the impact of oil prices on the German economy. Under fixed exchange rates, no bivariate or multivariate causal relationship can be detected. For the 1973-85 sample period, the bivariate tests indicate causality from oil prices to German industrial production, domestic credit, and nominal/real exchange rates. This result is confirmed by the multivariate tests where foreign output and oil prices as a block affect domestic output and credit. Additional results on the effects of oil prices on German prices and monetary aggregates are presented in tables 4.4 and 4.6.

German industrial production is exogenous with respect to most other domestic and foreign variables under both exchange rate regimes. In particular, the DM/$ nominal and real exchange rates do not Granger-cause domestic output, which is an indication of the relatively small role that U.S.-German trade plays for the German economy. However, the bivariate tests in table 4.1 detect causality in two cases. Under fixed exchange rates, the F-statistics for German consumer prices are significant. Under flexible exchange rates, real government spending influences industrial production. Based on the multivariate tests, German output is endogenous under flexible exchange rates where foreign variables (Y*, PO) and domestic policy variables (DC, G) exhibit significant F-statistics.

Next, the bivariate tests reveal the existence of causality from foreign to domestic prices under flexible exchange rates. This finding contradicts conventional wisdom about the international transmission of inflation - or lack thereof - under flexible exchange rates. It can only be explained if an omitted variable drives both

P* and P. In table 4.4, we investigate whether oil prices play a role in this context. For the fixed exchange rate period, no evidence for the phenomenon of imported inflation can be detected. The only variable causing domestic prices is real government spending. Similar results hold for the multivariate tests, where only Y* and P* as a block affect domestic prices for the flexible exchange rate period.

Changes in international reserves held by the Bundesbank are independent of individual or blocks of domestic and foreign variables under both exchange rate regimes. Of particular interest is the apparent lack of causality from domestic credit to international reserves under fixed exchange rates, which contradicts the implications of the monetary approach to the balance of payments for a given foreign money supply. The evidence points toward the active use of sterilization policy by the Bundesbank under fixed exchange rates, a conclusion which is confirmed by the causality from international reserves to domestic credit.

The bivariate tests for domestic credit as a dependent variable in table 4.1 support the sterilization assumption for the fixed exchange rate period. The sum of coefficients for IR (not reported here) is negative as expected. In addition, foreign prices matter for domestic credit growth in the four-lag specification. For the flexible period, foreign output and the nominal/real exchange rates are significant. The exchange rate result contradicts the monetary approach to the exchange rate, according to which changes in the domestic money supply (relative to the foreign money supply) induce exchange rate changes and not vice versa. On the other hand, it supports the view that the Bundesbank's reaction function includes the domestic currency price of foreign exchange. However, the bivariate tests suggest that other domestic variables are not included in such a reaction function for domestic credit. The multivariate tests in table 4.2 confirm the importance of foreign variables for domestic credit in the flexible subperiod. But the causality from exchange rates to domestic credit, detected with the bivariate tests, does not show up here.

Concerning the exogeneity of German real government expenditures, the bivariate and multivariate tests show that G is exogenous with respect to all other variables in both subperiods. The existence of a fiscal policy reaction function can thus be rejected for the entire sample period.

Finally, the evidence for nominal and real exchange rates indicates the existence of puzzling causal orderings for the fixed exchange rate regime. Domestic and foreign components of the German money supply (DC, IR) both "cause" nominal exchange rate changes. This puzzle, however, could be a methodological one since nominal exchange rates were not completely fixed under the Bretton Woods *adjustable* peg system. In particular, the Deutsche Mark was revalued twice, in 1961 and 1969, after periods of massive speculative capital flows which could account for the "causality" from international reserves to the exchange rate. Attempts by the Bundesbank to sterilize the capital flows prior to the revaluation could explain the "causality" from domestic credit to the exchange rate. For the flexible exchange rate period, the causal orderings are sensitive to the lag specification. The bivariate evidence suggests that the exchange rate is influenced by foreign prices, oil prices, and domestic credit. This result is confirmed by the multivariate causality tests in table 4.2 for the nominal exchange rate.

Table 4.3 reports the F-statistics concerning the causal relationship between domestic and foreign interest rates. The variables, all expressed as logarithmic first differences, are: RS German short-term interest rate (3-month money rate); RS^*_{us} U.S. short-term interest rate (3-month T-bill rate); RS^*_{eu} short-term (3-month) Eurodollar deposit rate; RL German long-term interest rate; RL^*_{us} U.S. long-term interest rate. The results underline the dichotomy between the two exchange rate regimes. The higher degree of international capital mobility and the resulting international financial interdependence also becomes apparent. Under fixed rates, changes in foreign interest rates do not affect German interest rates. Instead, a reverse influence from German to U.S. short-term rates exists, which can be interpreted as indirect evidence for the short-term monetary control retained by the Bundesbank under fixed exchange rates. Eurodollar and long-term interest rates are not affected by German rates. Our findings for the fixed exchange rate period are contrary to those of Cassese and Lothian (1982), who detect bidirectional causality

Table 4.3

The International Linkeage of Interest Rates

Causal Variable	Caused Variable			Fixed Rates (1960.1-1972.4)	Flexible Rates (1973.1-1985.4)
RS^*_{us}	RS	4	lags	1.20	<u>3.05</u>
		6	lags	1.29	1.88
RS^*_{eu}	RS	4	lags	1.24	<u>3.83</u>
		6	lags	1.06	<u>2.59</u>
RL^*_{us}	RL	4	lags	1.04	1.93
		6	lags	.89	*1.99*
RS	RS^*_{us}	4	lags	<u>5.55</u>	.39
		6	lags	<u>5.33</u>	.34
RS	RS^*_{eu}	4	lags	1.38	1.59
		6	lags	*2.25*	1.88
RL	RL^*_{us}	4	lags	1.78	1.05
		6	lags	1.16	.73

Note: **Boldface** (5% and 1%) and *italics* (10%) denote significant F-statistics. RS and RL denote short and long-term interest rates, respectively. Foreign interest rates (U.S. or Eurodollar rates) are denoted by the * superscript. All interest rates are expressed as logarithmic first differences. Data sources can be found at the end of the book.

Table 4.4

The International Transmission of Inflation

Causal Variable		Caused Variable					
		PGNE	PGNP	CPI	P*	PO	PI

Fixed Exchange Rates (1960.1-1972.4)

Causal Variable		PGNE	PGNP	CPI	P*	PO	PI
PGNE	4 lags	-	.36	.89	*2.33*	.77	<u>3.16</u>
	6 lags	-	.20	1.88	*2.03*	.60	1.08
PGNP	4 lags	.52	-	.91	*2.46*	.81	<u>3.08</u>
	6 lags	.37	-	1.87	*2.25*	.70	1.11
CPI	4 lags	<u>3.42</u>	<u>3.21</u>	-	1.68	.58	1.63
	6 lags	<u>2.58</u>	*2.33*	-	1.19	.49	1.91
P*	4 lags	.78	1.13	.65	-	1.15	*2.41*
	6 lags	.43	.78	.80	-	1.19	1.14
PO	4 lags	.30	.41	*2.09*	.42	-	.88
	6 lags	.39	.55	1.38	.18	-	.79
PI	4 lags	.23	.49	.29	.27	1.62	-
	6 lags	.65	.87	.84	.40	1.32	-

Flexible Exchange Rates (1973.1-1985.4)

Causal Variable		PGNE	PGNP	CPI	P*	PO	PI
PGNE	4 lags	-	1.98	1.37	.86	<u>2.72</u>	<u>4.07</u>
	6 lags	-	1.15	1.82	1.62	1.30	<u>5.13</u>
PGNP	4 lags	1.35	-	.70	1.33	<u>2.82</u>	<u>4.49</u>
	6 lags	.66	-	.78	1.28	1.52	<u>4.73</u>
CPI	4 lags	<u>5.06</u>	1.78	-	1.31	<u>2.60</u>	<u>2.59</u>
	6 lags	*2.37*	1.16	-	1.27	.33	1.12
P*	4 lags	<u>5.35</u>	*2.16*	<u>5.41</u>	-	.80	<u>2.85</u>
	6 lags	<u>4.99</u>	1.32	<u>4.24</u>	-	<u>2.86</u>	<u>4.78</u>
PO	4 lags	<u>5.37</u>	<u>3.70</u>	.41	.70	-	<u>15.8</u>
	6 lags	<u>3.54</u>	*2.13*	1.60	1.22	-	<u>5.12</u>
PI	4 lags	<u>3.83</u>	<u>2.65</u>	.56	.80	2.45	-
	6 lags	1.84	1.52	.76	1.05	.65	-

Note: **Boldface** (5% and 1%) and *italics* (10%) denote significant F-statistics. PGNE and PGNP are the deflators for gross national expenditures and GNP, respectively. CPI is the German consumer price index. P* denotes the foreign (U.S.) consumer price index. PO is a price index for imported crude oil, and PI measures the price of all imports. All variables are expressed as first differences in logs. Data sources are indicated at the end of the book.

between German and U.S. short-term interest rates. Under flexible rates, foreign interest rates cause domestic rates without feedback.

Detailed information about the phenomenon of imported inflation is presented in table 4.4, where we consider the bivariate relationships among various measures of domestic and foreign inflation. German inflation is measured, alternatively, by the GNP deflator (PGNP), the deflator of gross national expenditures (PGNE), and the consumer price index (CPI). Measures of foreign inflation include: P* U.S. consumer price index; PO price index for imported crude oil; PI import price index. For the fixed exchange rate period, no evidence for the international transmission of inflation can be detected at conventional significance levels. Cassese and Lothian (1982), on the other hand, discover causality from U.S. to German inflation over a similar sample period. For the flexible period, our tests indicate that domestic inflation in the implicit deflators is influenced by all three measures of foreign inflation. German inflation (based on the CPI) is caused only by U.S. consumer price inflation, but not by inflated oil prices or import price inflation in general. Surprisingly, no causal relationship between the German oil price index and U.S. inflation can be detected, which contradicts the findings of previous studies. Gisser and Goodwin (1985), for example, investigate the role of crude oil prices with St.Louis-type equations and multivariate Granger causality tests and find that oil prices contribute significantly to U.S. inflation. However, their results are derived for the (seasonally adjusted) U.S. GNP deflator whereas our study uses (seasonally unadjusted) CPI data. Finally, the finding that the measures of German inflation affect the import price index is hard to rationalize.

The causal role of money with respect to real output and inflation in Germany is analyzed in table 4.5. The monetary aggregates considered are: IR international reserves; DC domestic credit; MB monetary base; M1 narrow definition of the money supply; M2 wider definition of the money supply. Real output is measured by real GNP (RGNP) and real gross national expenditure (RGNE). Inflation rates are computed for the corresponding implicit deflators (PGNP, PGNE) and the consumer price index (CPI). The dichotomy between the two exchange rate regimes is obvious.

Table 4.5

The Causal Role of Money

Causal Variable		Caused Variable				
		RGNE	RGNP	PGNE	PGNP	CPI

Fixed Exchange Rates (1960.1-1972.4)

Causal Variable		RGNE	RGNP	PGNE	PGNP	CPI
IR	4 lags	.67	.99	.28	.24	.39
	6 lags	.61	.83	.22	.24	.86
DC	4 lags	.80	.84	.29	.32	.65
	6 lags	.48	.61	.40	.47	1.07
MB	4 lags	.33	.32	.71	.55	*3.27*
	6 lags	1.12	1.81	.35	.32	*2.25*
M1	4 lags	.97	1.01	.94	.86	*4.13*
	6 lags	.72	.47	.45	.43	*2.60*
M2	4 lags	.65	.58	.55	.63	1.04
	6 lags	.43	.75	.47	.56	.58

Flexible Exchange Rates (1973.1-1985.4)

Causal Variable		RGNE	RGNP	PGNE	PGNP	CPI
IR	4 lags	1.57	.98	1.48	.29	1.04
	6 lags	1.07	.68	*2.44*	.28	1.48
DC	4 lags	1.07	1.15	.78	.84	.29
	6 lags	1.18	1.93	.81	.80	.91
MB	4 lags	*4.99*	*3.87*	2.54	*2.87*	.13
	6 lags	*4.59*	*4.58*	*6.18*	*8.47*	.20
M1	4 lags	*7.71*	*2.89*	1.98	1.35	1.28
	6 lags	*4.99*	*3.28*	1.63	*2.87*	.78
M2	4 lags	1.94	*2.32*	1.10	1.22	1.18
	6 lags	.85	1.01	*2.79*	*3.04*	.95

Note: Significant F-statistics are indicated by **boldface** (5% and 1%) and *italics* (10%). The monetary variables are: IR international reserves; DC domestic credit; MB monetary base; M1 narrow money supply; M2 wider money supply. RGNE and RGNP denote real gross national expenditures and GNP, respectively. PGNE and PGNP are the corresponding deflators. CPI is the consumer price index. All variables are expressed as logarithmic first differences. Data sources are given at the end of the book.

For the period of fixed rates, no causality can be detected between the monetary aggregates, real output growth, and inflation computed for the implicit deflators. The rate of consumer price inflation is Granger-caused by the monetary base and the narrow money supply M1. Overall, these results are consistent with the monetary approach to the balance of payments which implies that domestic monetary policy is ineffective under fixed exchange rates in the absence of sterilization policies. However, this conclusion contradicts our findings in tables 4.1 and 4.2, which suggest that the Bundesbank systematically sterilized exogenous shifts in international reserves to maintain some degree of monetary independence. Two explanations can be given for this apparent inconsistency. First, sterilization policy may have been ineffective. Second, German money growth may affect real output and prices with longer lags than our causality tests allow for.

Under flexible exchange rates, the German monetary base causes both inflation (except for CPI-inflation) and real output growth. The money supply M1 causes real output, but does not affect inflation consistenly. The causality results for M2 are sensitive to the lag length. None of the monetary aggregates Granger-causes the rate of consumer price inflation. Overall, the money-output and money-inflation relationships are strongest for the monetary base, which is the monetary aggregate directly controlled by the central bank. Kohli and Rich (1986) discover similar relationships for the Swiss economy.[12]

Previous studies for the causal role of money in Germany report conflicting evidence. Cassese and Lothian (1982) detect causality from money to prices in the fixed exchange rate period. Scheide (1982,1984), on the other hand, finds only weak support for the money-inflation causality from 1960-80 while confirming the existence of money-output causality. Fitzgerald and Pollio (1983) show that money affects both real output and prices in the 1965-79 period.

The feedback from selected domestic variables to monetary aggregates is investigated in table 4.6. The F-statistics indicate that German monetary and fiscal

---

[12]Kohli and Rich's (1986) empirical methods differ from our approach. Instead of conducting causality tests, they simply regress nominal income growth and inflation on money growth lagged 4 to 19 quarters. A third-degree polynominal distributed lag with endpoint constraints is adopted for all cases.

Table 4.6

The Feedback from Domestic Variables to Monetary Aggregates

Causal Variable		Caused Variable				
		IR	DC	MB	M1	M2
Fixed Exchange Rates (1960.1-1972.4)						
RGNP	4 lags	.61	.56	.27	1.12	.63
	6 lags	.60	.74	.38	1.15	1.58
RGNE	4 lags	.23	.27	.86	.78	.21
	6 lags	.26	.25	.80	1.14	1.15
PGNP	4 lags	1.29	.88	.34	_2.70_	1.44
	6 lags	.96	1.17	.24	_2.23_	.78
PGNE	4 lags	1.27	.93	.19	_2.61_	1.33
	6 lags	1.08	1.27	.40	1.78	.68
CPI	4 lags	1.08	.65	1.11	.41	.85
	6 lags	1.17	.62	1.21	.21	.70
PO	4 lags	.97	1.47	.59	_2.12_	1.98
	6 lags	.96	1.50	_2.18_	_2.13_	_3.77_
PI	4 lags	.89	.41	.33	1.94	_5.67_
	6 lags	.57	.28	.69	1.45	_4.86_
G	4 lags	1.39	.43	.93	_2.18_	1.62
	6 lags	.85	.41	.42	.49	.49
Flexible Exchange Rates (1973.1-1985.4)						
RGNP	4 lags	.37	.12	.55	_3.17_	1.92
	6 lags	.44	.79	.80	1.62	.81
RGNE	4 lags	.70	.34	.40	2.06	_2.93_
	6 lags	.98	1.26	.84	1.05	1.26
PGNP	4 lags	.94	.74	1.10	.27	1.85
	6 lags	.70	1.19	.68	.33	.71
PGNE	4 lags	2.07	.53	_2.35_	.66	.95
	6 lags	1.23	.84	1.10	.95	.51
CPI	4 lags	1.32	.27	_4.22_	1.15	.53
	6 lags	1.21	.74	1.12	.68	.81
PO	4 lags	1.30	_2.42_	_2.86_	.80	1.38
	6 lags	1.26	_3.97_	_2.54_	1.76	_2.45_
PI	4 lags	_2.48_	2.04	_4.07_	1.24	.87
	6 lags	_1.99_	1.83	_2.54_	1.36	1.71
G	4 lags	.57	.33	1.16	1.88	_2.91_
	6 lags	.86	.35	1.11	.79	_2.56_

Note: **Boldface** (5% and 1%) and *italics* denote significant F-statistics. The monetary aggregates are: IR international reserves; DC domestic credit; MB monetary base; M1 narrow money supply; M2 wider money supply. RGNP and RGNE denote real GNP and gross national expenditures, respectively. The corresponding price deflators are PGNP and PGNE. CPI is the consumer price index. PO is a price index for imported crude oil, and PI is the price index for all imported goods. G represents real government spending. All variables are expressed as first differences in logs. Data sources can be found at the end of the book.

Table 4.7

Bivariate Relationships among Domestic
and Foreign Monetary Aggregates

Causal Variable		Caused Variable						
		MB*	M1*	IR	DC	MB	M1	M2

Fixed Exchange Rates (1960.1-1972.4)

Causal Variable		MB*	M1*	IR	DC	MB	M1	M2
MB*	4 lags	-	-	.75	.55	.32	.92	1.71
	6 lags	-	-	1.96	1.54	.74	1.31	**2.89**
M1*	4 lags	-	-	.64	.24	.14	*2.53*	**2.73**
	6 lags	-	-	**2.60**	**2.39**	.83	1.94	**3.10**
IR	4 lags	.38	.36	-	**2.84**	.93	.52	1.66
	6 lags	.59	.60	-	1.60	.71	.70	.94
DC	4 lags	.30	.46	.71	-	-	-	-
	6 lags	.33	.63	.54	-	-	-	-
MB	4 lags	.76	.48	**2.85**	-	-	-	-
	6 lags	.41	.22	**2.66**	-	-	-	-
M1	4 lags	1.87	.53	1.34	-	-	-	-
	6 lags	1.57	.31	1.00	-	-	-	-
M2	4 lags	.87	.25	1.95	-	-	-	-
	6 lags	1.16	.65	1.40	-	-	-	-

Flexible Exchange Rates (1973.1-1985.4)

Causal Variable		MB*	M1*	IR	DC	MB	M1	M2
MB*	4 lags	-	-	1.52	1 61	1.88	.90	.51
	6 lags	-	-	.99	*2.14*	.69	.68	.46
M1*	4 lags	-	-	1.80	.60	*2.09*	1.89	.70
	6 lags	-	-	1.04	.77	.77	1.22	.60
IR	4 lags	*2.25*	1.56	-	.78	1.79	1.32	.70
	6 lags	1.41	.88	-	*2.03*	.46	.68	.38
DC	4 lags	1.16	1.02	.44	-	-	-	-
	6 lags	1.41	.19	.66	-	-	-	-
MB	4 lags	1.18	1.53	1.50	-	-	-	-
	6 lags	.52	1.18	1.73	-	-	-	-
M1	4 lags	1.05	1.03	1.20	-	-	-	-
	6 lags	*1.96*	1.17	1.02	-	-	-	-
M2	4 lags	.78	1.49	1.52	-	-	-	-
	6 lags	1.68	*2.01*	1.67	-	-	-	-

Note: **Boldface** (5% and 1%) and *italics* (10%) denote significant F-statistics. The variables are: MB* foreign (U.S.) monetary base; M1* foreign (U.S.) narrow money supply; IR international reserves; DC domestic credit; MB monetary base; M1 narrow money supply; M2 wider money supply. All variables are expressed as first differences in logs. Data sources are given at the end of the book.

policies are independent of each other for the fixed exchange rate period. Under flexible rates, real government spending affects only the wider money supply M2. Feedback exists between the implicit price deflators and the narrow money supply M1 under fixed exchange rates. Measures of imported inflation, on the other hand, affect the wider money supply M2. For the flexible exchange rate period, we find support for the anti-inflationary Bundesbank policies after the first oil price shock. Oil prices affect domestic credit and the monetary base with significantly negative coefficients (not reported here). Similarly, import prices cause the monetary base. Depending on the lag specification, some support for a feedback relationship between real output and the money supplies M1 and M2 is detected.

Finally, table 4.7 presents the causal relationships among German and U.S. monetary aggregates.[13] The U.S. monetary aggregates are: MB* the adjusted monetary base; M1* the narrowly defined money supply. For the fixed exchange rate period, U.S. money growth primarily influences German M2, even though marginal effects of M1* on domestic credit and German M1 emerge for some lag specifications. In addition, six lags of M1* cause changes in German international reserves with significantly negative coefficients (not reported here). No feedback exists from German to U.S. monetary aggregates. Under flexible exchange rates, German and U.S. money growth are independent at standard significance levels.

3.4. Open Economy Macroeconomics and Reality: Where Do We Stand?

The causality tests conducted here cannot and shall not replace economic theories about the functioning of the open macroeconomy. After all, "causality" may simply be an indication of lagged relationships between variables and their predictive content, so that a "post-hoc-ergo-propter-hoc" argument may be misleading.

---

[13] Additional tests (not reported here) reject the hypothesis of causality from U.S. money growth to German real output and inflation.

The interpretation of the results is made even more difficult by the sensitivity of the causality tests with respect to lag specification, omitted variables, and linearization. Nevertheless, the tests constitute a useful tool to reveal the underlying causal orderings and check the validity of maintained hypotheses before they are incorporated in a structural model. Accepting these advantages and shortcomings of causality tests, let us summarize and evaluate the major findings about the dynamic relationships characterizing the German economy over the 1960-85 sample period. The major findings of the bivariate tests are presented in tables 4.8a and 4.8b.

Based on the bivariate test results, the small country assumption that German output and prices do not influence their foreign counterparts cannot be rejected for either subperiod (tables 4.1 and 4.4). Considering financial variables, causality from German to foreign short-term interest rates is detected only under fixed exchange rates and is sensitive to the measure of foreign interest rates (table 4.3). Foreign monetary aggregates are independent of German money growth under both exchange rate regimes (table 4.7).

The multivariate tests (table 4.2) for the flexible exchange rate period, on the other hand, detect feedback from blocks of German variables to foreign output and, in one of three cases, to foreign prices. Thus, the existence of spillover effects from the German economy to the rest of the world cannot be ruled out completely, although few German variables directly affect their foreign counterparts. It has been argued that this finding could be the result of the two oil price shocks in the 1970's which affected all major industrialized countries profoundly. With some reservations, then, the small country assumption can be defended in the German case.

The channels through which external impulses have been transmitted to the German economy differ for the two subperiods. Under fixed exchange rates, neither price nor interest arbitrage prevail since German prices and interest rates are independent of their foreign counterparts (tables 4.1, 4.3, and 4.4). In addition, foreign output has no direct effect on German economic growth (table 4.1). The only evidence for the transmission of foreign impulses is found in the monetary sector, where German M2

Table 4.8a

Summary of the Major Findings from Bivariate Causality Tests:
Open Economy Considerations

Null Hypothesis	Fixed Exchange Rates (1960.1-1972.4)	Flexible Exchange Rates (1973.1-1985.4)
Small Country Assumptions		
Y ↛ Y*	accept	accept
P ↛ P*	accept	accept
RS ↛ RS*	accept (Eurodollar rate) reject (U.S. rate)	accept
RL ↛ RL*	accept	accept
M ↛ M*	accept	accept
Channels of Transmission for Foreign Impulses		
Y* → Y	reject	reject
P* → P	reject	accept (PGNE,CPI) reject (PGNP)
RS* → RS	reject	accept
RL* → RL	reject	reject
M* → M	accept (M2 only)	reject
ER → Y	reject	reject
PO → Y	reject	accept (4 lags only)
PO → P	reject	accept (PGNP,PGNE) reject (CPI)
PI → P	reject	accept (PGNP,PGNE) reject (CPI)
Monetary Approach and Sterilization Policy		
DC → IR	reject	-
MB → IR	accept	-
IR → DC	accept (4 lags only)	-
IR → MB	reject	-
IR → E	-	reject
DC → E	-	reject

Note: For definitions of the variables see the text. Granger causality from X to Y is indicated by →. The absence of a causal relationship is denoted by ↛.

Table 4.8b

Summary of the Major Findings from Bivariate Causality Tests:
Domestic Policy Variables

Null Hypothesis	Fixed Exchange Rates (1960.1-1972.4)	Flexible Exchange Rates (1973.1-1985.4)
Causal Role of Money		
M → Y	reject	accept (MB,M1) reject (IR,DC,M2)
DC → P	reject	reject
MB → P	reject (except CPI)	accept (except CPI)
M1 → P	reject (except CPI)	reject
M2 → P	reject	reject (except PGNP,PGNE - 6 lags)
Exogeneity of Policy Variables		
G ↛ M	accept	accept (except M2)
exogenous G	accept	accept
exogenous DC	accept	accept (except PO,E,ER)
exogenous MB	accept	accept (except CPI,PO,PI)
exogenous M1	accept (except PGNP,PGNE - 4 lags)	accept
exogenous M2	accept (except PI)	accept

Note: For definitions of the variables see the text. Granger causality from X to Y is indicated by →. The absence of a causal relationship is denoted by ↛.

responds to changes in U.S. monetary aggregates (table 4.7).

Under flexible exchange rates, we find evidence for the transmission of foreign impulses via prices (tables 4.1 and 4.4). German short-term interest rates are caused by foreign rates without feedback (table 4.3), whereas German monetary aggregates are independent of U.S. money growth (table 4.7). Industrial production in the U.S. does not Granger-cause German economic growth (table 4.1). Nominal and real exchange rate changes do not affect domestic output under either exchange rate regime (table 4.1).

The multivariate tests (table 4.2) generally confirm these results. For the flexible exchange rate period, causality from blocks of foreign variables (Y*, P* or Y*, PO) to German output and prices is detected. Altogether, our findings indicate that the Bundesbank succeeded in maintaining some degree of monetary independence under fixed exchange rates. During the flexible exchange rate period, international shocks are transmitted primarily through capital markets and prices.

Turning to the degree of monetary (in)dependence and the existence of sterilization policies under fixed exchange rates, the evidence (table 4.1) rejects the monetary approach to the balance of payments since domestic credit does not Granger-cause international reserves. However, a significantly negative relationship exists between the monetary base and international reserves (table 4.7). Concerning the use of sterilization policies to assure short-term domestic monetary control, we find supportive evidence since fluctuations in international reserves induce opposite changes in domestic credit (table 4.1). No such relationship exists between international reserves and the monetary base (table 4.7).

For the flexible exchange rate period, the monetary approach to exchange rate determination must be rejected since changes in domestic credit do not lead to exchange rate changes (table 4.1). Instead, the Bundesbank's reaction function for domestic credit includes nominal and real exchange rate changes.

The existence of sterilization under fixed exchange rates implies that the Bundesbank preserved some degree of short-term monetary control. However, the evidence in table 4.5 indicates that domestic monetary control does not necessarily imply a causal role for money in terms of influencing domestic growth and inflation.

Under fixed exchange rates, none of the German monetary aggregates affects domestic output growth significantly. Monetary policy is simply ineffective, as the monetary approach to the balance of payments implies. One explanation is that the Bundesbank's sterilization efforts were ineffective. Another argument suggests that monetary policy under fixed exchange rates was simply accommodating the economic growth of the "Wirtschaftswunder". Of the various inflation measures, only the rate of consumer price inflation responds to changes in the monetary base or the narrow money supply. Beginning in 1973, with greater monetary independence guaranteed by flexible exchange rates, the monetary aggregates cause some measures of domestic growth and inflation.

Finally, domestic policy variables are not completely exogenous with respect to German and foreign variables. Based on bivariate and multivariate test results (tables 4.1 and 4.2), the existence of a fiscal policy reaction function must be rejected for the entire sample period. Similarly, monetary aggregates are exogenous with respect to most other variables under fixed exchange rates (tables 4.1, 4.2, and 4.6). One exception is the significant relationship between M1 and inflation measured by the implicit deflators. Under flexible rates, the reaction functions for the monetary aggregates directly controlled by the central bank include primarily foreign variables. Domestic credit responds to foreign output, oil prices, and nominal/real exchange rates (tables 4.1 and 4.2). The monetary base is influenced by domestic (CPI) and imported (PO, PI) inflation. The overall money supply (M1 or M2) is not influenced systematically by the variables considered (table 4.6). Domestic credit and real federal government spending are mutually independent over the entire sample period (table 4.1). Furthermore, causality from G to other monetary aggregates is detected only for the flexible exchange rate period and M2 (table 4.6), suggesting that German budget deficits were not systematically monetized.

In short, a structural model of the German economy consistent with the sample information should incorporate the small country assumption, allow for the sterilization of exogenous international reserve flows under fixed exchange rates, and include both trade and capital flows as transmission channels for foreign influences. Furthermore, the DM/$ exchange rate can be ignored as a determinant of aggregate spending. Finally, money can be expected to have different effects on output and inflation under the two exchange rate regimes. In chapter V, we specify a full dynamic model of the German economy on the basis of the causality tests presented here.

CHAPTER V

MONETARIST, KEYNESIAN, AND NEW CLASSICAL THEORIES

OF OUTPUT, UNEMPLOYMENT, AND INFLATION IN GERMANY: 1960 - 1985

1. INTRODUCTION

One of the recurring themes in the macroeconomic literature is the controversy about the short-term determinants of output, unemployment, and inflation. Much of the debate has focused on the specification and estimation of a *single* theory, judging the "success" or "failure" of each theory on the basis of the goodness of fit for the estimated reduced-form equation. The dispute among Monetarist, Keynesian, and New Classical economists, however, cannot be considered settled until their respective hypotheses are tested against each other *directly* by using the same data set and nested regression equations.

Recently, a number of authors have presented evidence on the explanatory power of alternative macroeconomic theories in the U.S. economy. Stein (1982b) puts forth a general macrodynamic framework from which the competing statistical hypotheses can be derived as special cases, given certain parameter specifications reflecting the propositions of each school of thought.[1] The results of his direct tests strongly support the Monetarist propositions, while the Keynesian and New Classical hypotheses are rejected by the U.S. data from 1958-79. However, Desai and Blake (1982) argue that the opposite results can be obtained from the same data set when

---

[1]Stein's (1982b) book is the synthesis and extension of many earlier contributions in which he has presented theoretical arguments and empirical evidence pertaining to the Monetarist-Keynesian debate. See Stein (1974,1976,1978,1979).

more appropriate estimation techniques are employed.[2]

In two important contributions, Mishkin (1982a,b) strongly rejects the Policy Ineffectiveness Proposition (PIP) associated with New Classical Economics (NCE). Both anticipated and unanticipated aggregate demand policy variables affect output and unemployment significantly.

Rea (1983) and Turnovsky and Wohar (1984) compare alternative theories of inflation and unemployment over longer time periods. While their models, methods, and estimation periods differ, their conclusions are generally consistent with each other. No single model can explain the U.S. evidence over the entire sample period. In both studies, the Monetarist propositions are strongly supported by the evidence for the later subperiods.[3] For the earlier period, Rea (1983) finds that his Keynesian model outperforms the Monetarist version. Turnovsky and Wohar (1984) report that, while some of the Monetarist propositions hold for the early period, the crucial long-run neutrality of money appears to be violated. In addition, their results reject the Policy Ineffectiveness Proposition for both subperiods.

McKenna and Zannoni (1984) contrast the predictive power of Monetarist and Keynesian explanations of inflation and conclude that the money wage hypothesis fits the data better. Finally, defying both Monetarist and Keynesian views, Benderly and Zwick (1985) find that U.S. inflation over the 1955-82 period was affected significantly by unemployment, money growth, and relative energy prices.

These contributions have advanced the debate among macroeconomists by focusing on the *substantial* disagreements while ignoring differences in the techniques of analysis favored by each school of thought. However, in light of the conflicting empirical evidence for the U.S. economy, the controversy about the short-term macrodynamics between steady states cannot be considered settled. The U.S. findings highlight the need for further research and point toward the importance of changing

---

[2]In an earlier paper, Desai (1981) tests the implications of the Stein (1974) model with data for the U.K. economy from 1881-1965. The results provide only weak evidence in favor of the Monetarist position since the system is found to be seriously misspecified.

[3]Rea (1983) considers the subperiods from 1895-1956 and 1957-79. Turnovsky and Wohar (1984) split their sample into two subperiods from 1923-60 and 1961-82.

policy regimes in trying to resolve the unsettled state of macroeconomics. Few empirical studies using *direct* tests of alternative theories exist, and their numbers are even smaller for economies other than the U.S. economy.

For the German economy, to our knowledge, no such study has been rigorously conducted to this date. In an early attempt, Trapp (1976) sets out to test the Monetarist and Keynesian hypotheses, but quickly refutes the Keynesian framework on theoretical grounds. Similarly, Risch (1980) rejects the Keynesian explanation of stagflation for theoretical reasons and proposes and estimates a Monetarist alternative. Scheide (1984), contrasting Keynesian and New Classical models, rejects the Keynesian specification when it fails the structural stability test. Darrat (1985) compares the relative effects of anticipated and unanticipated money growth on real output, but does not consider Monetarist or Keynesian explanations. Other studies [Gschwendtner (1977), König (1978), Neumann (1981), Batchelor (1982), Hansen (1986)] are concerned with tests of a *single* theory of output, unemployment, or inflation only. Most impulse-theoretic studies focus on the Monetarist-Keynesian controversy about the dominant impulses [Läufer (1975,1977), Dewald and Marchon (1978,1979), Dewald and Gavin (1981), Batten and Hafer (1983)], while Neumann (1978) tests the accelerationist hypothesis by considering anticipated and unanticipated impulses for the determination of output and inflation.

As an important contribution to the ongoing macroeconomic debate, we propose to analyze the aggregate German economy from 1960-85. During this period, the maturing "Wirtschaftswunder" - the economic miracle - of the 1960's turned into a stagflation-ridden economy in the early 1970's. Furthermore, the international monetary system changed fundamentally when the Bretton Woods system of fixed exchange rates was replaced by the current system of managed floating in 1973. Today, Germany continues to experience sluggish output growth accompanied by moderate inflation and record unemployment rates, thus posing the "Wirtschaftsfrage" - the economic riddle - of the 1980's.

Incorporating the evidence from chapter IV, which provides information on the dynamic structure and causal orderings among macrovariables over the 1960-85 sample period, we specify a structural model of the German economy in the tradition of the closed economy versions of Stein (1982b) and Turnovsky and Wohar (1984).

A summary of the model is presented in section 2. The structural equations of the general framework are rationalized and, in some cases, derived explicitely. We discuss the cyclical relationship of output and unemployment. This relationship, also known as "Okun's Law", is crucial for the derivation of the output equations. Section 3 summarizes the key propositions of the competing schools of thought and derives the reduced-form regression equations for output, unemployment, and inflation under Monetarist, Keynesian, and New Classical parameter specifications. Empirical tests of the competing statistical hypotheses are conducted in section 4, using different specifications (money definitions, data frequency, lag length, etc.) of the nested regression equations to check the robustness of the results. In addition, several unanticipated money growth series are generated from univariate and multivariate forecasting equations. The last section contains concluding remarks and proposes an agenda for further research.

2. THE GENERAL THEORETICAL FRAMEWORK

This section outlines the general macrodynamic model used in our subsequent empirical analysis of the short-run dynamics of output, unemployment, and inflation in Germany. The general model implies the competing macroeconomic theories and their respective statistical hypotheses as special cases, which can be derived under certain parameter specifications reflecting each school's key propositions. Apart from open economy modifications, our structural model is similar to the frameworks of Stein (1982b) and Turnovsky and Wohar (1984).[4]

---

[4]Stein's (1982b) model expresses all structural equations in real per capita terms. His empirical analysis, however, considers a non-growing economy where physical capital accumulation and population growth are ignored.

The following equations describe the general framework:

$$y(t) = A(t) \cdot F[K(t), L(t)] \tag{5.1}$$

$$U(t) = \beta_0 t + \beta_1 \ln w(t) \tag{5.2}$$

$$\dot{W}(t) = \omega + \dot{p}*(t) - h \cdot [U(t) - U_e] \tag{5.3a}$$

$$\dot{w}(t) = \omega + \dot{p}*(t) - \dot{p}(t) - h \cdot [U(t) - U_e] \tag{5.3b}$$

$$r(t) = r[y(t), m(t), r_w(t), \dot{e}*(t)] \tag{5.4}$$

$$\dot{p}(t) = \dot{W}(t) + \gamma \cdot ED[y(t), r(t) - \dot{p}*(t), g(t), q(t)] \tag{5.5}$$

$$\dot{p}_\tau^*(t) = E_\tau[\dot{p}(t)/I(\tau)] \quad \text{and} \quad \dot{p}(t) - \dot{p}_\tau^*(t) = \eta(t) \tag{5.6a}$$

$$D\dot{p}*(t) = \delta \cdot [\dot{M}(t) - \dot{p}*(t)] \tag{5.6b}$$

The symbols are: y real output; A level of Hicks-neutral technology; K capital stock; $L = L^S(1-U)$ employment, where L^S is the labor supply, U the unemployment rate; t time trend; W nominal wage rate; $w = W/p$ real wage rate; $\dot{W} = D\ln W$ wage inflation, where $D = d/dt$; $\omega = D\ln A$ Hicks-neutral technical progress; $\dot{p} = D\ln p$ rate of inflation; $\dot{p}* = D\ln p* = \ln p* - \ln p_{-1}$ anticipated inflation rate; r domestic nominal interest rate; r_w foreign nominal interest rate; $r - \dot{p}*$ domestic (ex-ante) real interest rate; $\dot{e}*$ anticipated rate of depreciation, where e is the domestic currency price of foreign exchange; $m = M/p$ real balances, where M is the money stock; $\dot{M} = D\ln M$ money growth; ED excess demand function; g real government purchases of goods and services; $q = e p_w/p$ real exchange rate, where e is the exchange rate, p_w the foreign price level, and p the domestic price level; E_τ expectations operator, where expectations are taken at time τ; $p_\tau^*(t)$ price level anticipated at time τ to prevail at a later time t; $I(\tau)$ information set including all relevant information up to time τ; η white noise error term.

A brief description and explanation of the structural equations is given in the next section. The cyclical relationship between unemployment and output is used in section 2.2 to derive the output supply equation implied by the general model.

2.1. The Structural Equations of the General Model

Real output supply in equation (5.1) depends upon the level of Hicks-neutral technology, the capital stock, and employment. The production function satisfies the usual neoclassical properties of positive and diminishing marginal products:

$$\partial F/\partial K > 0, \quad \partial F/\partial L > 0$$
$$\partial^2 F/(\partial K)^2 < 0, \quad \partial^2 F/(\partial L)^2 < 0$$

Real capacity output $\bar{y}$ is defined as the level of real output consistent with full employment, i.e., the unemployment rate is at its equilibrium value.

$$\bar{y}(t) = A(t) \cdot F[K(t), L_e(t)] = A(t) \cdot F[K(t), L^S(t) \cdot (1-U_e)] \tag{5.1'}$$

where U_e is the natural rate of unemployment.

Our output supply equation does not incorporate the supply side effects of foreign (oil) price shocks. As Leiderman (1980a) shows, equation (5.1) implicitely considers such effects if the underlying labor supply function, derived from utility maximization, includes the relative price of domestic and imported goods as an explanatory variable. Our labor supply function abstracts from foreign price influences for simplicity, so that foreign price shocks can affect the domestic economy only from the demand side.

The labor market is summarized by equations (5.2) and (5.3a,b). The unemployment equation (5.2) can be derived from the relationship between the unemployment rate and the unobservable (percentage) excess supply of labor. Since the measured unemployment rate is non-negative for both positive and negative excess supplies of labor, it must be written as a *function* of the excess supply of labor.

$$U(t) = U\left[\frac{L^S(t) - L(t)}{L^S(t)}\right] \tag{5.2'}$$

where $\partial U/\partial L^S > 0$ and $\partial U/\partial L < 0$, and $U(t) = U_e$ with full employment.

The labor demand function $L(t) = L[w(t), A(t), K(t)]$, with $\partial L/\partial w < 0$, $\partial L/\partial A < 0$, and $\partial L/\partial K > 0$, follows from marginal productivity theory. Utility maximization yields the labor supply function $L^S(t) = L^S[w(t), A(t)]$, where wealth effects and foreign price influences are assumed to be negligible.[5] We postulate that the substitution effect of real wage changes dominates the income effect, i.e., $\partial L^s/\partial w > 0$. In addition, the condition $\partial L^s/\partial A < 0$ implies that technical progress increases the value of leisure time.

After substituting the labor supply and demand functions for L^s and L in equation (5.2'), it can be shown that the unemployment rate depends upon the level of technology, wealth variables, and the real wage rate. In the linear version, technology and the wealth variables are represented by a time trend.

$$U(t) = U[A(t),K(t),w(t)] = \beta_0 t + \beta_1 \ln w(t) \tag{5.2}$$

Deviations of the unemployment rate from the natural rate can be expressed as

$$u(t) = U(t) - U_e = \beta \cdot \ln w(t) \tag{5.7}$$

where the equilibrium real wage w_e is normalized to unity and $\beta = \beta_1$.

Equations (5.3a) and (5.3b) describe the expectations-augmented Phillips curve for nominal and real wage rate changes, respectively. Wages adjust in response to technical change, the state of the labor market, and anticipated or unanticipated inflation. Differencing equation (5.7) and substituting for $D\ln w(t) = \dot{w}(t)$ from (5.3b) results in

$$Du(t) = \beta \cdot D\ln w(t) = \beta\omega - \beta h \cdot u(t) - \beta \cdot [\dot{p}(t) - \dot{p}*(t)] \tag{5.8}$$

so that deviations of unemployment from its equilibrium rate are given by

$$u(t) = \rho\beta\omega + \rho \cdot u(t-1) - \rho\beta \cdot [\dot{p}(t) - \dot{p}*(t)] \tag{5.8'}$$

with $\rho = 1/(1+\beta h)$. It is shown in the next section that equation (5.8) implies a Lucas aggregate supply function.

Equation (5.4), which can be derived from the LM-curve, assumes that the nominal interest rate adjusts quickly to clear the domestic money market. Allowing for currency substitution, the domestic money demand depends positively on real income, and negatively on the opportunity cost of holding domestic and foreign real balances

---

[5]The underlying utility function depends on technology, leisure, and consumption of domestic and imported goods. Foreign prices are assumed to be constant for simplicity and, hence, do not appear in the labor supply function. Leiderman (1980a) relaxes this assumption.

measured by domestic and foreign interest rates and exchange rate expectations.[6] For convenience, the real interest rate is assumed to be constant, so that the negative effect of (expected) domestic inflation on money demand can be captured by the nominal interest rate.

Under fixed exchange rates, exchange rate expectations do not systematically and continuously affect the demand for real balances and, thus, can be ignored. For the flexible exchange rate period, we follow Gutierrez-Camara and Vaubel (1981) and assume that uncovered interest rate parity (UIP) holds in a stochastic version. Expected exchange rate changes can thus be represented by the international interest differential.[7] The interest equation (5.4) simplifies to

$$r(t) - r[y(t),m(t),r_w(t)] \qquad (5.4')$$

If uncovered interest parity is violated due to the existence of a time-variant serially correlated risk premium, the specification of (5.4)' can still be defended by introducing serially correlated error terms.

The inflation rate in equation (5.5) depends on the rate of change of nominal wages, given by equation (5.3a), and the excess demand for domestic output. It is assumed that inflation is the result of cost-push and demand-pull pressures transmitted from one sector of the economy to another. Note that (5.5) can easily be expanded to distinguish between traded and nontraded goods. If import prices are exogenously determined, the overall rate of inflation is a weighted average of

---

[6]Several authors have presented evidence in support of the currency substitution hypothesis for the German money demand function. See Hamburger (1977), Akhtar and Putnam (1980), Vaubel (1980), Boughton (1981), Buscher (1984), and Batten and Hafer (1984). Their measures of international influences on the German money demand include foreign nominal interest rates, the international interest rate differential, the DM/$ forward premium/discount, the DM/$ swap rate, or the spot exchange rate variability.

[7]Empirical support for uncovered interest rate parity is, of course, weak since the question of a non-zero risk premium has not been settled. See Dooley and Isard (1982) for evidence supporting a non-zero risk premium on the DM/$ exchange rate, and Cumby and Obstfeld (1981), Frankel (1983), and Mishkin (1984) for the opposite results.

inflation for "home goods" (i.e., nontraded and export goods) and imported goods.[8] Our specification of equation (5.5) is supported, however, by the findings of Spitäller (1978) and Argy and Spitäller (1980) who report that import price inflation did not contribute significantly to Germany's overall rate of inflation over the 1958-76 sample period.

In an open economy, $ED[\cdot]$ is the excess of planned consumption, investment, government spending, and net exports over actual output (all in real terms). Ignoring wealth effects, consumption $c(t)$ depends positively on real income and negatively on the real interest rate. Investment $i(t)$ fluctuates inversely with the real interest rate. Finally, net exports $nx(t)$ depend negatively on domestic income and positively on the real exchange rate. The latter assumption implies that the Marshall-Lerner condition is satisfied, so that a J-curve effect does not exist. Repercussion effects are ignored in our version of $nx(t)$ since foreign real income is not included as a determinant of the real demand for exports.[9]

Substituting for nominal wage changes from equation (5.3a), the inflation equation can be rewritten as

$$\dot{p}(t) = \omega + \dot{p}*(t) - h \cdot u(t) + \gamma \cdot ED[y(t), r(t) - \dot{p}*(t), g(t), q(t)] \tag{5.5'}$$

where $\omega = DlnA(t)$ is technical progress and $u = U - U_e$.

Equation (5.6a) describes the Muth Rational Expectations (MRE) hypothesis which states that the subjectively anticipated rate of inflation is equal to the mathematical expectation, given all currently available and relevant information. The forecast error η has a zero mean, is serially uncorrelated and independent of any other current variables.

Equation (5.6b) describes the Asymptotically Rational Expectations (ARE) hypothesis which argues that rational economic agents facing risk and uncertainty

---

[8] Spitäller (1978), Aghevli and Rodriguez (1979), Myhrman (1979), and Argy and Spitäller (1980), for example, specify inflation equations in which import prices are considered explicitly.

[9] The causality studies in chapter IV confirm the absence of such repercussion effects.

> "...form an estimate of the equilibrium rate of inflation on the basis of the current monetary input. If the current ... rate of monetary expansion $\mu(0)$ remains constant, and there are no permanent real shocks, the price level will grow at rate $\mu(0)$-n from the current price level $p(0)$. Economic agents do not know if the current rate of monetary expansion will continue, or if real shocks affecting the price level are transitory or permanent. Consequently, they adjust their anticipated rate of inflation slowly towards the current rate of monetary expansion *per capita*, that is, the rate of inflation that will occur if the current rate of monetary expansion *per capita* were to continue."(Stein, 1982b, p. 22)

Asymptotically Rational Expectations (ARE) describe the inability of economic agents to estimate the objective mean of the price distribution in the short term. This "Bayesian error" is serially correlated, but converges to zero with repeated sampling.[10] Thus, in the steady state, Asymptotically Rational Expectations (ARE) converge to Muth Rational Expectations (MRE).

2.2. The Relationship of Output and Unemployment[11]

The production function (5.1) establishes a link between real output and the unemployment rate since employment can be written as $L(t) = L^s(t) \cdot [1-U(t)]$, where L^s is the labor supply and U the unemployment rate. The neoclassical property of

---

[10]The forecast error between the realized price level and its subjective expectation can be decomposed into two parts. The "unavoidable error" is the difference between the realized price level and its mathematical expectation. The "Bayesian error" reflects the difference between the objective mean of the distribution and the subjective estimate of the mean. See Stein (1985, p. 5).

[11]This section grew out of an exchange with Professor Krelle about the theoretical and empirical validity of "Okun's Law." We acknowledge his insightful comments and suggestions. The usual disclaimer for any remaining errors applies.

positive and diminishing marginal products implies $\partial F/\partial L^s = (\partial F/\partial L) \cdot (1-U) > 0$ and $\partial F/\partial U = (\partial F/\partial L) \cdot (-L^s) < 0$, so that output is inversely related to the unemployment rate for a given capital stock, labor supply, and technology.

Define real capacity output $\bar{y}$ as the level of output for which unemployment is at its equilibrium (natural) rate U_e.

$$\bar{y}(t) = A(t) \cdot F[K(t), L^s(t) \cdot (1-U_e)] \qquad (5.1')$$

Consequently, for any production function, the ratio of actual to capacity output is inversely related to the unemployment rate relative to its equilibrium value.

$$y(t)/\bar{y}(t) = \tilde{\tilde{F}}\left[\frac{1-U(t)}{1-U_e}\right] \quad \text{with} \quad \partial\tilde{\tilde{F}}/\partial U < 0 \qquad (5.1'')$$

Consider the Cobb-Douglas production function: $y = (A \cdot K)^a \cdot [L^s(1-U)]^b$, where $a > 0$ and $b > 0$. The ratio of actual to capacity output is $y/\bar{y} = [(1-U)/(1-U_e)]^b$, or, in a log-linear version, $\tilde{\tilde{F}} = (\ln y - \ln \bar{y}) = b \cdot [\ln(1-U) - \ln(1-U_e)]$, where $\partial\tilde{\tilde{F}}/\partial U < 0$, $\partial^2\tilde{\tilde{F}}/(\partial U)^2 < 0$ satisfy the neoclassical properties. Using a first-order Taylor series expansion of the log-linear function $\tilde{\tilde{F}}$ around the equilibrium unemployment rate $U = U_e$, we obtain as an approximation $(\ln y - \ln \bar{y}) \approx -\left[\frac{b}{1-U_e}\right](U-U_e) = G(U-U_e)$, where the ratio of actual to capacity output is negatively related to unemployment deviations from the natural rate. This approximation is valid for any homogenous production function since $\partial G/\partial U < 0$ and $\partial^2 G/(\partial U)^2 = 0$, so that the transformed function continues to be (weakly) concave.

Based on these theoretical considerations about the nature of the relationship between real output and unemployment, Okun (1970) argues that the elasticity of the ratio of actual to capacity output with respect to temporary deviations of the unemployment rate from its equilibrium level is a constant α, which he estimates to be roughly equal to 3.0 for the U.S. economy. This statistical relationship, widely known as "Okun's Law," provides a crude estimate of the output loss associated with a short-run increase in unemployment.[12] Because of the approximation above, a generalized version of the "Law" can be written as

$$\ln y(t) - \ln \bar{y}(t) = -\alpha \cdot [U(t) - U_e] \qquad (5.9)$$

---

[12] See Pearce (1983) for a definition of "Okun's Law."

where $\alpha = b/(1-U_e)$ for the Cobb-Douglas case. Recall that $u(t) = U(t) - U_e$. When unemployment rises above the natural rate by one percentage point, real output will fall relative to capacity output by a factor of α.

Alternatively, "Okun's Law" states that the unemployment rate is positively related to the percentage gap between potential and actual real output in the short term.

$$U(t) = U_e + \frac{1}{\alpha} \cdot [\ln\overline{y}(t) - \ln y(t)] \qquad (5.9')$$

It should be clear that the Okun parameter α is not time-invariant since the "Law" describes a short-term *empirical* relationship which may break down in the long run. The structural instability of α can be interpreted as evidence in favor of the "decoupling" hypothesis which maintains that the relationship between output and unemployment fluctuations changed in the aftermath of the first oil price shock.[13] In recent years, the "hysteresis" debate has focused on the structure of labor markets to explain the persistence of high (European) unemployment rates during the 1980's.

The "Law" furthermore ignores that deviations of output from capacity are also related to fluctuations in labor productivity and in the number of hours worked. Given the relative rigidity of unemployment rates, changes in these omitted variables could explain the breakdown of the Okun relationship in the long run.

If one is willing to accept the generalized version of "Okun's Law," where the parameter α is allowed to change over time, then this short-run link between real output and the unemployment rate can be used to analyze the real sector of the economy in terms of either variable. Combining the "Law" with the unemployment equation (5.8) implied by our structural model, a Lucas aggregate supply curve can be derived.

Taking first differences of equation (5.9) and holding U_e constant, we obtain

$$Dlny(t) = Dln\overline{y}(t) - \alpha \cdot [U(t) - U(t-1)] \qquad (5.10)$$

where $Dlny(t) = lny(t) - lny(t-1)$ is the growth rate of real output. Equivalently,

$$U(t) - U(t-1) = \frac{1}{\alpha} \cdot [Dln\overline{y}(t) - Dlny(t)] \qquad (5.10')$$

---

[13] Reineke (1986), for instance, interprets the slower adjustment of German unemployment in response to output fluctuations during the post-1973 period as

If real capacity output grows exponentially at rate s, then $D\ln\bar{y}(t)=s$ and $\ln\bar{y}(t)=\ln[e^{st}\cdot\bar{y}(0)]=st+\ln\bar{y}(0)$. Since $u(t)=U(t)-U_e$ by definition and, therefore, $Du(t)=U(t)-U(t-1)$, we can use equations (5.9') and (5.10') to substitute for $Du(t)$ and $u(t)$ in the unemployment equation (5.8). Rearranging terms, we obtain

$$D\ln y(t) = \mu + \beta hst - \beta h \cdot \ln y(t) + \alpha\beta \cdot [\dot{p}(t)-\dot{p}*(t)] \qquad (5.11)$$

where $\mu=s-\alpha\beta\omega+\beta h\cdot\ln\bar{y}(0)$. The Lucas supply function is given by

$$\ln y(t) = \rho\mu + \rho\beta hst + \rho\cdot\ln y(t-1) + \rho\alpha\beta\cdot[\dot{p}(t)-\dot{p}*(t)] \qquad (5.11')$$

where $\rho=1/(1+\beta h)$. Real output depends upon its own past, a linear time trend capturing potential output, and unanticipated inflation. Note that the Okun parameter α contributes to the coefficient on unanticipated inflation and is allowed to vary over time.

While equation (5.11') is not a "true" reduced form in the sense of following *directly* from the structural model, it can be viewed as the output-equivalent to the unemployment equation (5.8) in empirical tests. Given the specification of the Phillips curve equations (5.3a) and (5.3b) with *unemployment* deviations as proxy for the state of the labor market, our structural model necessarily implies a Lucas-type *unemployment* equation as the reduced form for the real sector. McCallum (1980), on the other hand, specifies a Phillips curve where wages respond positively to lagged real *output*, presumably a proxy for labor market conditions. When combined with a markup pricing equation, which also includes contemporaneous real output, the Lucas supply function can be derived without the explicit use of "Okun's Law." Implicitely, however, McCallum's Phillips curve is based on the "Law's" inverse relationship between real output and unemployment deviations in the short run.

To conclude this section, consider the empirical evidence regarding the much debated "Law" for the German economy. Bombach (1988) shows that the nature of the output-unemployment relationship changed in the late 1960's or early 1970's, a finding supported by our own estimates. Estimation of equation (5.9') with annual data for real GNP - actual and potential - and the unemployment rate yields the following results:

1960-72: $\quad$ U(t) = .66 + .15 [ln$\overline{y}$(t)-lny(t)] $\qquad$ $\overline{R}^2$ = .401
$\qquad\qquad$ (t=) (4.55) (3.01) $\qquad\qquad\qquad\qquad$ DW = 1.07

1973-85: $\quad$ U(t) = 1.67 + .93 [ln$\overline{y}$(t)-lny(t)] $\qquad$ $\overline{R}^2$ = .537
$\qquad\qquad$ (t=) (1.52) (3.86) $\qquad\qquad\qquad\qquad$ DW = .50

1960-85: $\quad$ U(t) = .32 + .92 [ln$\overline{y}$(t)-lny(t)] $\qquad$ $\overline{R}^2$ = .454
$\qquad\qquad$ (t=) (.43) (4.66) $\qquad\qquad\qquad\qquad$ DW = .38

The estimates indicate that an increase in the output gap during the 1973-85 period implied a much higher increase in the unemployment rate than during the 1960's. The instability of the Okun parameter α is confirmed by the Chow-test result of $F(2,22)=23.09$ (significant at the 1% level). The low Durbin-Watson (DW) statistics indicate that the estimated equation is probably misspecified due to omitted variables and/or nonlinearity.

When estimated in growth form, the misspecification problems are less prominent. Annual regression results for equation (5.10) are presented below. Note that the constant term $s=Dln\overline{y}$ capture the well-documented slowdown in the growth rate of potential real GNP in the 1970's and 1980's.

1960-72: $\quad$ $\dot{y}$(t) = 4.21 - 3.19 [U(t)-U(t-1)] $\qquad$ $\overline{R}^2$ = .746
$\qquad\qquad$ (t=) (14.9) (5.77) $\qquad\qquad\qquad\qquad$ DW = 2.25

1973-85: $\quad$ $\dot{y}$(t) = 3.21 - 1.93 [U(t)-U(t-1)] $\qquad$ $\overline{R}^2$ = .750
$\qquad\qquad$ (t=) (9.04) (6.08) $\qquad\qquad\qquad\qquad$ DW = 2.19

1960-85: $\quad$ $\dot{y}$(t) = 3.85 - 2.40 [U(t)-U(t-1)] $\qquad$ $\overline{R}^2$ = .758
$\qquad\qquad$ (t=) (15.9) (8.72) $\qquad\qquad\qquad\qquad$ DW = 1.66

Again, the Okun parameter α is structurally unstable across the two subperiods based on the Chow-test result of $F(2,21)=3.63$ (significant at the 5% level).

1960-72: $\quad$ [U(t)-U(t-1)] = 1.01 - .24 $\dot{y}$(t) $\qquad$ $\overline{R}^2$ = .746
$\qquad\qquad$ (t=) (5.25) (5.77) $\qquad\qquad\qquad\qquad$ DW = 2.37

1973-85: $\quad$ [U(t)-U(t-1)] = 1.43 - .40 $\dot{y}$(t) $\qquad$ $\overline{R}^2$ = .750
$\qquad\qquad$ (t=) (7.66) (6.08) $\qquad\qquad\qquad\qquad$ DW = 1.60

1960-85: $\quad$ [U(t)-U(t-1)] = 1.31 - .32 $\dot{y}$(t) $\qquad$ $\overline{R}^2$ = .758
$\qquad\qquad$ (t=) (9.38) (8.72) $\qquad\qquad\qquad\qquad$ DW = 1.44

Finally, the results for equation (5.10′) indicate that the sensitivity of unemployment fluctuations with respect to real GNP growth decreased significantly in the 1970's and 1980's.

3. ALTERNATIVE VIEWS OF UNEMPLOYMENT, OUTPUT, AND INFLATION

The general theoretical framework outlined in the previous section implies competing macroeconomic theories about the short-run dymamics of unemployment, output, and inflation as special cases, which can be derived under certain parameter specifications reflecting the propositions of the alternative schools of thought. The key propositions of the opposing views - Montarist [M], Keynesian [K], and New Classical Economics [NCE] - for an open economy are summarized under the following categories:

A. *Money Growth and Inflation*

[M]   Inflation is primarly a monetary phenomenon. A rise in the rate of money growth will increase inflation even when unemployment exceeds the equilibrium rate. Under fixed exchange rates without sterilization policies, the domestic rate of money growth will be endogenously determined.

[K]   Inflation is determined by the "underlying rate of inflation" of unit labor costs and exogenous (supply) disturbances. Unit labor costs, in turn, respond sluggishly to excess demand pressures in the labor market - measured by the "Okun gap" between potential and actual real GNP or, equivalently, by unemployment deviations from the natural rate. If unemployment exceeds the "non-accelerating inflation rate of unemployment" (NAIRU), a monetary (or fiscal) expansion has no effect on the rate of inflation.

[NCE]   Anticipated changes in money growth affect inflation contemporaneously.

B. Money Growth, Unemployment, and Real Output

[M]   Changes in the rate of money growth have significant short-run effects on unemployment and output; under fixed exchange rates, however, this holds only in the presence of sterilization and/or imperfect capital mobility. The equilibrium rate of unemployment is independent of money growth.

[K]   Expansionary monetary and fiscal policies are effective in eliminating an "Okun gap" since wages and prices are sticky in the short run. Since monetary policy affects aggregate demand only indirectly, its primary role is the stabilization of nominal interest rates.

[NCE] Anticipated changes in monetary growth have no real effects independent of the degree of capital mobility and/or the exchange rate regime. Only surprises in the rate of money growth matter.

C. Phillips Curve

[M]   In the short run, a tradeoff exists between accelerations or decelerations of inflation and temporary changes in the unemployment rate; in the long run, however, no such tradeoff exists.

[K]   A negatively sloped Phillips curve exists and is stable over time.

[NCE] There exists no exploitable tradeoff between unemployment and inflation at any time, that is, the Phillips curve is vertical.

D. Effectiveness of Fiscal Policy

[M]   Fiscal policy which is not money-financed has negligible effects on inflation, unemployment, and output because it crowds out private investment spending and/or the export sector.

[K]   Fiscal policy has a direct effect on unemployment and real output since wages
      and prices are sticky in the short run. Under flexible exchange rates and
      perfect capital mobility, however, a fiscal expansion only leads to the
      crowding-out of exports due to an appreciating domestic currency.

[NCE] On average, deviations of unemployment and output from their equilibrium
      values are totally insensitive to demand management policies.

E. Inflationary Expectations

[M]   Inflationary expectations are asymptotically rational in a world
      characterized by risk and uncertainty.

[K]   Due to wage and price stickiness, inflationary expectations change slowly in
      response to changes in the rate of money growth.

[NCE] Expectations are formed rationally on the basis of currently available and
      relevant information. The forecast errors are serially uncorrelated with a
      zero mean.

We will now derive regression equations for inflation, unemployment, and real
output under Monetarist, Keynesian, and New Classical parameter specifications.

3.1. The Monetarist Specification

The reduced-form inflation equation is derived from equations (5.4'), (5.5'),
and (5.6a) of the general model. Substituting (5.4') for the nominal interest rate,
the inflation equation (5.5') can be written as

$$\dot{p}(t) = \omega + \dot{p}*(t) + P[u(t),m(t),\dot{p}*(t),g(t),r_w(t),q(t)] \qquad (M1)$$

$$\text{where } P[\cdot] = -h \cdot u(t) + \gamma \cdot ED(t)$$

A linear version of (M1) is equation (M2), where real balances and the real exchange rate enter logarithmically.

$$\dot{p}(t) = \omega + \dot{p}^*(t) + P_1 u(t) + P_2 \ln m(t) + P_3 \dot{p}^*(t) \tag{M2}$$
$$+ P_4 g(t) + P_5 r_w(t) + P_6 \ln q(t)$$

The Monetarist propositions from above, together with two additional assumptions, impose the following restrictions:

(i)   The "Okun gap," measured by unemployment deviations from the natural rate, has only weak effects on inflation, i.e., $P_1 \approx 0$.

(ii)   Pure (bond-financed) fiscal policy has no real effects since it completely crowds out investment spending and/or exports. Hence, the inflation rate is not affected: $P_4 \approx 0$.

(iii)   Inflationary expectations are asymptotically rational, i.e., equation (5.6b) holds: $D\dot{p}^*(t) = \delta \cdot [\dot{M}(t) - \dot{p}^*(t)]$.

(iv)   It is convenient, but not necessary, to assume a full Fisher-effect. The real interest rate is relatively constant and has only weak effects on excess demand and inflation: $P_3 \approx 0$.

(v)   Trade between Germany and the U.S. and, thus, the DM/$ real exchange rate have little effect on German real spending and inflation.[14] Formally: $P_6 \approx 0$.

Differentiating equation (M2), while imposing the above restrictions, the change in the inflation rate is given by

$$D\dot{p}(t) = D\dot{p}^*(t) + P_2 D\ln m(t) + P_5 \dot{r}_w(t) \tag{M3}$$
$$= \delta \cdot [\dot{M}(t) - \dot{p}^*(t)] + P_2 \cdot [\dot{M}(t) - \dot{p}(t)] + P_5 \dot{r}_w(t)$$

Equation (M3) implicitly assumes that the rate of Hicks-neutral technical progress $\omega = D\ln A(t)$ does not change over time. To relax this assumption, a constant term is required in (M3) and all subsequent inflation equations.

The unobservable anticipated inflation rate can be eliminated by first letting

---

[14] Chapter II presents data on the share of U.S.-German trade. Over the 1960-85 sample period, German exports to the U.S. account for 8.2% of total exports. German imports from the U.S. amount to 9.5% of total imports. In addition, our causality tests in chapter IV indicate that the DM/$ real exchange rate does not contribute significantly to changes in any of the German macrovariables considered.

$\dot{p}*(0)-\dot{p}(0)$ at time $t=0$ and then approximating for $t>0$.[15]

$$D\dot{p}(t) = (\delta+P_2)\cdot[\dot{M}(t)-\dot{p}(t)] + P_5\dot{r}_w(t) \qquad (M4)$$

Letting $D\dot{p}(t)=\dot{p}(t+1)-\dot{p}(t)$ in discrete time and solving for $\dot{p}(t+1)$, inflation can be expressed as a weighted sum of lagged inflation, money growth, and foreign interest rate changes.

$$\dot{p}(t+1) = (1-\delta-P_2)\cdot\dot{p}(t) + (\delta+P_2)\cdot\dot{M}(t) + P_5\dot{r}_w(t) \qquad (M5)$$

Correspondingly,

$$\dot{p}(t) = (1-\delta-P_2)\cdot\dot{p}(t-1) + (\delta+P_2)\cdot\dot{M}(t-1) + P_5\dot{r}_w(t-1) \qquad (M5')$$

where $\dot{p}(t-1)$ represents the lagged inflation rate. Note that the coefficients of lagged inflation and lagged money growth sum to unity. The Monetarist reduced-form inflation equation is consistent with the propositions from above.

Next, the regression equations for unemployment and real output are derived. Equation (5.8'), repeated here as (M6), describes deviations of the unemployment rate from its equilibrium level.

$$u(t) = \rho\beta\omega + \rho\cdot u(t-1) - \rho\beta\cdot[\dot{p}(t)-\dot{p}*(t)] \qquad (M6)$$

Equation (4.11'), repeated here as (M7), is the output equation.

$$\ln y(t) = \rho\mu + \rho\beta hst + \rho\cdot\ln y(t-1) + \rho\alpha\beta\cdot[\dot{p}(t)-\dot{p}*(t)] \qquad (M7)$$

where $\rho=1/(1+\beta h)$, $\mu=s-\alpha\beta\omega+\beta h\cdot\ln\bar{y}(0)$, and t is a time trend. Equations (M6) and (M7) are quasi-reduced form equations for unemployment and output which contain the unobservable unanticipated rate of inflation.

For an approximation of $[\dot{p}(t)-\dot{p}*(t)]$ by observable variables, consider the following. An increase in the rate of money growth will accelerate inflation by raising the excess demand for goods. Given asymptotically rational expectations, the anticipated rate of inflation will rise slowly due to the uncertainty whether the monetary change is transitory or permanent.[16] As the rate of inflation converges to the steady state, the unanticipated component goes to zero. Accordingly, the

---

[15] The approximation loses its validity as $\dot{p}*(t)$ approaches $\dot{p}(t)$.

[16] Stein (1982b, pp. 50-51) argues that there is also a lag between the *expected* rate of inflation and the *risk-adjusted* anticipated rate.

unanticipated rate of inflation can be approximated by

$$\dot{p}(t) - \dot{p}*(t) = \lambda \cdot [\dot{M}(t-1) - \dot{p}(t-1)] = \lambda \cdot \dot{m}(t-1) \tag{M8}$$

where $\dot{m} = \dot{M} - \dot{p}$ is the percentage change in real balances.

Substitution of equation (M8) into (M6) and (M7) yields the regression equations for unemployment and output.

$$u(t) = \rho\beta\omega + \rho \cdot u(t-1) - \rho\beta\lambda \cdot \dot{m}(t-1) \tag{M9}$$

$$\ln y(t) = \rho\mu + \rho \cdot \ln y(t-1) + \rho\alpha\beta\lambda \cdot \dot{m}(t-1) + \rho\beta hst \tag{M10}$$

Recall that $\rho = 1/(1+\beta h)$ and $\mu = s - \alpha\beta\omega + \beta h \cdot \overline{\ln y}(0)$. These reduced-form equations adequately describe the Monetarist propositions discussed earlier.

3.2. The New Classical Specification

When Muth Rational Expectations (MRE) are invoked in equations (5.8') and (5.11'), the New Classical regression equations for unemployment and output can be derived.

$$u(t) = \rho\beta\omega + \rho \cdot u(t-1) - \rho\beta \cdot \eta(t) \tag{NCE1}$$

$$\ln y(t) = \rho\mu + \rho\beta hst + \rho \cdot \ln y(t-1) + \rho\alpha\beta \cdot \eta(t) \tag{NCE2}$$

The key proposition of New Classical Economics (NCE), the Policy Ineffectiveness Proposition (PIP), then follows directly. Taking the mathematical expectation E_{t-1}, unemployment deviations depend only on their own past. Real output depends on a time trend and its own past values.

The forecast error $\eta(t)$ can be shown to be a function of unanticipated money growth, unanticipated fiscal and exogenous disturbances, and the structure of the model. Substituting (5.4') for the nominal interest rate, the inflation equation (5.5') can be written as

$$\dot{p}(t) = \omega + \dot{p}*(t) + P[u(t), m(t), \dot{p}*(t), z(t)] \tag{NCE3}$$

where $P[\cdot] = -h \cdot u(t) + \gamma \cdot ED(t)$ and $z(t)$ is a vector subsuming real government expenditures and foreign variables, such as the interest rate, the real exchange rate, or real exports. Note that (NCE3) corresponds to (M1) derived in the previous section. Assuming that the real interest rate is constant and does not affect excess demand and inflation, a linear version of (NCE3) is

$$\dot{p}(t) = \omega + \dot{p}*(t) + P_1 u(t) + P_2 \ln m(t) + P_3 z(t) \qquad \text{(NCE3')}$$

where real balances enter logarithmically and $P_1 < 0$. Taking expectations E_{t-1} of (NCE3'), the rationally expected rate of inflation $E_{t-1}\dot{p}(t) = \dot{p}*(t)$ is derived:

$$\dot{p}*(t) = \omega + \dot{p}*(t) + P_1 u*(t) + P_2 \ln m*(t) + P_3 z*(t) \qquad \text{(NCE4)}$$

where $*$ indicates the rationally expected value of any variable. Subtracting (NCE4) from (NCE3') yields the unexpected rate of inflation $[\dot{p}(t) - \dot{p}*(t)]$, which corresponds to the forecast error $\eta(t)$ under Muth Rational Expectations (MRE).

$$\eta(t) = P_1[u(t) - u*(t)] + P_2[\ln m(t) - \ln m*(t)] + P_3[z(t) - z*(t)] \qquad \text{(NCE5)}$$

Equation (NCE1) implies that $u*(t) = E_{t-1}u(t) = \rho\beta\omega + \rho \cdot u(t-1)$ and, consequently, $[u(t) - u*(t)] = -\rho\beta \cdot \eta(t)$. By definition, unanticipated real balances can be written as $[\ln m(t) - \ln m*(t)] = [\dot{M}(t) - \dot{M}*(t)] - [\dot{p}(t) - \dot{p}*(t)] = [\dot{M}(t) - \dot{M}*(t)] - \eta(t)$. Substituting these expressions for unanticipated unemployment deviations and real balances in (NCE5) and rearranging terms, the forecast error $\eta(t)$ can be expressed as a function of unanticipated money growth, unanticipated changes in fiscal and foreign variables, and the structural parameters of the model.

$$\eta(t) = \frac{1}{1+\rho\beta P_1 + P_2} \left[P_2[\dot{M}(t) - \dot{M}*(t)] + P_3[z(t) - z*(t)] \right] \qquad \text{(NCE5')}$$

Using (NCE5') in equations (NCE1) and (NCE2), it follows that unemployment and real output only respond to unanticipated changes in domestic policy variables and foreign impulses.

$$u(t) = \rho\beta\omega + \rho \cdot u(t-1) - \frac{\rho\beta}{1+\rho\beta P_1 + P_2} \left[P_2 \cdot U\dot{M}(t) + P_3 \cdot Uz(t) \right] \qquad \text{(NCE1')}$$

$$\ln y(t) = \rho\mu + \rho\beta hst + \rho \cdot \ln y(t-1) + \frac{\rho\alpha\beta}{1+\rho\beta P_1 + P_2} \left[P_2 \cdot U\dot{M}(t) + P_3 \cdot Uz(t) \right] \qquad \text{(NCE2')}$$

where $U\dot{M}(t) = \dot{M}(t) - \dot{M}*(t)$ and $Uz(t) = z(t) - z*(t)$ represent the unanticipated variables.

The regression equation for inflation follows from (NCE4), where $\dot{p}*(t)$ appears on both sides of the equation. Given the definition $\ln m*(t) = \ln M*(t) - \ln p*(t)$, equation (NCE4) can be solved for

$$\ln p*(t) = \frac{1}{P_2}\left[\omega + P_1 u*(t) + P_2 \ln M*(t) + P_3 z*(t)\right] \tag{NCE6}$$

where $u*(t)=E_{t-1}u(t)=\rho\beta\omega+\rho\cdot u(t-1)$ according to (NCE1). Subtracting $\ln p(t-1)$ on both sides of equation (NCE6) yields

$$\ln p*(t)-\ln p(t-1) = \dot{p}*(t) - \dot{p}(t)-\eta(t) \tag{NCE7}$$

$$= \frac{1}{P_2}\left[\omega\cdot(1+\rho\beta P_1) + \rho P_1\cdot u(t-1) + P_3 z*(t)\right] + \ln M*(t) - \ln p(t-1).$$

Since $[\ln M*(t)-\ln p(t-1)]=[\ln M*(t)-\ln M(t-1)]+[\ln M(t-1)-\ln p(t-1)]=\dot{M}*(t)+\ln m(t-1)$, the inflation equation can be derived as

$$\dot{p}(t) = \frac{\omega\cdot(1+\rho\beta P_1)}{P_2} + \rho\,\frac{P_1}{P_2}\cdot u(t-1) + \ln m(t-1) + \dot{M}*(t) + \frac{P_3}{P_2}\,z*(t) + \eta(t) \tag{NCE8}$$

Anticipated money growth as well as anticipated fiscal and foreign impulses affect inflation contemporaneously, given lagged real balances and lagged deviations of the unemployment rate. Recall that $P_1<0$. Note that the reduced-form equation conforms to the NCE propositions listed at the beginning of this section.

3.3. The Keynesian Specification

By differentiating equation (5.5) of the structural model, the Keynesian inflation equation is derived as

$$D\dot{p}(t) = D\dot{w}(t) + \nu_1(t) \tag{K1}$$

where changes in the inflation rate depend on changes in the rate of wage inflation and exogenous disturbances subsumed under $\nu_1(t)$. This formulation stresses the key Keynesian proposition that inflation is directly determined by the "underlying rate of inflation." Changes in monetary and fiscal policy variables affect inflation only indirectly. By influencing the "Okun gap" between potential and actual output, these demand management policies affect the rate of nominal wage inflation. This occurs with a lag, however, given the Keynesian scenario of sticky wages and prices. Using the Phillips curve equation (5.3a), it can be shown that nominal wages respond slowly to changes in unemployment.

$$D\dot{W}(t) = D\dot{p}^*(t) - h \cdot Du(t) \tag{K2}$$

The Keynesian proposition of nominal wage rigidity implies that the coefficient h is relatively small. Furthermore, in a Keynesian world, inflationary expectations adjust slowly to changes in the rate of money growth. The coefficient δ in the ARE-equation (5.6b) of the structural model is relatively small. Thus,

$$D\dot{W}(t) = -h \cdot Du(t) + \nu_2(t) \tag{K2'}$$

where the slow adjustment of inflationary expectations to a new rate of money growth is reflected by $\nu_2(t)$. Combining (K1) and (K2') yields

$$D\dot{p}(t) = -h \cdot Du(t) + \nu_3(t) \tag{K3}$$

where $\nu_3(t) = \nu_1(t) + \nu_2(t)$. Letting $D\dot{p}(t) = \dot{p}(t+1) - \dot{p}(t)$ in discrete time, and solving (K2') for $\dot{p}(t+1)$, we obtain

$$\dot{p}(t+1) = \dot{p}(t) - h \cdot [u(t) - u(t-1)] + \nu_3(t) \tag{K4}$$

and, correspondingly,

$$\dot{p}(t) = \dot{p}(t-1) - h \cdot [u(t-1) - u(t-2)] + \nu_3(t-1) \tag{K4'}$$

The inflation rate thus depends on its own past, lagged changes in unemployment deviations (i.e., the "Okun gap," which affects the "underlying rate of inflation" in money wages), and lagged disturbances reflecting the slow adjustment of inflationary expectations and other exogenous factors.

The regression equations for unemployment and output are obtained from equations (5.8), (5.4'), and (5.5) of the structural model. It follows from (5.8) that changes in unemployment deviations can be expressed as

$$Du(t) = \beta \cdot Dlnw(t) = \beta \cdot [DlnW(t) - Dlnp(t)] \tag{K5}$$

where $DlnW(t) = \dot{W}(t)$ and $Dlnp(t) = \dot{p}(t)$ are the rates of nominal wage and price inflation, respectively. Under the assumption of constant real interest rates, substitution of (5.4') into (5.5) yields

$$\dot{p}(t) = \dot{W}(t) + \gamma \cdot ED[y(t), m(t), r_w(t), g(t), q(t)] \tag{K6}$$

Using (K6) in (K5), we obtain

$$Du(t) = -\beta\gamma \cdot ED[m(t), g(t), z(t)] \tag{K7}$$

where the exogenous factors such as shifts in the foreign export demand are subsumed under z(t). Given the Keynesian scenario of price stickiness, monetary and fiscal policies directly influence real output/excess demand and, hence, the "Okun gap." The output gap, in turn, affects the rates of wage and price inflation with a lag. Solving equation (K7) for u(t), we obtain

$$u(t) = u(t-1) - \beta\gamma \cdot ED[m(t),g(t),z(t)] \tag{K7'}$$

in which the deviations of the unemployment rate from its equilibrium value are negatively related to the excess demand function. Unemployment and real output are linked empirically by "Okun's Law" (5.9) and (5.10'). Note that Du(t)=DU(t) for a constant equilibrium rate U_e. If potential output grows exponentially at rate s, substitution of (5.10') into (K7) gives the output equations.

$$Dlny(t) = s + \alpha\beta\gamma \cdot ED[m(t),g(t),z(t)] \tag{K8}$$

$$lny(t) = s + lny(t-1) + \alpha\beta\gamma \cdot ED[m(t),g(t),z(t)] \tag{K8'}$$

These reduced-form equations for the real sector are consistent with the Keynesian propositions put forth earlier.

4. EMPIRICAL EVIDENCE

The regression equations derived in the previous section will be estimated with quarterly and annual German data from 1960-85, with special consideration to the two subperiods corresponding to the fixed exchange rate regime (1960.1-72.4) and the period of "dirty" floating since the first quarter of 1973. Our analysis of the causal relationships among macrovariables in chapter IV reveals that the nature of these relations in the pre- and post-floating periods differs substantially.

To avoid the observational equivalence problem, we conduct our tests of the competing macroeconomic theories using nested regression equations. Sargent (1976) shows that the existence of deterministic feedback rules for monetary policy causes "natural" (i.e., New Classical) and "unnatural" (i.e., Monetarist and Keynesian) reduced-form equations to be observationally equivalent. Under these circumstances, the policy debate between opposing schools of thought cannot be settled by merely comparing the goodness of fit for each school's equation. A *direct* test of each school's propositions requires nesting their crucial hypotheses in a single regression equation, which allows the data to "speak" unambiguously.

The reduced-form unemployment equations derived for each school of thought are

$$u(t) = \rho\beta\omega + \rho \cdot u(t-1) - \rho\beta\lambda \cdot \dot{m}(t-1) \tag{M9}$$

$$u(t) = \rho\beta\omega + \rho \cdot u(t-1) - \left[\frac{\rho\beta P_2}{1+\rho\beta P_1+P_2}\right] \cdot \dot{UM}(t) - \left[\frac{\rho\beta P_3}{1+\rho\beta P_1+P_2}\right] \cdot Uz(t) \tag{NCE1'}$$

$$u(t) = u(t-1) - \beta\gamma \cdot ED[m(t),g(t),z(t)] \tag{K7'}$$

The Monetarist and NCE specifications are directly opposed due to each school's assumption about the formation of inflationary expectations. Only minor differences exist between the Monetarist and Keynesian specifications, deriving from the debate about the relative effectiveness of monetary and fiscal policies. Emphasizing *substantial* rather than minor differences, we propose the nested unemployment equation:

$$u(t) = a_0 + a_1 u(t-1) + a_2 \dot{m}(t-1) + a_3 \dot{UM}(t-1) + \epsilon_1(t) \tag{R1}$$

where $\dot{UM}=(\dot{M}-\dot{M}\star)=(\dot{M}-E_{-1}\dot{M})$ is unanticipated money growth, and $\dot{m}=\dot{M}-\dot{p}$ denotes the percentage change in real balances. Unanticipated fiscal policy and exogenous real shocks are subsumed under ϵ_1. A direct test of Monetarist versus NCE theories of unemployment amounts to statistical tests of the coefficient estimates in the nested equation (R1). The Monetarist propositions imply $a_2<0$ and $a_3=0$; the NCE view postulates $a_2=0$ and $a_3<0$.

The reason for considering only lagged unanticipated money growth in the nested equation is the nature of the statistical tests to discriminate between competing macro-hypotheses. These direct tests focus on the relative significance of each school's coefficients and their predictive content with respect to the dependent variable. In a recent paper, Granger (1988) argues that "the cause occurs before the effect" (p. 200) and refutes the concept of "instantaneous causation," except when attributable to temporal aggregation of the data or missing causal variables. Consequently, regression equations which test the predictive content of alternative variables in the sense of Granger causality tests should include only lagged regressors.

The reduced-form equations for real output follow directly from the unemployment equations if "Okun's Law" is applied.

$$lny(t) = \rho\mu + \rho \cdot lny(t-1) + \rho\alpha\beta\lambda \cdot \dot{m}(t-1) + \rho\beta hst \qquad (M10)$$

$$lny(t) = \rho\mu + \rho \cdot lny(t-1) + \left[\frac{\rho\alpha\beta}{1+\rho\beta P_1 + P_2}\right] \cdot [P_2 \cdot U\dot{M}(t) + P_3 \cdot Uz(t)] + \rho\beta hst \qquad (NCE2')$$

$$lny(t) = s + lny(t-1) + \alpha\beta\gamma \cdot ED[m(t), g(t), z(t)] \qquad (K8')$$

Again, the Monetarist specification stands in sharp contrast to the NCE version, whereas the Monetarist and Keynesian equations differ only with respect to the role of fiscal policy. The nested output equation can be written as

$$lny(t) = b_0 + b_1 lny(t-1) + b_2\dot{m}(t-1) + b_3 U\dot{M}(t-1) + b_4 t + \epsilon_2(t) \qquad (R2)$$

where unanticipated fiscal policy and exogenous real shocks are represented by ϵ_2. The Monetarist propositions imply $b_2 > 0$ and $b_3 = 0$; the NCE view can be summarized by $b_2 = 0$ and $b_3 > 0$.

Finally, consider the reduced-form inflation equations derived from the general model for each school of thought:

$$\dot{p}(t) = (1-\delta-P_2) \cdot \dot{p}(t-1) + (\delta+P_2) \cdot \dot{M}(t-1) + P_5 \cdot \dot{r}_w(t-1) \qquad (M5')$$

$$\dot{p}(t) = \frac{\omega \cdot (1+\rho\beta P_1)}{P_2} + \dot{M}*(t) + \frac{P_3}{P_2} \cdot z*(t) + lnm(t-1) + \rho \cdot \frac{P_1}{P_2} \cdot u(t-1) + \eta(t) \qquad (NCE8)$$

$$\dot{p}(t) = \dot{p}(t-1) - h \cdot [u(t-1) - u(t-2)] + \nu_3(t-1) \qquad (K4')$$

The Monetarist and Keynesian specifications represent two extreme views of the rate of inflation. To Monetarists, inflation is essentially a monetary phenomenon - apart from foreign influences in the open economy case. Keynesians focus instead on the labor market, which determines the "underlying rate of inflation" in nominal wages independently of the rate of money growth. The NCE version incorporates elements of both extreme views: anticipated money growth affects inflation contemporaneously for given (lagged) unemployment deviations, real balances, and anticipated fiscal and real disturbances. Focusing on the areas of substantial disagreement, the nested inflation equation can be expressed as

$$\dot{p}(t) = c_0 + c_1\dot{p}(t-1) + c_2\dot{M}(t-1) + c_3[u(t-1) - u(t-2)] + c_4\dot{r}_w(t-1) + \epsilon_3(t) \qquad (R3)$$

where ϵ_3 reflects the slow adjustment of inflationary expectations and exogenous demand disturbances. The Monetarist view implies $c_2 > 0$, $c_3 = 0$, and also $c_1 + c_2 = 1$; the Keynesian hypotheses are summarized by $c_2 = 0$ and $c_3 < 0$.

An alternative version of the nested inflation equation incorporates the "underlying rate of inflation" in nominal wages, which responds to changes in the "Okun gap" with a lag according to the Keynesian view.

$$\dot{p}(t) = c_0 + c_1 \dot{p}(t-1) + c_2 \dot{M}(t-1) + c_3 [\dot{W}(t-1) - \dot{W}(t-2)] + c_4 \dot{r}_w(t-1) + \epsilon_3(t) \qquad (R4)$$

Finally, both Monetarists and Keynesians have an argument for considering the phenomenon of imported inflation even though the structural model does not consider foreign rates of inflation explicitly. If foreign nominal interest rates reflect (ex-post) changes in foreign inflation, the nested equations (R3) and (R4) can be re-estimated with lagged foreign inflation $\dot{p}_w$ instead of $\dot{r}_w$. Furthermore, the Keynesian inflation equation (K4') includes the demand side effects of foreign inflation in the error term ν_3. The explicit consideration of $\dot{p}_w$ does not contradict the Keynesian propositions.

4.1. The Unanticipated Money Growth Series

Estimation of the nested regression equations (R1) and (R2) which include both actual variables and unanticipated rates of money growth requires a two-step procedure. First, a forecasting equation for money growth is estimated by ordinary least squares (OLS) and the residuals are calculated. Second, the residuals are used as the unanticipated money growth variable in the nested unemployment and output regression equations.[17]

---

[17]Mishkin (1983, pp. 24-25) argues that joint estimation of the forecasting and reduced-form equations is superior since it results in more efficient estimates and allows tests of both the rationality and neutrality (i.e., policy ineffectiveness) propositions.

The specification of an appropriate unanticipated money growth series is of extreme importance to tests of the New Classical propositions. Barro's (1977,1978) original results for the U.S. economy, for example, have been questioned on the basis of his methodological approach to decomposing actual money growth into its anticipated and unanticipated components [Small (1979), Mishkin (1983)]. In particular, his inclusion of a contemporaneous variable ($FEDV_t$) in the forecasting equation violates the principle of rational expectations that anticipated values should be optimal, one-step-ahead forecasts conditional on available information. Thus, an appropriate forecasting equation should include only lagged explanatory variables.

We adopt Mishkin's (1982a,b,1983) approach for the specification of an anticipated money growth equation. His atheoretical statistical procedure suggests that any particular macrovariable available at time t-1 may be helpful in predicting monetary policy - even if there are no strong theoretical reasons explaining its predictive content.

Several issues relating to the specification and actual estimation of the forecasting equation need to be addressed. First, theory does not indicate whether economic agents rely on seasonally adjusted or unadjusted data when forming their rational expectations. Therefore, we generate unanticipated money growth series from both data sets, which allows us to check the robustness of the results on competing macroeconomic hypotheses later on. Given our seasonally unadjusted data base, the "seasonally adjusted" money growth series are obtained from regressions which include seasonal dummies. Inspection of the residual autocorrelation functions and a plot of their correlograms shows no apparent seasonal pattern, indicating that this method of seasonal adjustment is sufficient.

Second, the move from fixed to flexible exchange rates in 1973 amounts to a monetary regime break for the non-reserve-currency countries, enabling them - in principle - to pursue domestic monetary policies independent of balance of payments considerations. Thus, it is conceivable that the anticipated money growth equations are structurally unstable across the two exchange rate regimes, a hypothesis confirmed by the significant Chow F-tests for all four specifications of the forecasting equation considered below. Hence, we estimate separate forecasting equations for the two subperiods and also for the entire sample period.[18]

Third, the robustness of the results from the atheoretical unanticipated money growth series can be checked by employing several specifications of the forecasting equation. The simplest version is a univariate autoregressive model of the following form:

$$\dot{M}(t) = \alpha_0 + \sum_{i=1}^{N} \alpha_i \dot{M}(t-i) + \epsilon(t)$$

where $\dot{M}$ is the quarterly rate of money growth. Using two alternative money definitions, regression results for the univariate model are reported below.

The version with seasonally unadjusted data (table 5.1a) uses six autoregressive terms to guarantee white noise residuals. In addition to the Box-Pierce Q-test, which has been proven unreliable for sample sizes larger than ours (Chatfield, 1980, p. 79), we report the residual autocorrelation functions r_k up to lag $k=20$ in table 5.1b. Under the null hypothesis of white noise residuals, r_k is distributed asymptotically normal with an approximate 95% confidence limit of $+/-(2/\sqrt{T})$, where T is the number of observations. Thus, as Chatfield (1980, p. 25) points out: "One can expect to find one 'significant' value on average [among the first twenty autocorrelation coefficients] even when the time series really is random." Our data reveal only one marginally significant autocorrelation coefficient at an arbitrary non-seasonal lag, so the residuals are considered white noise for this particular forecasting equation.

The "seasonally adjusted" version (table 5.2) simply adds seasonal dummies to the univariate model described above and continues to use seasonally unadjusted data. A fourth-order autoregressive process is sufficient to generate white noise residuals, as the Q-test and an inspection of the sample autocorrelation functions (not reported here) indicate.

---

[18]These considerations were inspired by the comments of an anonymous referee, which are hereby gratefully acknowledged.

Table 5.1a

Univariate Money Growth Equations:
Seasonally Unadjusted (NSA) Data

$$\dot{M}(t) = \alpha_0 + \sum_{i=1}^{6} \alpha_i \dot{M}(t-i) + \epsilon(t)$$

	Monetary Base (MB)			Money Supply (M1)		
	Fixed Rates	Flexible Rates	Entire Period	Fixed Rates	Flexible Rates	Entire Period
Constant	.65 (.74)	.55 (*1.87*)	1.19 (**2.88**)	1.09 (*1.90*)	1.28 (**2.65**)	1.46 (**4.13**)
$\dot{M}(-1)$	-.41 (**2.53**)	.64 (**4.57**)	-.14 (1.35)	.33 (**2.12**)	.33 (**2.15**)	.33 (**3.19**)
$\dot{M}(-2)$	.11 (.64)	-.48 (**3.78**)	.17 (*1.69*)	-.08 (.55)	-.03 (.19)	-.05 (.51)
$\dot{M}(-3)$	.11 (.70)	.53 (**3.65**)	.01 (.08)	-.13 (1.59)	-.20 (**2.41**)	-.23 (**4.08**)
$\dot{M}(-4)$	.66 (**4.17**)	.11 (.76)	.43 (**4.71**)	.84 (**10.47**)	.79 (**9.53**)	.76 (**13.67**)
$\dot{M}(-5)$	.36 (*1.94*)	.13 (.97)	.10 (.97)	-.48 (**3.19**)	-.48 (**3.28**)	-.51 (**5.26**)
$\dot{M}(-6)$	-.12 (.70)	-.27 (**2.53**)	-.25 (**2.46**)	-.03 (.17)	-.17 (1.07)	-.13 (1.19)
$\bar{R}^2$	.375	.582	.217	.873	.829	.842
Q	12.08	6.00	34.36	19.92	11.56	27.06
DW	2.05	2.04	2.10	2.05	2.05	2.02
Dh	-	-.47	-	-	-	-
CHOW	-	-	**10.25**	-	-	**3.38**

Note: $\dot{M}(-i)$ is the rate of money growth for the i-th lagged quarter. Absolute values of t-statistics are given in parantheses below the coefficient estimates. Significance at the 5% (or higher) level is indicated by **boldface**, at the 10% level by *italics*. The Q-statistic provides a crude test of the null hypothesis that the residuals are white noise. The Durbin-Watson statistic (DW) tests for the absence of first-order serial correlation; Durbin's h-statistic (Dh) provides a correct test for first-order autocorrelation when the list of regressors includes lagged dependent variables. CHOW reports the results of the Chow F-test for structural stability of the coefficient estimates across different subperiods.

Table 5.1b

Sample Autocorrelation Coefficients for
Unanticipated Univariate Money Growth Series
(Based on NSA Data)

Lag	Monetary Base (MB) Fixed Rates	Flexible Rates	Entire Period	Money Supply (M1) Fixed Rates	Flexible Rates	Entire Period
1	-.057	-.059	-.067	-.033	-.061	-.010
2	.173	.132	.085	.007	.050	.022
3	.183	-.025	.068	.199	.101	.094
4	-.111	.108	-.154	-.262	-.107	-.190
5	.147	-.017	.064	.070	.113	.099
6	-.026	-.112	-.037	.123	-.021	.061
7	-.113	.114	-.075	.059	.103	.090
8	.136	.061	.189	-.004	-.123	-.068
9	-.215	-.015	-.160	-.013	.048	-.085
10	-.027	.018	-.002	-.153	.165	.028
11	-.076	.040	-.127	-.058	.200	.119
12	.091	.098	.169	.051	-.135	-.045
13	.045	-.056	.043	-.090	-.031	.108
14	.040	.035	-.067	.310	.023	.071
15	.096	-.094	.139	.076	-.171	-.018
16	.070	.112	-.114	-.067	.055	-.072
17	-.031	-.017	-.002	.076	.019	.021
18	-.049	-.016	.110	-.195	.000	-.074
19	-.050	.125	-.198	-.070	-.133	-.155
20	-.020	-.023	.146	-.011	.137	.186
S.E.	.298	.295	.203	.298	.295	.203
Observations	45	46	97	45	46	97

Note: The 95% confidence interval is computed as S.E. = +/-(2/$\sqrt{T}$), where T is the number of observations. **Boldface** indicates significant autocorrelation coefficients.

Table 5.2

Univariate Money Growth Equations:
Seasonally Adjusted (SA) Data

$$\dot{M}(t) = \alpha_0 + \sum_{i=1}^{4} \alpha_i \dot{M}(t-i) + \sum_{j=1}^{3} s_j SEAS(j) + \epsilon(t)$$

	Monetary Base (MB)			Money Supply (M1)		
	Fixed Rates	Flexible Rates	Entire Period	Fixed Rates	Flexible Rates	Entire Period
Constant	-2.27 (**2.96**)	-.38 (.94)	-.35 (.76)	-5.47 (**4.71**)	-6.11 (**4.55**)	-4.50 (**5.61**)
$\dot{M}(-1)$	-.32 (**2.01**)	.46 (**2.94**)	-.14 (1.31)	.43 (**2.82**)	.48 (**2.98**)	.38 (**3.66**)
$\dot{M}(-2)$	.61 (**3.84**)	-.01 (.05)	.32 (3.03)	.01 (.04)	-.07 (.41)	.004 (.04)
$\dot{M}(-3)$	.43 (**2.40**)	.17 (1.05)	.12 (1.16)	.13 (.74)	.01 (.07)	-.08 (.74)
$\dot{M}(-4)$	-.10 (.58)	-.01 (.07)	.15 (1.41)	.05 (.30)	.10 (.64)	.20 (*1.87*)
SEAS(2)	3.45 (**3.65**)	.74 (*1.75*)	1.26 (**2.70**)	10.38 (**5.45**)	11.28 (**4.50**)	8.88 (**6.53**)
SEAS(3)	5.17 (**6.47**)	2.05 (**4.59**)	2.28 (**4.57**)	5.99 (**4.24**)	5.77 (**4.33**)	5.28 (**5.57**)
SEAS(4)	3.76 (**5.31**)	1.18 (**2.92**)	1.80 (**4.02**)	8.74 (**4.15**)	10.90 (**4.15**)	7.52 (**5.07**)
$\bar{R}^2$	.668	.531	.332	.906	.868	.856
Q	14.49	22.29	23.39	16.65	14.62	*36.67*
DW	1.92	2.01	1.97	1.95	1.93	1.85
Dh	-	-	-	-	-	-
CHOW	-	-	**18.48**	-	-	**6.53**

Note: $\dot{M}(-i)$ is the rate of money growth for the i-th lagged quarter. Absolute values of t-statistics are given in parantheses below the coefficient estimates. Significance at the 5% (or higher) level is indicated by **boldface**, at the 10% level by *italics*. SEAS(j) represents a seasonal dummy for the j-th quarter. See table 5.1a for further notes. Visual inspection of the autocorrelation coefficients (not reported here) confirms that all unanticipated money growth series are white noise.

Alternatively, multivariate forecasting models are specified by using the Granger "causality" test to ascertain the predictive content of information for several plausible macrovariables. By definition (Granger, 1969), a variable Y is Granger-caused by another variable X if predictions of Y based on past values of X *and* Y are better than predictions based on past values of Y alone. If X Granger-causes Y, it should be included as an explanatory variable in a forecasting equation for Y. Note that Granger "causality" is not interpreted here in the sense of economic causality, but rather as a concept of predictive content.

The Granger-criterion involves regressing money growth on a constant and its own four lags (to ensure white noise residuals) as well as four lagged values of the following nine macrovariables: real GNP growth, inflation, import price inflation, the growth of real government expenditures, the real federal budget deficit, the unemployment rate, a short-term interest rate, the balance on current account, and the DM/$ spot exchange rate. Data for these macrovariables are easily and cheaply available to economic agents and researchers trying to predict monetary policy. The multivariate forecasting equation is:

$$\dot{M}(t) = \alpha_0 + \sum_{i=1}^{4} \alpha_i \dot{M}(t-i) + \sum_{j=1}^{N} \sum_{i=1}^{4} \beta_{ji} X_j(t-i) + \epsilon(t)$$

where the X_j's represent the N macrovariables with possible predictive content. Only variables that are jointly significant at the 5% (or higher) significance level are retained in the forecasting equation.

The F-statistics for the predictive content test are reported in table 5.3. Since the Mishkin-procedure, applied to a list of nine macrovariables, quickly depletes degrees of freedom available for estimation, the significant macrovariables have to be identified from causality tests for the entire sample period. Estimation of the resulting forecasting equations, however, proceeds separately for the two subperiods to allow for the monetary regime break in 1973. A stepwise procedure, which would avoid the degrees of freedom problem, is inferior to the Mishkin-procedure since the order in which the macrovariables are added to the forecasting equation might bias the results of the predictive content test.

Table 5.3

Multivariate Money Growth Equations:
F-Statistics for Significant Predictive Content

$$\dot{M}(t) = \alpha_0 + \sum_{i=1}^{4} \alpha_i \dot{M}(t-i) + \sum_{j=1}^{9} \sum_{i=1}^{4} \beta_{ji} X_j(t-i) + \epsilon(t)$$

Potential Money Growth Predictors	Monetary Base (MB)		Money Supply (M1)	
	NSA Data	SA Data	NSA Data	SA Data
Money Growth	**9.47**	**9.10**	**5.25**	1.11
Real GNP Growth	**5.62**	**4.57**	*2.79*	*3.78*
Inflation Rate	*2.09*	2.00	1.87	*2.66*
Import Price Inflation	.62	.64	1.27	1.14
Growth of Gvt. Spending	**3.55**	**2.80**	.83	.31
Unemployment Rate	**4.51**	**2.99**	*2.05*	1.07
Short-Term Interest Rate	**8.22**	**8.08**	**13.41**	**13.02**
Real Budget Deficit	1.43	1.32	1.90	1.16
Current Acct. Balance	1.70	1.73	.41	1.67
Exchange Rate (DM/$)	1.56	1.44	**2.52**	**2.26**
$\bar{R}^2$	.634	.623	.920	.936
Q	24.56	27.91	29.40	31.02
DW	2.12	2.09	1.76	1.78
Dh	-	-	-	-
Dm(AR1)	.66	.25	2.10	*2.84*
Dm(AR4)	1.22	.99	.87	1.26

Note: The F-statistics test the hypothesis that the coefficients of the four lagged values of each macrovariable are jointly equal to zero. Significance at the 5% (or higher) level is indicated by **boldface**, at the 10% level by *italics*. Durbin's m-statistic (Dm) tests the hypothesis of no first (AR1) or fourth-order (AR4) autocorrelation. The sample period is 1962.1-1985.4. The regressions for SA data use seasonally unadjusted data and include three seasonal dummies in the forecasting equation. See table 5.1a for further notes.

The F-tests indicate that the monetary base equation should include real GNP growth, the growth of real government spending, the unemployment rate, and the interest rate as money growth predictors. This specification evolves for both seasonally adjusted and unadjusted data. The F-tests for the seasonally unadjusted M1-equation identify real GNP growth, the unemployment rate, and the exchange rate as significant predictors. In the "seasonally adjusted" version, the inflation rate must be added to this list of predictive content variables.

Using seasonally unadjusted data, the multivariate forecasting equations for money growth are estimated, and the results are reported in tables 5.4a and 5.4b. The resulting unanticipated series are all white noise, as shown by the Box-Pierce Q-statistics and the residual autocorrelation functions (not reported here). The null hypothesis of structural stability across the two exchange rate regimes must be rejected in every case. When compared to the corresponding univariate models in table 5.1a, the multivariate forecasting equations exhibit a higher coefficient of determination.

The same statements can be made for the "seasonally adjusted" versions of the multivariate equations in tables 5.5a and 5.5b. Caution should be exercised, however, when interpreting individual coefficient estimates. Variables are included in the forecasting equations for their *predictive content* only, without any implication for the complex issue of economic causality. The critical reader might object to the inclusion of lagged inflation rates in the M1-equation (table 5.5b), since they exhibit significantly *positive* coefficients at most lags. One interpretation suggests that a "perverse" central bank responds to increased inflation by accelerating the rate of money growth. Yet, as Sims (1980) mentions, the interpretation of individual coefficients is difficult due to the reduced-form nature of the estimated model.

Table 5.4a

Multivariate NSA Money Growth Equations:
Monetary Base (MB)

Money Growth Predictors	Lag	Fixed Rates (1961.2-1972.4)	Flexible Rates (1974.1-1985.4)	Entire Period (1961.2-1985.4)
Constant		.616 (.35)	7.551 (__4.51__)	.887 (1.35)
Money Growth	1	-.499 (__2.60__)	-.291 (1.59)	-.389 (__3.49__)
(MB)	2	.548 (__2.55__)	-.280 (1.39)	.454 (__3.76__)
	3	.523 (__2.49__)	.033 (.16)	.417 (__3.82__)
	4	-.005 (.03)	-.172 (1.24)	.099 (.89)
Real GNP Growth	1	.084 (.65)	-.054 (.58)	.038 (.50)
	2	.028 (.21)	-.124 (1.49)	-.099 (1.39)
	3	.118 (.87)	-.052 (.58)	.056 (.71)
	4	.178 (*1.69*)	-.103 (1.38)	.127 (__2.02__)
Growth of Real	1	-.025 (.68)	-.034 (1.30)	.007 (.28)
Gvt. Spending	2	-.058 (1.40)	-.054 (*1.85*)	-.017 (.65)
	3	-.067 (*1.92*)	-.063 (__2.39__)	-.053 (__2.19__)
	4	-.027 (.93)	-.033 (1.47)	-.019 (.91)
Unemployment Rate	1	-.503 (.56)	-.318 (.95)	-.571 (*1.71*)
	2	-.208 (.20)	.179 (.43)	-.184 (.46)
	3	1.554 (1.49)	.474 (1.14)	.985 (__2.48__)
	4	-1.116 (1.30)	-.674 (*1.86*)	-.304 (.86)
Short-Term	1	-.514 (*1.89*)	-.606 (__4.47__)	-.536 (__4.04__)
Interest Rate	2	.107 (.27)	.302 (1.28)	.165 (.72)
	3	.570 (1.43)	-.047 (.20)	.341 (1.57)
	4	-.099 (.32)	-.053 (.36)	.052 (.34)

Statistics:				
	$\bar{R}^2$	.689	.758	.610
	Q-test	11.39	22.99	31.52
	DW	2.11	1.83	2.03
	Dh	-	-	-
	CHOW	-	-	__11.13__

Note: The figures in parantheses are absolute values of t-statistics. Significance at the 5% level (or higher) is indicated by __boldface__, at the 10% level by *italics*. See table 5.1a for additional notes. Visual inspection of the autocorrelation coefficients (not reported here) confirms that the series for unanticipated monetary base growth are white noise.

Table 5.4b

Multivariate NSA Money Growth Equation:
Money Supply (M1)

Money Growth Predictors	Lag	Fixed Rates (1961.2-1972.4)	Flexible Rates (1974.1-1985.4)	Entire Period (1961.2-1985.4)
Constant		1.407 (.22)	2.883 (1.16)	.826 (.91)
Money Growth (M1)	1	-.170 (1.11)	-.155 (.87)	-.121 (1.56)
	2	.113 (.74)	-.007 (.04)	-.113 (1.51)
	3	-.192 (1.40)	-.248 (*1.91*)	-.275 (**3.87**)
	4	.424 (**2.74**)	.397 (**3.41**)	.535 (**7.29**)
Real GNP Growth	1	.222 (**2.51**)	-.082 (.58)	.100 (1.42)
	2	.078 (.85)	-.256 (1.62)	.094 (1.27)
	3	.144 (*1.70*)	-.183 (1.08)	.103 (1.41)
	4	.253 (**3.05**)	.145 (.90)	.224 (**3.22**)
Short-Term Interest Rate	1	-.538 (**2.39**)	-1.044 (**3.23**)	-.723 (**5.39**)
	2	.032 (.09)	1.109 (**2.39**)	.372 (1.61)
	3	.055 (.16)	-.685 (1.43)	-.293 (1.28)
	4	.521 (**2.03**)	.514 (*1.83*)	.690 (**4.64**)
Exchange Rate (DM/$)	1	1.625 (.53)	-1.488 (.77)	-1.499 (1.21)
	2	-7.950 (1.65)	-1.521 (.57)	-1.482 (.74)
	3	4.752 (.95)	1.799 (.75)	1.230 (.61)
	4	1.345 (.38)	1.059 (.63)	1.815 (1.44)
Statistics:	$\bar{R}^2$	.913	.917	.907
	Q-test	20.52	9.33	16.36
	DW	1.95	1.82	1.80
	Dh	-	-	1.60
	CHOW	-	-	**5.65**

Note: The figures in parantheses are absolute values of t-statistics. Significance at the 5% (or higher) level is indicated by **boldface**, at the 10% level by *italics*. See table 5.1a for additional notes. Visual inspection of the autocorrelation coefficients (not reported here) confirms that the series for unanticipated money growth are white noise.

Table 5.5a

Multivariate SA Money Growth Equation:
Monetary Base (MB)

Money Growth Predictors	Lag	Fixed Rates (1961.2-1972.4)	Flexible Rates (1974.1-1985.4)	Entire Period (1961.2-1985.4)
Constant		-1.004 (.43)	6.609 (**3.10**)	1.514 (1.55)
Money Growth	1	-.471 (**2.39**)	-.257 (1.31)	-.378 (**3.33**)
(MB)	2	.589 (**2.67**)	-.217 (1.02)	.457 (**3.72**)
	3	.523 (**2.44**)	-.072 (.31)	.406 (**3.67**)
	4	-.024 (.12)	-.135 (.90)	.094 (.83)
Real GNP Growth	1	.063 (.45)	-.033 (.33)	.030 (.38)
	2	.108 (.75)	-.046 (.42)	-.079 (.99)
	3	.108 (.75)	-.049 (.42)	.044 (.50)
	4	.122 (.93)	-.119 (1.13)	.154 (*1.90*)
Growth of Real	1	-.024 (.62)	-.045 (1.50)	.002 (.07)
Gvt. Spending	2	-.047 (1.06)	-.053 (*1.75*)	-.017 (.62)
	3	-.085 (**2.11**)	-.062 (**2.12**)	-.061 (**2.36**)
	4	-.039 (1.25)	-.038 (1.54)	-.016 (.74)
Unemployment Rate	1	-.196 (.20)	.192 (.37)	-.498 (1.01)
	2	-.772 (.70)	-.371 (.52)	-.393 (.59)
	3	2.083 (*1.79*)	.246 (.35)	1.442 (**2.16**)
	4	-1.363 (1.42)	-.401 (.83)	-.630 (1.30)
Short-Term	1	-.456 (1.49)	-.644 (**4.21**)	-.539 (**3.88**)
Interest Rate	2	.204 (.45)	.369 (1.30)	.208 (.85)
	3	.314 (.72)	-.105 (.39)	.279 (1.21)
	4	-.012 (.04)	-.031 (.20)	.066 (.42)
SEAS(2)		1.783 (.68)	.302 (.24)	-.748 (.73)
SEAS(3)		4.089 (1.43)	2.172 (1.22)	-.273 (.22)
SEAS(4)		-.007 (.002)	.974 (.65)	-1.356 (1.01)
Statistics:	$\bar{R}^2$	.685	.748	.601
	Q-test	10.96	15.85	31.91
	DW	2.10	1.83	2.02
	Dh	-	-	-
	CHOW	-	-	11.59

Note: The figures in parantheses are absolute values of t-statistics. Significance at the 5% (or higher) level is indicated by **boldface**, at the 10% level by *italics*. See table 5.1a for more notes. Visual inspection of the autocorrelation coefficients (not reported here) confirms that the series for unanticipated monetary base growth are white noise. SEAS(i) represents a seasonal dummy for the i-th quarter.

Table 5.5b

Multivariate SA Money Growth Equation:
Money Supply (M1)

Money Growth Predictors	Lag	Fixed Rates (1961.2-1972.4)	Flexible Rates (1974.1-1985.4)	Entire Period (1961.2-1985.4)
Constant		2.971 (.53)	-2.317 (.72)	-1.718 (1.43)
Money Growth (M1)	1	-.111 (.59)	-.337 (1.41)	-.131 (1.11)
	2	-.380 (2.13)	-.304 (1.41)	-.155 (1.30)
	3	.073 (.39)	.224 (1.41)	-.006 (.05)
	4	-.248 (1.39)	-.162 (1.08)	.105 (1.10)
Real GNP Growth	1	.203 (2.16)	.211 (1.51)	.119 (1.87)
	2	.205 (2.47)	-.451 (2.78)	.039 (.60)
	3	.203 (2.24)	-.078 (.43)	.194 (2.95)
	4	.222 (2.43)	-.185 (1.03)	.160 (2.33)
Inflation Rate (GNP Deflator)	1	.254 (2.24)	1.121 (3.73)	.240 (2.32)
	2	.407 (3.42)	.377 (1.16)	.355 (3.35)
	3	.435 (3.79)	-.163 (.48)	.302 (3.01)
	4	.360 (3.41)	.278 (.93)	.293 (3.19)
Short-Term Interest Rate	1	-.805 (3.74)	-1.474 (4.92)	-.907 (6.57)
	2	.124 (.41)	1.150 (2.78)	.460 (1.93)
	3	-.044 (.15)	-.236 (.56)	-.005 (.02)
	4	.352 (1.53)	.118 (.49)	.282 (1.81)
Exchange Rate (DM/$)	1	-1.174 (.48)	-.884 (.50)	-.318 (.30)
	2	-4.779 (1.21)	-.852 (.38)	-1.692 (.99)
	3	5.489 (1.25)	.970 (.50)	1.537 (.90)
	4	-1.058 (.36)	.270 (.18)	.386 (.35)
SEAS(2)		8.311 (2.99)	13.848 (3.20)	3.958 (2.42)
SEAS(3)		4.544 (2.18)	3.916 (1.75)	2.480 (2.39)
SEAS(4)		10.308 (3.62)	13.065 (3.29)	7.822 (4.99)

Statistics:				
	$\bar{R}^2$	.952	.951	.935
	Q-test	23.38	10.29	21.56
	DW	2.15	2.02	1.87
	Dh	-	-	-
	CHOW	-	-	10.51

Note: The figures in parantheses are absolute values of t-statistics. Significance at the 5% (or higher) level is indicated by **boldface**, at the 10% level by *italics*. See table 5.1a for more notes. Visual inspection of the autocorrelation coefficients (not reported here) confirms that the series for unanticipated money growth are white noise. SEAS(i) represents a seasonal dummy for the i-th quarter.

4.2. Technical Notes

The nested regression equations (R1), (R2), (R3), and (R4) are tested with annual and seasonally unadjusted quarterly data. The quarterly equations include three seasonal dummies in addition to the listed explanatory variables. This method of seasonal adjustment is found to be sufficient in eliminating any seasonal spikes in the residual autocorrelation functions.

In addition, the quarterly regressions include four lags of all explanatory variable instead of just one, as shown for the reduced-form equations. This approach can be justified on several grounds. First, the existence of long and variable lags in the effects of money on inflation and the real sector is well-documented.[19] Second, all studies of competing macroeconomic hypotheses for the U.S. have been conducted with annual data. By including four quarterly lags, we allow for similar dynamics in the German case. Finally, the structural model was conceived as an annual model, so that quarterly regressions with only one quarterly lag cannot be expected to yield sensical parameter estimates.

The percentage changes in variables are computed as quarter-to-quarter changes which generally have a poor signal-to-noise ratio. This problem could be avoided by computing overlapping changes between corresponding quarters of consecutive years. However, this procedure generates a moving average process in the residual and reduces the degrees of freedom available for estimation. Hence we re-estimate all equations with annual data, including only one lag for each explanatory variable. Due to the limited number of annual observations, the annual regressions are run over the entire sample period only. A dummy variable REGIME is included to capture the transition from fixed to flexible exchange rates in 1973.

Estimation proceeds using ordinary least squares (OLS). Since all regression equations contain lagged dependent variables as regressors, the Durbin-Watson (DW)

---

[19] See, for example, our findings on the causal relationship between monetary aggregates and prices in chapter IV.

test has reduced power and is biased against the detection of first-order serial correlation. A correct test for autocorrelation is Durbin's h-test (Dh), which has a standard normal asymptotic distribution N(0,1) under the null hypothesis of no serial correlation.

$$Dh = \rho_1 \left[\frac{T}{1 - T \cdot Var(\beta_1)} \right]^{1/2} \approx N(0,1)$$

The symbols are: ρ_1 estimated first-order correlation coefficient; T number of observations; $Var(\beta_1)$ estimated variance of the coefficient on the lagged dependent variable. The h-statistic is not defined when $T \cdot Var(\beta_1) > 1$. In addition, the test cannot detect fourth order autocorrelation often associated with quarterly data. An alternative procedure, Durbin's m-test (Dm), involves regressing the estimated residuals on their own lagged values as well as all regressors included in the original equation. The significance of the lagged first and fourth residual coefficients can then be tested using standard least squares methods.[20]

When the presence of serial correlation is detected, we re-estimate the equation using Hatanaka's (1974) two-step estimator (HAT). The standard procedures to correct for first-order autocorrelation (e.g., Cochrane-Orcutt) may generate inconsistent estimates since the initial OLS estimates will be inconsistent. The Hatanaka procedure, which involves instrumental variables regression to instrument out the lagged dependent variable, guarantees asymptotically efficient estimates. But for the instrumental variable results, Durbin's h-test is no longer recommended as a test for serial correlation.[21]

The validity of competing statistical hypotheses is evaluated on the basis of the significance of estimated coefficients. For quarterly data, we also consider the significance of the sum of estimated coefficients as well as F-tests (χ^2-tests for the Hatanaka two-step procedure) of the null hypothesis that the lags of any variable as a group are not significantly different from zero.

---

[20]This test is asymptotically equivalent to Durbin's h-test. See, for example, Judge et.al. (1985, pp. 326-327) and Kmenta (1986, p. 333).

4.3. The Unemployment Equation: Monetarist versus New Classical Theories

The regression results for the nested unemployment equation (R1) are summarized in tables 5.6 (annual data) and 5.7a,b (quarterly data). The validity of Monetarist versus New Classical propositions depends upon the significance of the relevant coefficient estimates. The Monetarist view is supported if the unemployment rate is negatively related to lagged changes in real balances $\dot{m}$, but independent of lagged unanticipated money growth $U\dot{M}$. The NCE view implies significantly negative coefficients for unanticipated money growth, though changes in real balances should not matter.

To check the robustness of our findings, we consider four alternative models of unanticipated money growth $U\dot{M}$ for each of the monetary aggregates - the monetary base (MB) and the money supply narrowly defined (M1). Note that the quarterly regressions use separate $U\dot{M}$-series for the fixed and flexible exchange rate periods since the hypothesis of structural stability across the two subperiods must be rejected.[22] However, the qualitative results are unchanged when the $U\dot{M}$-series are taken from forecasting equations estimated for the entire sample period.

In general, the evidence favors the Monetarist over NCE propositions because changes in real balances $\dot{m}$ affect the unemployment rate with significantly negative coefficients. Unanticipated money growth $U\dot{M}$, on the other hand, is insignificantly different from zero in most specifications.

Using annual data (table 5.6) for the entire sample period, these findings are robust across all eight specifications. In addition, the dummy variable for the exchange rate regime break REGIME is significant at the 5% or 10% level in every case. This result, however, is not necessarily due to the shift from fixed to flexible exchange rates in 1973 since the German economy suffered the first of two oil-related supply shocks at approximately the same time.

---

[22] See the regression results in section 4.1.

Table 5.6

Nested Annual Unemployment Equations:
Results for Different Models of Unanticipated Money Growth

$$u(t) = a_0 + a_1 u(t-1) + a_2 \dot{m}(t-1) + a_3 U\dot{M}(t-1) + a_4 REGIME + \epsilon(t)$$

| | Univariate Models of UṀ | | | | Multivariate Models of UṀ | | | |
| | NSA Data | | SA Data | | NSA Data | | SA Data | |
Variable	MB	M1	MB	M1	MB	M1	MB	M1
constant	1.691	.739	1.676	.761	2.346	.788	2.351	.762
(t=)	(1.52)	(**3.67**)	(1.53)	(**3.71**)	(1.51)	(**4.03**)	(1.56)	(**4.01**)
u(t-1)	.620	.919	.630	.926	.547	.914	.541	.905
(t=)	(**4.71**)	(**16.92**)	(**4.72**)	(**16.98**)	(**3.62**)	(**16.13**)	(**3.56**)	(**16.53**)
ṁ(t-1)	-.193	-.175	-.191	-.184	-.199	-.187	-.199	-.181
(t=)	(**4.01**)	(**4.92**)	(**3.93**)	(**5.19**)	(**3.88**)	(**6.02**)	(**3.89**)	(**5.92**)
UṀ(t-1)	-.283	-.122	-.293	-.065	-.244	.140	-.258	-.373
(t=)	(*1.79*)	(.83)	(1.70)	(.39)	(1.01)	(.69)	(1.03)	(1.32)
REGIME	1.431	.784	1.366	.752	1.489	.784	1.496	.845
(t=)	(**2.15**)	(**2.67**)	(*2.06*)	(**2.55**)	(*1.99*)	(**2.64**)	(*2.01*)	(**2.89**)
RHO1	.729	-	.721	-	.860	-	.849	-
(t=)	(**7.51**)	-	(**7.28**)	-	(**39.97**)	-	(**32.08**)	-
R̄²	.704	.973	.705	.973	.586	.973	.593	.975
DW	1.93	1.76	1.95	1.78	2.02	1.80	2.01	1.83
Dh	*	.59	*	.54	*	.50	*	.43
Dm(AR1)	*	.09	*	.04	*	.02	*	.04
Method	HAT	OLS	HAT	OLS	HAT	OLS	HAT	OLS
Period	64-85	63-85	64-85	63-85	64-85	63-85	64-85	63-85

Note: The figures in parantheses are absolute values of t-statistics. Significance at the 5% (or higher level) is indicated by **boldface**, at the 10% level by *italics*. The Monetarist view cannot be rejected if $a_2 < 0$ and $a_3 = 0$; the NCE hypothesis must be accepted if $a_2 = 0$ and $a_3 < 0$. REGIME is a dummy variable for the the exchange rate regime break in 1973. In the presence of serial correlation, the equations are re-estimated using Hatanaka's (1974) two-step estimator (HAT); the estimated serial correlation coefficient is RHO1. * indicates that Durbin's h-test is not recommended as a test for autocorrelation with instrumental variables results (see Turnovsky and Wohar, 1984, footnote 18).

Table 5.7a

Nested Quarterly Unemployment Equations:
Monetary Base (MB)
Summary of Results for Different Models of Unanticipated Money Growth

$$u(t) = a_0 + \sum_{i=1}^{4} a_{1i} u(t-i) + \sum_{i=1}^{4} a_{2i} \dot{m}(t-i) + \sum_{i=1}^{4} a_{3i} \dot{UM}(t-i) + \sum_{j=1}^{3} s_j SEAS(j) + \epsilon(t)$$

| Variable | Univariate Models of $\dot{UM}$ | | | | Multivariate Models of $\dot{UM}$ | | | |
| | NSA Data | | SA Data | | NSA Data | | SA Data | |
	Fix	Flex	Fix	Flex	Fix	Flex	Fix	Flex
constant	1.080	1.088	1.114	1.207	1.114	1.246	1.089	1.597
(t=)	(4.96)	(3.23)	(5.13)	(3.32)	(5.46)	(3.72)	(5.25)	(1.72)
$\Sigma u(t-i)$	.740	.993	.756	.996	.707	.986	.719	.892
(t=)	(7.12)	(57.41)	(7.53)	(51.07)	(7.12)	(61.64)	(7.17)	(6.15)
$\Sigma \dot{m}(t-i)$	.030	-.364	.015	-.404	.027	-.250	.025	-.073
(t=)	(.42)	(2.62)	(.21)	(2.49)	(.42)	(3.30)	(.38)	(.38)
F-test	.235	6.457	.051	3.997	.098	6.839	.074	6.134
$\Sigma \dot{UM}(t-i)$	-.039	.205	.005	.269	-.155	-.004	-.156	-.292
(t=)	(.56)	(.91)	(.05)	(.98)	(1.15)	(.02)	(1.11)	(.64)
F-test	.272	2.190	.050	1.635	.770	1.893	.518	1.588
RHO1	-	-	-	-	-	-	-	.573
(t=)	-	-	-	-	-	-	-	(2.50)
$\bar{R}^2$	.804	.992	.804	.991	.823	.991	.817	.927
DW	2.04	2.13	2.07	2.12	2.05	2.30	2.08	1.99
Dh	-	-	-	-	-	-	-	*
Dm(AR1)	.000	.27	1.68	1.94	.99	3.29	.41	*
Dm(AR4)	.001	1.00	1.21	.08	1.05	.07	.35	*
CHOW	3.92		3.79		4.07		-	
Method	OLS	OLS	OLS	OLS	OLS	OLS	OLS	HAT

Note: The F-statistics (χ^2 with HAT-method) test the hypothesis that the lagged coefficients are jointly equal to zero. The Monetarist view cannot be rejected if $\Sigma a_{2i}<0$ and $\Sigma a_{3i}=0$; the NCE hypothesis must be accepted if $\Sigma a_{2i}=0$ and $\Sigma a_{3i}<0$. Significance at the 5% (or higher) level is indicated by **boldface**, at the 10% level by *italics*. The figures in parantheses are absolute values of t-statistics. In the presence of serial correlation the equations are re-estimated using Hatanaka's (1974) two-step estimator (HAT). RHO1 is the estimated serial correlation coefficient. * indicates that Durbin's h-test is not recommended with instrumental variables results. Due to space limitations, estimates for the seasonal dummies SEAS(j) are not reported here.

Table 5.7b

Nested Quarterly Unemployment Equations:
Money Supply (M1)
Summary of Results for Different Models of Unanticipated Money Growth

$$u(t) = a_0 + \sum_{i=1}^{4} a_{1i} u(t-i) + \sum_{i=1}^{4} a_{2i} \dot{m}(t-i) + \sum_{i=1}^{4} a_{3i} U\dot{M}(t-i) + \sum_{j=1}^{3} s_j SEAS(j) + \epsilon(t)$$

| | Univariate Models of UṀ | | | | Multivariate Models of UṀ | | | |
| | NSA Data | | SA Data | | NSA Data | | SA Data | |
Variable	Fix	Flex	Fix	Flex	Fix	Flex	Fix	Flex
constant	1.112	1.260	.895	-.029	1.125	1.084	1.040	1.118
(t=)	(4.67)	(3.91)	(3.39)	(.04)	(5.08)	(3.36)	(5.37)	(3.41)
$\Sigma u(t-i)$	.768	1.003	.800	.969	.671	.988	.772	.984
(t=)	(7.66)	(49.23)	(8.28)	(27.20)	(6.27)	(43.25)	(8.42)	(51.09)
$\Sigma \dot{m}(t-i)$	-.009	-.260	-.021	.382	-.019	-.132	-.046	-.124
(t=)	(.10)	(3.02)	(.27)	(1.12)	(.32)	(2.61)	(.89)	(2.63)
F-test	.402	2.551	.316	12.030	.210	2.149	.483	2.864
$\Sigma U\dot{M}(t-i)$	-.093	.192	-.080	-.577	-.284	.008	-.344	-.039
(t=)	(.94)	(1.64)	(.66)	(1.26)	(2.27)	(.07)	(1.70)	(.27)
F-test	.383	.846	.575	11.130	1.460	.208	3.188	.341
RHO1	-	-	-	-.541	-	-	-	-
(t=)	-	-	-	(1.63)	-	-	-	-
$\bar{R}^2$	.815	.989	.827	.978	.845	.988	.872	.988
DW	2.05	2.04	2.14	2.29	2.24	2.16	2.21	2.18
Dh	-	-	-	*	-	-	-	-
Dm(AR1)	.004	1.44	2.01	*	.79	1.52	3.37	2.28
Dm(AR4)	.06	.36	.01	*	.03	1.31	.01	.25
CHOW	2.55		-		2.98		3.42	
Method	OLS	OLS	OLS	HAT	OLS	OLS	OLS	OLS

Note: See table 5.7a.

With quarterly data (tables 5.7a,b), the findings in favor of the Monetarist view are less robust. For the fixed exchange rate period, neither the Monetarist nor the NCE parameters, as a group, are significant in six out of eight cases. In the remaining two cases (M1-version with multivariate models of UM), the coefficients on unanticipated money growth are jointly significant. However, for the seasonally unadjusted version, the hypothesis that the UM-coefficients can be excluded from the equation cannot be rejected. The F-statistics (χ^2-statistics for the Hatanaka procedure) test the hypothesis that the Monetarist or NCE parameters as a group are not significantly different from zero.

For the flexible exchange rate period, the sum of unanticipated money growth coefficients is insignificant in every case and the F-tests indicate that the hypothesis of jointly insignificant UM-coefficients cannot be rejected in all but one case. By contrast, the Monetarist parameter estimates m̀ are significantly negative (at the 10% level in two cases) for six of the eight specifications. For the remaining two versions, both estimated with the Hatanaka procedure, the sums of coefficients and/or the χ^2-tests are found to be insignificant.

Detailed quarterly regression results, using the multivariate NSA model of unanticipated money growth, are presented in tables 5.8a (MB-version) and 5.8b (M1-version).[23] Inspection of the coefficient estimates reveals that the first lag of the unemployment rate is not significantly different from one, an indication that the underlying time series is not stationary. While stationarity is not required for the classical linear regression model, it has been a common practice in time series analysis to impose stationarity by differencing the series before estimation. Recent econometric studies, however, argue that differencing might introduce several anomalies, including spurious relationships.[24]

---

[23]The complete quarterly results for the remaining univariate and multivariate models of unanticipated money growth are available from the author upon request.

[24]See Tsay (1984) for a discussion and references.

Table 5.8a

Nested Quarterly Unemployment Equation:
Monetary Base (MB)
Complete Results for the Multivariate NSA Model
of Unanticipated Money Growth

$$u(t) = a_0 + \sum_{i=1}^{4} a_{1i}u(t-i) + \sum_{i=1}^{4} a_{2i}\dot{m}(t-i) + \sum_{i=1}^{4} a_{3i}\dot{UM}(t-i) + \sum_{j=1}^{3} s_j SEAS(j) + \epsilon(t)$$

Method	Lag	constant	$u(t-i)$	$\dot{m}(t-i)$	$\dot{UM}(t-i)$	SEAS(j)
			Fixed Exchange Rates (1962.2-1972.4)			
OLS	1	1.114 (_5.46_)	1.055 (_5.85_)	.003 (.16)	.012 (.20)	-1.632 (_8.37_)
	2		-.368 (1.37)	.001 (.05)	-.022 (.35)	-.859 (_2.82_)
	3		.374 (1.41)	.011 (.49)	-.055 (.92)	-.891 (_2.80_)
	4		-.354 (_2.03_)	.012 (.55)	-.091 (1.47)	
	Sum		.707 (_7.12_)	.027 (.42)	-.155 (1.15)	
	F-test		21.540	.098	.770	
		$\bar{R}^2 = .823$	DW = 2.05	Dm(AR1) = .99		
			Dh = -	Dm(AR4) = 1.05		
			Flexible Exchange Rates (1975.1-1985.4)			
OLS	1	1.246 (_3.72_)	1.204 (_6.77_)	-.115 (_2.59_)	-.011 (.10)	-2.548 (_5.29_)
	2		.085 (.30)	-.050 (1.02)	.085 (.66)	-.626 (1.46)
	3		-.541 (_1.91_)	.064 (1.51)	-.267 (_2.41_)	-.450 (.64)
	4		.237 (1.47)	-.149 (_3.76_)	.189 (_1.83_)	
	Sum		.986 (_61.64_)	-.250 (_3.30_)	-.004 (.02)	
	F-test		977.345	6.839	1.893	
		$\bar{R}^2 = .991$	DW = 2.30	Dm(AR1) = _3.29_		
			Dh = -	Dm(AR4) = .07		

Note: The figures in parantheses are absolute values of t-statistics. **Boldface** denotes significance at the 5% (or higher) level, _italics_ at the 10% level. The F-statistics test the hypothesis that the four lagged coefficients are jointly equal to zero. The Monetarist view cannot be rejected if $\Sigma a_{2i} < 0$ and $\Sigma a_{3i} = 0$; the NCE hypothesis must be accepted if $\Sigma a_{2i} = 0$ and $\Sigma a_{3i} < 0$. SEAS(j) represents a seasonal dummy for the j-th quarter. Durbin's m-statistic (Dm) tests the hypothesis of no first (AR1) or fourth-order (AR4) autocorrelation.

Table 5.8b

Nested Quarterly Unemployment Equation:
Money Supply (M1)
Complete Results for the Multivariate NSA Model
of Unanticipated Money Growth

$$u(t) = a_0 + \sum_{i=1}^{4} a_{1i}u(t-i) + \sum_{i=1}^{4} a_{2i}^{*}\dot{m}(t-i) + \sum_{i=1}^{4} a_{3i}U\dot{M}(t-i) + \sum_{j=1}^{3} s_j SEAS(j) + \epsilon(t)$$

Method	Lag	constant	u(t-i)	ṁ(t-i)	UṀ(t-i)	SEAS(j)
			Fixed Exchange Rates (1962.2-1972.4)			
OLS	1	1.125 (5.08)	.976 (5.56)	-.014 (.74)	-.086 (1.53)	-1.520 (6.76)
	2		-.426 (1.69)	-.004 (.22)	-.087 (1.55)	-.744 (2.12)
	3		.404 (1.62)	.005 (.27)	-.055 (.98)	-.811 (2.37)
	4		-.283 (1.68)	-.006 (.30)	-.056 (1.01)	
	Sum		.671 (6.27)	-.019 (.32)	-.284 (2.27)	
	F-test		15.144	.210	1.460	
		$\bar{R}^2$ = .845	DW = 2.24	Dm(AR1) = .79		
			Dh = -	Dm(AR4) = .03		
			Flexible Exchange Rates (1975.1-1985.4)			
OLS	1	1.084 (3.36)	1.201 (6.89)	-.052 (1.51)	.011 (.21)	-2.388 (9.95)
	2		.141 (.51)	-.051 (1.35)	-.035 (.72)	-1.093 (2.01)
	3		-.372 (1.24)	.011 (.32)	.014 (.29)	.015 (.03)
	4		.017 (.10)	-.041 (1.12)	.018 (.36)	
	Sum		.988 (43.25)	-.132 (2.61)	.008 (.07)	
	F-test		562.233	2.149	.208	
		$\bar{R}^2$ = .988	DW = 2.16	Dm(AR1) = 1.52		
			Dh = -	Dm(AR4) = 1.31		

Note: See table 5.8a.

Table 5.9a

Preferred Quarterly Unemployment Equation:
Monetary Base (MB)

$$u(t) = a_0 + \sum_{i=1}^{4} a_{1i}u(t-i) + \sum_{i=1}^{4} a_{2i}\dot{m}(t-i) + \sum_{j=1}^{3} s_j SEAS(j) + \epsilon(t)$$

Method	Lag	constant	u(t-i)	ṁ(t-i)	SEAS(j)
Fixed Exchange Rates (1961.2-1972.4)					
OLS	1	1.087 (*5.81*)	1.105 (*7.04*)	-.005 (.33)	-1.667 (*9.64*)
	2		-.370 (1.57)	-.000 (.01)	-.854 (*3.13*)
	3		.407 (*1.74*)	.008 (.46)	-.911 (*3.13*)
	4		-.375 (*2.38*)	.004 (.28)	
	Sum		.766 (*8.75*)	.007 (.13)	
	F-test		*35.098*	.123	
		$\bar{R}^2$ = .831	DW = 2.12	Dm(AR1) = .54	
			Dh = -	Dm(AR4) = .31	
Flexible Exchange Rates (1975.1-1985.4)					
HAT	1	.571 (*1.84*)	1.508 (*6.98*)	-.087 (*2.79*)	-1.902 (*7.20*)
	2		.862 (*4.09*)	.136 (*2.44*)	-.860 (*2.26*)
	3		-2.044 (*5.22*)	.087 (*2.21*)	2.588 (*3.59*)
	4		.561 (*3.37*)	-.020 (.64)	
	Sum		.887 (*26.38*)	.116 (.99)	
	χ^2-test		*1483.114*	*28.668*	
		$\bar{R}^2$ = .981	DW = 2.00	Dm(AR1) = *	RHO1 = -.455
			Dh = *	Dm(AR4) = *	(*2.16*)

Note: The figures in parantheses are absolute values of t-statistics. Significance at the 5% (or higher) level is indicated by **boldface**, at the 10% level by *italics*.

The F-statistics (χ^2 with HAT-method) test the hypothesis that the four lagged coefficients are jointly equal to zero. Durbin's m-test (Dm) tests the hypothesis of no first (AR1) or fourth-order (AR4) autocorrelation. In the presence of serial correlation, the equations are re-estimated using Hatanaka's (1974) two-step estimator (HAT); the estimated serial correlation coefficient is RHO1. * indicates that Durbin's h-test is not recommended as a test for autocorrelation when based on instrumental variables results.

Table 5.9b

Preferred Quarterly Unemployment Equation:
Money Supply (M1)

$$u(t) = a_0 + \sum_{i=1}^{4} a_{1i} u(t-i) + \sum_{i=1}^{4} a_{2i} \dot{m}(t-i) + \sum_{j=1}^{3} s_j SEAS(j) + \epsilon(t)$$

Method	Lag	constant	u(t-i)	ṁ(t-i)	SEAS(j)

Fixed Exchange Rates (1961.2-1972.4)

Method	Lag	constant	u(t-i)	ṁ(t-i)	SEAS(j)
OLS	1	1.123 (_5.86_)	1.088 (_6.93_)	-.025 (1.55)	-1.682 (_8.44_)
	2		-.362 (1.57)	-.019 (1.13)	-.876 (_2.96_)
	3		.398 (_1.75_)	-.005 (.31)	-.855 (_2.82_)
	4		-.334 (_2.15_)	-.010 (.61)	
	Sum		.790 (_9.17_)	-.059 (1.11)	
	F-test		_36.027_	.669	
		$\bar{R}^2$ = .841	DW = 2.15	Dm(AR1) = .43	
			Dh = -	Dm(AR4) = .16	

Flexible Exchange Rates (1974.1-1985.4)

Method	Lag	constant	u(t-i)	ṁ(t-i)	SEAS(j)
OLS	1	.870 (_3.40_)	1.242 (_7.77_)	-.037 (1.23)	-2.21 (_10.3_)
	2		.166 (.62)	-.050 (1.58)	-.868 (_1.86_)
	3		-.557 (_2.05_)	.020 (.66)	.469 (1.06)
	4		.136 (.87)	-.044 (1.55)	
	Sum		.986 (_61.18_)	-.111 (_2.94_)	
	F-test		_1010.709_	_2.964_	
		$\bar{R}^2$ = .989	DW = 2.09	Dm(AR1) = _3.16_	
			Dh = -	Dm(AR4) = .58	

Note: See table 5.9a.

Table 5.10

Preferred Annual Unemployment Equations

$$u(t) = a_0 + a_1 u(t-1) + a_2 \dot{m}(t-1) + a_4 REGIME + \epsilon(t)$$

Variable	Monetary Base (MB)	Money Supply (M1)
constant	1.899 (1.46)	.776 (*4.23*)
u(t-1)	.616 (*4.39*)	.926 (*17.84*)
$\dot{m}$(t-1)	-.211 (*4.20*)	-.190 (*6.46*)
REGIME	1.356 (*1.90*)	.756 (*2.72*)
RHO1	.868 (*14.78*)	-
$\bar{R}^2$	.601	.975
DW	2.13	1.91
Dh	*	.22
Dm(AR1)	*	.02
Method	HAT	OLS
Period	1963-85	1962-85

Note: The figures in parantheses are absolute values of t-statistics. Significance at the 5% (or higher level) is indicated by **boldface**, at the 10% level by *italics*. REGIME is a dummy variable for the exchange rate regime break in 1973. In the presence of serial correlation, the equations are re-estimated using Hatanaka's (1974) two-step estimator (HAT); RHO1 is the estimated serial correlation coefficient. * indicates that the Durbin's h-test is not recommended as a test for autocorrelation with instrumental variables results.

Since the stationarity versus nonstationarity debate cannot be considered settled at this time, we re-estimate our nested equations using stationary first differences of the unemployment rate as the dependent variable. The results are summarized in tables A5.6 (annual data) and A5.7a,b (quarterly data) in the appendix to this chapter. The complete quarterly results for the multivariate NSA model of $\dot{U}M$ are given in tables A5.8a,b. It is sufficient to say that the evidence in favor of the Monetarist view is even stronger, although the quarterly results for the fixed exchange rate period support neither view.

The preferred unemployment equation for Germany thus excludes unanticipated money growth from the list of explanatory variables. The regression results for the preferred Monetarist equation are presented in tables 5.9a,b (quarterly data) and 5.10 (annual data). The corresponding results using stationary first differences of the unemployment rate can be found in tables A5.9a,b (quarterly data) and A5.10 (annual data) in the appendix.

4.4. The Output Equation: Monetarist versus New Classical Theories

The empirical evidence for the nested output equation (R2) is summarized in tables 5.11 (annual data) and 5.12a,b (quarterly data). Recall that the output equation for each school of thought can be viewed as equivalent to the unemployment equation, given the inverse empirical relationship - better known as "Okun's Law" - between output relative to capacity and deviations of the unemployment rate from its equilibrium level. Thus, if we accept "Okun's Law" and estimate the implied output equations, a Monetarist would predict significantly positive coefficients for lagged changes in real balances $\dot{m}$, but insignificant coefficients for lagged unanticipated money growth $\dot{U}M$; a New Classical economist would expect the opposite.

Table 5.11

Nested Annual Output Equations:
Results for Different Models of Unanticipated Money Growth

$$lny(t) = b_0 + b_1 lny(t-1) + b_2 \dot{m}(t-1) + b_3 U\dot{M}(t-1) + b_4 t + b_5 REGIME + \epsilon(t)$$

	Univariate Models of UṀ				Multivariate Models of UṀ			
	NSA Data		SA Data		NSA Data		SA Data	
Variable	MB	M1	MB	M1	MB	M1	MB	M1
constant	.609	.233	.568	.194	.517	.194	.516	.362
(t=)	(1.27)	(.54)	(1.25)	(.46)	(.88)	(.40)	(.85)	(.82)
lny(t-1)	.887	.959	.895	.967	.906	.966	.906	.935
(t=)	(*9.73*)	(*11.67*)	(*10.36*)	(*12.04*)	(*8.10*)	(*10.55*)	(*7.91*)	(*11.17*)
$\dot{m}$(t-1)	.003	.004	.003	.004	.004	.005	.004	.004
(t=)	(*1.86*)	(**3.25**)	(*1.92*)	(**3.30**)	(*1.93*)	(**4.14**)	(*1.93*)	(**4.02**)
UṀ(t-1)	.018	.006	.021	.008	.012	.003	.011	.015
(t=)	(**2.87**)	(1.35)	(**3.26**)	(1.47)	(1.00)	(.45)	(.86)	(1.65)
TREND	.005	.002	.004	.002	.004	.002	.004	.003
(t=)	(*1.81*)	(.93)	(*1.77*)	(.80)	(1.15)	(.73)	(1.12)	(1.17)
REGIME	-.036	-.030	-.035	-.028	-.033	-.028	-.032	-.028
(t=)	(**2.17**)	(**2.17**)	(**2.19**)	(**2.07**)	(1.67)	(*1.94*)	(1.63)	(**2.08**)
$\bar{R}^2$	.993	.994	.993	.994	.990	.994	.990	.995
DW	1.71	2.05	1.77	2.13	1.67	2.12	1.67	2.12
Dh	.78	-.12	.61	-.35	.93	-.31	.94	-.31
Dm(AR1)	.59	.03	.40	.14	1.18	.17	1.14	.21
Method	OLS	OLS	OLS	OLS	OLS	OLS	OLS	OLS
Period	63-85	63-85	63-85	63-85	63-85	63-85	63-85	63-85

Note: The figures in parantheses are absolute values of t-statistics. Significance at the 5% (or higher level) is indicated by **boldface**, at the 10% level by *italics*. The Monetarist view cannot be rejected if $b_2 > 0$ and $b_3 = 0$; the NCE hypothesis must be accepted if $b_2 = 0$ and $b_3 > 0$. REGIME is a dummy variable for the exchange rate regime break in 1973.

Table 5.12a

Nested Quarterly Output Equations:
Monetary Base (MB)
Summary of Results for Different Models of Unanticipated Money Growth

$$\ln y(t) = b_0 + \sum_{i=1}^{4} b_{1i} \ln y(t-i) + \sum_{i=1}^{4} b_{2i} \dot{m}(t-i) + \sum_{i=1}^{4} b_{3i} \dot{UM}(t-i) + b_4 t + \sum_{j=1}^{3} s_j SEAS(j) + \epsilon(t)$$

| | Univariate Models of UM | | | | Multivariate Models of UM | | | |
| | NSA Data | | SA Data | | NSA Data | | SA Data | |
Variable	Fix	Flex	Fix	Flex	Fix	Flex	Fix	Flex
constant	2.839	-.694	2.144	.826	2.078	.396	1.943	.396
(t−)	(3.22)	(1.25)	(2.33)	(1.86)	(2.42)	(.98)	(2.29)	(.96)
$\Sigma \ln y(t-i)$	.443	1.104	.570	.844	.585	.918	.613	.918
(t−)	(2.60)	(11.22)	(3.20)	(10.49)	(3.52)	(12.46)	(3.72)	(12.19)
$\Sigma \dot{m}(t-i)$	-.015	.001	-.006	.021	-.001	.013	-.001	.013
(t−)	(2.39)	(.17)	(.89)	(3.26)	(.18)	(2.84)	(.28)	(2.91)
F-test	2.699	8.870	1.680	2.728	1.138	2.808	.899	2.564
$\Sigma \dot{UM}(t-i)$	.019	.008	.012	-.020	.019	-.011	.020	-.010
(t−)	(3.00)	(.85)	(1.40)	(1.69)	(2.08)	(1.12)	(2.13)	(.96)
F-test	2.693	3.683	1.622	1.428	1.678	1.755	1.692	1.506
TREND	.005	.0001	.004	.001	.004	.001	.004	.001
(t−)	(3.00)	(.27)	(2.43)	(1.81)	(2.50)	(1.59)	(2.36)	(1.57)
RHO1	-	-1.202	-	-	-	-	-	-
(t−)	-	(2.34)	-	-	-	-	-	-
$\bar{R}^2$	.987	.987	.987	.982	.987	.983	.987	.983
DW	1.70	1.74	1.88	2.16	1.94	2.47	1.90	2.45
Dh	-	*	-	-	-	-	-	-
Dm(AR1)	.45	*	2.45	.73	.63	1.42	.04	1.12
Dm(AR4)	.11	*	2.53	.001	.59	.04	.07	.003
CHOW	-		3.41		3.82		3.77	
Method	OLS	HAT	OLS	OLS	OLS	OLS	OLS	OLS

Note: The F-statistics (χ^2 with HAT-method) test the hypothesis that the lagged coefficients are jointly equal to zero. The Monetarist view cannot be rejected if $\Sigma b_{2i} > 0$ and $\Sigma b_{3i} = 0$; the NCE hypothesis must be accepted if $\Sigma b_{2i} = 0$ and $\Sigma b_{3i} > 0$. Significance at the 5% (or higher) level is indicated by **boldface**, at the 10% level by *italics*. The figures in parantheses are absolute values of t-statistics. In the presence of serial correlation, the equations are re-estimated using Hatanaka's (1974) two-step estimator (HAT); the estimated autocorrelation coefficient is RHO1. * indicates that Durbin's h-test is not recommended with instrumental variables results. Due to space limitations, estimates for the seasonal dummies SEAS(j) are not reported here.

Table 5.12b

Nested Quarterly Output Equations:
Money Supply (M1)
Summary of Results for Different Models of Unanticipated Money Growth

$$\ln y(t) = b_0 + \sum_{i=1}^{4} b_{1i} \ln y(t-i) + \sum_{i=1}^{4} b_{2i} \dot{m}(t-i) + \sum_{i=1}^{4} b_{3i} \dot{UM}(t-i) + b_4 t + \sum_{j=1}^{3} s_j SEAS(j) + \epsilon(t)$$

| | Univariate Models of UM | | | | Multivariate Models of UM | | | |
| | NSA Data | | SA Data | | NSA Data | | SA Data | |
Variable	Fix	Flex	Fix	Flex	Fix	Flex	Fix	Flex
constant	1.920	-.600	1.766	-.212	2.345	-.512	2.036	-.278
(t=)	(2.22)	(.69)	(2.00)	(.43)	(2.47)	(.78)	(2.24)	(.49)
$\Sigma \ln y(t-i)$	.612	1.091	.641	1.028	.529	1.082	.590	1.038
(t=)	(3.64)	(6.90)	(3.73)	(11.46)	(2.88)	(9.05)	(3.55)	(9.97)
$\Sigma \dot{m}(t-i)$	-.008	.003	-.005	.018	-.004	.009	-.001	.008
(t=)	(1.27)	(.42)	(.75)	(2.95)	(.77)	(2.74)	(.30)	(2.62)
F-test	2.562	7.179	1.979	2.218	1.968	2.696	1.587	2.640
$\Sigma \dot{UM}(t-i)$	.012	.002	.007	-.019	.014	-.006	.022	-.005
(t=)	(1.50)	(.30)	(.65)	(2.09)	(1.60)	(1.06)	(1.58)	(.84)
F-test	1.273	1.726	.849	1.549	1.125	.398	.762	.699
TREND	.004	-.0001	.004	-.0001	.005	-.0003	.004	-.0001
(t=)	(2.22)	(.12)	(2.11)	(.25)	(2.57)	(.50)	(2.33)	(.13)
RHO1	-	-.330	-	-	-	-	-	-
(t=)	-	(.72)	-	-	-	-	-	-
$\bar{R}^2$	.986	.962	.986	.982	.987	.979	.986	.980
DW	1.89	2.18	1.83	2.29	1.94	2.50	1.87	2.55
Dh	-	*	-	-	-	-	-	-
Dm(AR1)	1.05	*	1.93	2.85	.47	.33	.17	1.94
Dm(AR4)	.08	*	.66	1.92	.09	.02	.26	.55
CHOW	-		3.50		3.68		3.47	
Method	OLS	HAT	OLS	OLS	OLS	OLS	OLS	OLS

Note: See table 5.12a.

As before, we consider four different models of unanticipated money growth and two monetary aggregates (MB, M1) to check the robustness of our results. The UM-series in the quarterly regressions for the fixed and flexible exchange rate periods come from separate forecasting equations.

To summarize, the evidence supports the Monetarist propositions while rejecting the NCE view. However, the findings for the output equation are sensitive to the choice of monetary aggregate and UM-model and, therefore, less robust than the unemployment results.

Consider the annual results for the entire sample period (table 5.11). The M1-version of the output equation clearly favors the Monetarist view in that the changes in real balances are significantly positive in all four specifications, whereas unanticipated money growth does not matter. In the MB-version, the ṁ-coefficients are marginally significant at the 10% level in every case. In addition, the unanticipated money growth coefficients are positive and significant for two of the four cases (univariate models of UM). Hence, the NCE interpretation is not as easily rejected.

Based on quarterly data (tables 5.12a,b), the NCE propositions are usually rejected, yet the results in favor of the Monetarist view are not uniformly strong. For the fixed exchange rate period, neither school of thought is strongly favored by the evidence. The ṁ-coefficients are either insignificant or significantly *negative* (in one of the eight cases). Similarly, the unanticipated money growth coefficients are not significantly different from zero in five specifications. In the MB-version, we find significantly positive sums of UM-coefficients in three cases, which is consistent with the NCE view. The F-tests do not confirm these findings.

For the flexible exchange rate period, the NCE-hypothesis is unambiguously rejected since the UM-coefficients are either insignificant or significantly *negative* (in one of the eight cases). The Monetarist parameters are significantly positive in six of the eight specifications, even though in three cases the corresponding F-tests are only marginally significant. For the remaining specifications, the ṁ-coefficients are insignificantly different from zero.

Table 5.13a

Nested Quarterly Output Equation:
Monetary Base (MB)
Complete Results for the Multivariate NSA Model
of Unanticipated Money Growth

$$lny(t) = b_0 + \sum_{i=1}^{4} b_{1i}lny(t-i) + \sum_{i=1}^{4} b_{2i}\dot{m}(t-i) + \sum_{i=1}^{4} b_{3i}U\dot{M}(t-i) + b_4 t + \sum_{j=1}^{3} s_j SEAS(j) + \epsilon(t)$$

Method	Lag	constant	lny(t-i)	$\dot{m}$(t-i)	U$\dot{M}$(t-i)	TREND
			Fixed Exchange Rates (1962.2-72.4)			
OLS	1	2.078 (<u>2.42</u>)	.638 (<u>2.92</u>)	.0002 (.09)	-.0000 (.00)	.004 (<u>2.50</u>)
	2		-.241 (.87)	-.0000 (.02)	.0068 (1.62)	
	3		.294 (1.14)	.0001 (.09)	.0064 (1.47)	
	4		-.106 (.54)	-.0012 (.74)	.0061 (1.40)	
	Sum		.585 (<u>3.52</u>)	-.0009 (.18)	.0193 (<u>2.08</u>)	
	F-test		<u>4.028</u>	1.138	1.678	
		$\overline{R}^2$ = .987	DW = 1.94	Dm(AR1) = .63		
			Dh = -	Dm(AR4) = .59		
			Flexible Exchange Rates (1975.1-1985.4)			
OLS	1	.396 (.98)	.611 (<u>3.59</u>)	.0047 (<u>2.47</u>)	-.0092 (*1.83*)	.001 (1.59)
	2		.041 (.24)	.0012 (.64)	.0071 (1.33)	
	3		.279 (1.66)	.0045 (<u>2.46</u>)	-.0105 (<u>2.22</u>)	
	4		-.013 (.08)	.0022 (1.15)	.0020 (.37)	
	Sum		.918 (<u>12.5</u>)	.0127 (<u>2.84</u>)	-.0107 (1.12)	
	F-test		<u>45.854</u>	<u>2.808</u>	1.755	
		$\overline{R}^2$ = .983	DW = 2.47	Dm(AR1) = 1.42		
			Dh = -	Dm(AR4) = .04		

Note: The figures in parantheses are absolute values of t-statistics. **Boldface** denotes significance at the 5% (or higher) level, *italics* at the 10% level. The F-statistics test the hypothesis that the four lagged coefficients are jointly equal to zero. The Monetarist view cannot be rejected if $\Sigma b_{2i} > 0$ and $\Sigma b_{3i} = 0$; the NCE hypothesis must be accepted if $\Sigma b_{2i} = 0$ and $\Sigma b_{3i} > 0$. Durbin's m-statistic (Dm) tests the hypothesis of no first (AR1) or fourth-order (AR4) autocorrelation. Due to space limitations, estimates for the seasonal dummies SEAS(j) are not reported here.

Table 5.13b

Nested Quarterly Output Equation:
Money Supply (M1)
Complete Results for the Multivariate NSA Model
of Unanticipated Money Growth

$$\ln y(t) = b_0 + \sum_{i=1}^{4} b_{1i} \ln y(t-i) + \sum_{i=1}^{4} b_{2i} \dot{m}(t-i) + \sum_{i=1}^{4} b_{3i} U\dot{M}(t-i) + b_4 t + \sum_{j=1}^{3} s_j SEAS(j) + \epsilon(t)$$

Method	Lag	constant	$\ln y(t-i)$	$\dot{m}(t-i)$	$U\dot{M}(t-i)$	TREND
\multicolumn{7}{c}{Fixed Exchange Rates (1962.2-1972.4)}						
OLS	1	2.345 (_2.47_)	.657 (_3.22_)	-.0013 (.82)	.0028 (.68)	.005 (_2.57_)
	2		-.110 (.44)	.0004 (.25)	.0009 (.21)	
	3		.142 (.56)	.0003 (.19)	.0035 (.90)	
	4		-.160 (.76)	-.0029 (_1.79_)	.0066 (_1.69_)	
	Sum		.529 (_2.88_)	-.0035 (.77)	.0138 (1.60)	
	F-test		_3.888_	1.968	1.125	
		$\bar{R}^2 = .987$	DW = 1.94	Dm(AR1) = .47		
			Dh = -	Dm(AR4) = .09		
\multicolumn{7}{c}{Flexible Exchange Rates (1975.1-1985.4)}						
OLS	1	-.512 (.78)	.761 (_4.87_)	.0037 (_2.22_)	-.0022 (.95)	-.0003 (.50)
	2		.007 (.04)	.0003 (.17)	-.0011 (.53)	
	3		.418 (_2.37_)	.0030 (_1.91_)	-.0017 (.82)	
	4		-.104 (.63)	.0022 (1.30)	-.0005 (.24)	
	Sum		1.082 (_9.05_)	.0091 (_2.74_)	-.0056 (1.06)	
	F-test		_37.920_	_2.696_	.398	
		$\bar{R}^2 = .979$	DW = 2.50	Dm(AR1) = .33		
			Dh = -	Dm(AR4) = .02		

Note: See table 5.13a.

Table 5.14a

Preferred Quarterly Output Equation:
Monetary Base (MB)

$$\ln y(t) = b_0 + \sum_{i=1}^{4} b_{1i} \ln y(t-i) + \sum_{i=1}^{4} b_{2i} \dot{m}(t-i) + b_4 t + \sum_{j=1}^{3} s_j SEAS(j) + \epsilon(t)$$

Method	Lag	constant	$\ln y(t-i)$	$\dot{m}(t-i)$	TREND	SEAS(j)
Fixed Exchange Rates (1961.2-1972.4)						
OLS	1	1.519 (*1.88*)	.723 (**4.13**)	.0006 (.44)	.003 (**2.00**)	.113 (**5.33**)
	2		-.160 (.72)	.0002 (.14)		.128 (**3.87**)
	3		.180 (.81)	.0004 (.30)		.087 (**2.85**)
	4		-.051 (.27)	-.0010 (.77)		
	Sum		.692 (**4.41**)	.0002 (.05)		
	F-test		**7.581**	1.686		
	$\bar{R}^2 = .988$		DW = 1.92	Dm(AR1) = .01		
			Dh = -	Dm(AR4) = .29		
Flexible Exchange Rates (1975.2-1985.4)						
HAT	1	.926 (*1.90*)	.678 (**2.26**)	.0016 (.97)	.001 (*1.87*)	.060 (**2.15**)
	2		.156 (1.01)	.0013 (.57)		.076 (**2.76**)
	3		.119 (.65)	.0008 (.38)		.108 (**4.60**)
	4		-.133 (.69)	.0028 (**2.12**)		
	Sum		.821 (**9.18**)	.0064 (1.24)		
	χ^2-test		**102.306**	5.391		
	$\bar{R}^2 = .972$		DW = 2.42	Dm(AR1) = *	RHO1 = -.26	
			Dh = *	Dm(AR4) = *	(.84)	

Note: The figures in parantheses are absolute values of t-statistics. Significance at the 5% (or higher) level is indicated by **boldface**, at the 10% level by *italics*.

The F-statistics (χ^2 with HAT-method) test the hypothesis that the four lagged coefficients are jointly equal to zero. Durbin's m-statistic (Dm) tests the hypothesis of no first (AR1) or fourth-order (AR4) autocorrelation. In the presence of serial correlation, the equations are re-estimated using Hatanaka's (1974) two-step estimator (HAT); the estimated correlation coefficient is RHO1. * indicates that Durbin's h-test is not recommended as a test for autocorrelation with instrumental variables results.

Table 5.14b

Preferred Quarterly Output Equation:
Money Supply (M1)

$$\ln y(t) = b_0 + \sum_{i=1}^{4} b_{1i} \ln y(t-i) + \sum_{i=1}^{4} b_{2i} \dot{m}(t-i) + b_4 t + \sum_{j=1}^{3} s_j SEAS(j) + \epsilon(t)$$

Method	Lag	constant	$\ln y(t-i)$	$\dot{m}(t-i)$	TREND	SEAS(j)
			Fixed Exchange Rates (1961.2-1972.4)			
OLS	1	1.353 (*1.67*)	.729 (<u>4.32</u>)	.0007 (.57)	.003 (*1.82*)	.118 (<u>5.24</u>)
	2		-.165 (.78)	.0009 (.72)		.130 (<u>3.94</u>)
	3		.192 (.89)	.0014 (1.17)		.097 (<u>3.19</u>)
	4		-.034 (.18)	-.0008 (.69)		
	Sum		.723 (<u>4.60</u>)	.0022 (.56)		
	F-test		<u>8.407</u>	*2.419*		
		$\bar{R}^2 = .989$	DW = 1.81	Dm(AR1) = *3.77*		
			Dh = -	Dm(AR4) = .16		
			Flexible Exchange Rates (1974.1-1985.4)			
OLS	1	.053 (.09)	.644 (<u>4.03</u>)	.0016 (1.06)	.0002 (.34)	.049 (<u>2.92</u>)
	2		.129 (.66)	.0002 (.11)		.060 (<u>3.84</u>)
	3		.190 (1.02)	.0015 (1.02)		.083 (<u>5.27</u>)
	4		.018 (.11)	.0028 (<u>2.03</u>)		
	Sum		.981 (<u>9.01</u>)	.0061 (<u>2.65</u>)		
	F-test		<u>25.760</u>	*2.119*		
		$\bar{R}^2 = .974$	DW = 2.17	Dm(AR1) = 1.68		
			Dh = -	Dm(AR4) = .74		

Note: See table 5.14a.

Table 5.15

Preferred Annual Output Equations

$$\ln y(t) = b_0 + b_1 \ln y(t-1) + b_2 \dot{m}(t-1) + b_4 t + b_5 \text{REGIME} + \epsilon(t)$$

Variable	Monetary Base (MB)	Money Supply (M1)
constant	.272 (.54)	.157 (.41)
lny(t-1)	.952 (**9.97**)	.974 (**13.20**)
$\dot{m}$(t-1)	.004 (**2.19**)	.005 (**4.57**)
TREND	.003 (.87)	.002 (.73)
REGIME	-.032 (*1.71*)	-.028 (**2.16**)
$\bar{R}^2$	.992	.995
DW	1.83	2.37
Dh	.46	-.96
Dm(AR1)	.22	.94
Method	OLS	OLS
Period	1962-85	1962-85

Note: The figures in parantheses are absolute values of t-statistics. Significance at the 5% (or higher level) is indicated by **boldface**, at the 10% level by *italics*. REGIME is a dummy variable for the exchange rate regime break in 1973.

The complete quarterly regression results, using the multivariate NSA model of unanticipated money growth, are given in the following tables 5.13a (MB-version) and 5.13b (M1-version).[25] The coefficients on the first lag of real output do not exhibit the unit-root property, even though the corresponding time series is known to be nonstationary. For the debate about the stationarity and nonstationarity of time series, we refer the reader to the previous section. When re-estimated with stationary first differences of real GNP as the dependent variable, the results for the output equation (not reported here) are qualitatively robust.

Abstracting from two cases in which the NCE-specification is slightly favored by the (annual) data, the preferred German output equation excludes unanticipated money growth. Regression results for the resulting Monetarist equation are given in tables 5.14a,b (quarterly data) and 5.15 (annual data).

4.5. The Inflation Equation: Monetarist versus Keynesian Theories

The nested inflation equation (R3) is the most controversial of the regression equations derived from the structural model. Our empirical section, therefore, considers several modifications of (R3) in an effort to adequately represent alternative views and check the robustness of our findings. The proposed modifications and extension of (R3), however, are not made on an ad hoc basis. Instead, these "other" determinants of inflation in the short run are "hidden" in the error term of (R3) and follow directly from the structural model.

First, as argued earlier, the Keynesian explanation of inflation can be interpreted in terms of the "underlying rate of inflation" in nominal wages. This view follows from the inflation equation (5.5) of the structural model and the

---

[25] The complete quarterly results for the remaining univariate and multivariate models of unanticipated money growth are available from the author upon request.

Keynesian equation (K1). Hence, we estimate another nested equation (R4) where lagged rates of wage inflation replace the unemployment rate.

Second, the reduced-form equations (R3) and (R4) include changes in foreign interest rates as the only indirect foreign influence on German inflation. To allow for more direct channels of transmission and the phenomenon of imported inflation, we also consider the role of foreign inflation (measured by percentage changes in the U.S. consumer price index) for both specifications.[26] Recall that all three schools of thought can account for foreign rates of inflation in their respective reduced forms. To a Monetarist, changes in nominal (long-term) interest rates may simply reflect changes in the inflation rate designed to keep the real rate of interest constant. A Keynesian views foreign inflation as an exogenous (supply) disturbance which affects domestic inflation directly. Finally, a New Classical economist would argue that anticipated foreign shocks and, hence, anticipated foreign inflation affect the domestic rate of inflation.

Thirdly, it is questionable whether a lag structure of four quarterly lags is sufficient to capture the influence of money growth on inflation. After all, the stylized facts for the German economy point to the existence of long and variable lags between money growth and inflation. To avoid this bias against the Monetarist propositions due to insufficient lags, we re-estimate all quarterly specifications of the nested inflation equation with six lagged values of money growth.

Finally, the NCE inflation equation combines elements of both the Keynesian and Monetarist views and offers an additional test of the opposing views. The NCE view postulates that anticipated money growth affects inflation contemporaneously. Since univariate and multivariate series for anticipated money growth already exist, we estimate the NCE equation with annual data.

---

[26] Two other foreign variables were also tested. U.S. money growth does not contribute significantly to German inflation, a result which is consistent with our findings in chapter IV. The effects of changes in the relative price of oil are qualitatively similar to those of U.S. inflation, yet somewhat weaker. Thus, we only report the findings for U.S. inflation.

The Original Inflation Equation (R3)

The regression results for the nested inflation equation (R3) are summarized in tables 5.16 (quarterly data) and 5.18 (annual data). Note that the coefficients of lagged unemployment are estimated separately rather than in first difference form. The validity of the Monetarist and Keynesian propositions depends on the significance of the relevant coefficient estimates. The Monetarist view is supported if money growth contributes significantly to inflation *independently of the unemployment rate*. The Keynesian view, on the other hand, implies that inflation varies inversely with unemployment, but is not affected by money growth in the short run.

In the quarterly regressions, coefficient estimates at individual lags are often insignificant, although the sums of coefficients and the F-tests are significant at conventional significance levels. We focus on the summary results in our discussion, but the complete quarterly results are presented in tables A5.16a-d at the end of the chapter. All nested equations are estimated for two alternative money definitions - the monetary base (MB) and the narrow money supply (M1) - to check the robustness of the results.

In general, the evidence favors the Keynesian over Monetarist propositions. The unemployment rate affects inflation with significantly negative coefficients, and money growth is not significantly different from zero in most specifications.

Using quarterly data (table 5.16), the conclusions for the two subperiods differ slightly, but are robust across different lag lengths and money definitions. For the fixed exchange rate period, none of the regressors except various own lags of inflation matter. Lagged unemployment, lagged money growth, and lagged foreign interest rate changes are all insignificantly different from zero at conventional levels. The Monetarist hypotheses must be rejected. Under the MB-specification, there is weak support for the Keynesian view since the negative sum of unemployment coefficients is marginally significant at the 10% level.

For the flexible exchange rate period, the data reject the Monetarist view and

Table 5.16

Quarterly Nested Inflation Equations:
Summary of Results for the Original Version (R3)

$$\dot{p}(t) = c_0 + \sum_{i=1}^{4} c_{1i}\dot{p}(t-i) + \sum_{i=1}^{N} c_{2i}\dot{M}(t-i) + \sum_{i=1}^{4} c_{3i}u(t-i) + \sum_{i=1}^{4} c_{4i}\dot{r}_w(t-i) + \epsilon(t)$$

| Variable | Monetary Base (MB) | | | | Money Supply (M1) | | | |
| | 4 $\dot{M}$-Lags | | 6 $\dot{M}$-Lags | | 4 $\dot{M}$-Lags | | 6 $\dot{M}$-Lags | |
	Fix	Flex	Fix	Flex	Fix	Flex	Fix	Flex
constant	2.297	1.560	2.423	.209	-1.402	.938	-3.271	2.458
(t=)	(1.16)	(.93)	(1.00)	(.14)	(.44)	(.55)	(.71)	(1.47)
$\Sigma\dot{p}(t-i)$	-.685	-1.022	-.792	-.505	-.685	-.582	-.241	-.605
(t=)	(1.23)	(2.52)	(1.20)	(1.28)	(1.17)	(.96)	(.41)	(1.14)
$\Sigma\dot{M}(t-i)$	-.676	-.163	-.748	.044	-.083	-.055	-.344	-.205
(t=)	(1.34)	(1.23)	(1.24)	(.17)	(.22)	(.51)	(.85)	(1.65)
F-test	.77	15.77	.43	5.00	1.07	.32	9.16	1.39
$\Sigma u(t-i)$	-1.356	-.234	-1.451	-.154	-.587	-.188	-.543	-.217
(t=)	(1.84)	(3.97)	(1.70)	(2.11)	(.89)	(2.11)	(.91)	(2.65)
F-test	1.70	23.50	1.49	2.05	1.79	1.74	6.89	2.56
$\Sigma\dot{r}_w(t-i)$	-.084	.009	-.095	.009	-.118	.016	-.095	.014
(t=)	(1.46)	(.86)	(1.29)	(.66)	(1.84)	(.78)	(1.17)	(.80)
F-test	.66	7.98	.50	.48	1.11	.95	6.76	.94
RHO1	-	-.241	-	-	-	-	.323	-
(t=)	-	(1.03)	-	-	-	-	(1.42)	-
$\bar{R}^2$	.915	.942	.894	.967	.918	.929	.754	.945
DW	2.15	1.77	2.11	1.89	2.13	1.82	1.91	2.05
Dh	-	*	-	-	-	-	*	-
Dm(AR1)	.94	*	.36	1.02	.37	2.61	*	.10
Dm(AR4)	.32	*	.45	.18	.34	3.65	*	.55
CHOW	-		1.34		1.34		-	
Method	OLS	HAT	OLS	OLS	OLS	OLS	HAT	OLS

Note: The F-statistics (χ^2 with HAT-method) test the hypothesis that the lagged coefficients are jointly equal to zero. The Monetarist view cannot be rejected if $\Sigma c_{2i} > 0$ and $\Sigma c_{3i} = 0$; the Keynesian propositions are $\Sigma c_{2i} = 0$ and $\Sigma c_{3i} < 0$. In the presence of serial correlation, the equations are re-estimated using Hatanaka's (1974) two-step estimator (HAT); the estimated autocorrelation coefficient is RHO1. * indicates that Durbin's h-test is not recommended with instrumental variables results. The regressions also include three seasonal dummies, but the coefficient estimates are not reported due to space limitations.

favor the Keynesian interpretation of inflation. Lagged unemployment significantly affects inflation with the postulated negative coefficient and lagged money growth shows insignificant coefficients in the M1-version. In the MB-version, the insignificant coefficient sums stand in contrast to the significant F-tests.

The annual regression results (table 5.18, columns 1 and 3) support the conclusions in favor of Keynesian theories. Lagged unemployment affects inflation with a negative coefficient, whereas money growth is insignificant. The regime break dummy REGIME is significant in both specifications. Note that the coefficient of determination is considerably lower with annual data compared to the quarterly regressions: the estimated annual equations explain between 30% and 33% of the variation in German inflation.

The "Underlying Rate of Inflation" Equation (R4)

Keynesians argue that the "underlying rate of inflation" of nominal wages, which responds to the state of the labor market, is the major determinant of the rate of price inflation. We investigate this proposition by estimating the nested inflation equation (R4) that includes lagged rates of wage inflation instead of lagged unemployment rates. Keynesians now predict a *positive* coefficient since nominal wages are negatively related to fluctuations in unemployment. The Monetarist position that inflation is primarily a monetary phenomenon is unchanged.

A summary of the regression results for equation (R4), based on foreign interest rate changes, is given in tables 5.17 (quarterly data) and 5.18 (annual data). Complete quarterly regressions for the alternative money definitions and lag specifications are reported in the appendix in tables A5.17a-d.

For quarterly data (table 5.17), the inclusion of lagged wage inflation strengthens the support for the Keynesian hypothesis in both subperiods. This result is robust across different lag specifications and money definitions. As a group, the wage inflation coefficients are significant and positive in six out of eight cases. In one case, the coefficient sum and the χ^2-test are marginally significant at the

Table 5.17

Quarterly Nested Inflation Equations:
The "Underlying Rate of Inflation" Version (R4)
Summary of Results

$$\dot{p}(t) = c_0 + \sum_{i=1}^{4} c_{1i}\dot{p}(t-i) + \sum_{i=1}^{N} c_{2i}\dot{M}(t-i) + \sum_{i=1}^{4} c_{3i}\dot{W}(t-i) + \sum_{i=1}^{4} c_{4i}\dot{r}_w(t-i) + \epsilon(t)$$

| | Monetary Base (MB) | | | | Money Supply (M1) | | | |
| | 4 Ṁ-Lags | | 6 Ṁ-Lags | | 4 Ṁ-Lags | | 6 Ṁ-Lags | |
Variable	Fix	Flex	Fix	Flex	Fix	Flex	Fix	Flex
constant	-.563	-1.458	-1.175	-2.008	-.232	-1.224	-1.253	-.436
(t-)	(.48)	(1.09)	(.82)	(2.27)	(.08)	(1.32)	(.34)	(.44)
Σṗ(t-i)	-2.169	.039	-2.208	.224	-2.004	-.291	-1.953	-.345
(t-)	(2.75)	(.09)	(2.62)	(.55)	(2.32)	(.60)	(2.08)	(.71)
ΣṀ(t-i)	-.580	-.032	-.701	.004	-.019	-.021	-.034	-.102
(t-)	(1.34)	(.27)	(1.43)	(.03)	(.05)	(.23)	(.07)	(1.01)
F-test	.92	3.91	.76	3.38	.33	.04	.24	.82
ΣẆ(t-i)	2.166	.266	2.295	.193	1.795	.574	1.788	.597
(t-)	(3.38)	(1.05)	(3.35)	(.74)	(2.62)	(2.12)	(2.37)	(2.07)
F-test	3.06	7.14	2.99	1.16	2.05	3.73	1.76	2.30
Σṙ$_w$(t-i)	.048	.026	.082	.015	.009	.022	.020	.028
(t-)	(.96)	(2.04)	(1.33)	(1.11)	(.15)	(1.40)	(.26)	(1.77)
F-test	.70	4.68	.82	.43	.10	.75	.07	1.06
RHO1	-	-.102	-	-	-	-	-	-
(t-)	-	(.27)	-	-	-	-	-	-
R̄²	.927	.926	.912	.963	.921	.942	.901	.943
DW	1.99	1.70	1.98	1.43	1.87	1.90	1.87	1.93
Dh	-	*	-	-	-	-	-	-
Dm(AR1)	.25	*	.01	3.62	2.59	.05	2.96	.33
Dm(AR4)	3.55	*	2.40	.84	.04	.78	1.45	.21
CHOW	-		1.21		.85		.74	
Method	OLS	HAT	OLS	OLS	OLS	OLS	OLS	OLS

Note: See table 5.16. The Monetarist view cannot be rejected if $\Sigma c_{2i} > 0$ and $\Sigma c_{3i} = 0$; the Keynesian propositions are $\Sigma c_{2i} = 0$ and $\Sigma c_{3i} > 0$.

Table 5.18

Annual Nested Inflation Equations:
The Original and "Underlying Rate of Inflation" Versions
Complete Results

$$\dot{p}(t) = c_0 + c_1\dot{p}(t-1) + c_2\dot{M}(t-1) + c_3X(t-1) + c_4\dot{r}_w(t-1) + c_5REGIME + \epsilon(t)$$

| Variable | Monetary Base (MB) | | Money Supply (M1) | |
	U-Version	$\dot{W}$-Version	U-Version	$\dot{W}$-Version
constant	4.429 (_2.71_)	.850 (.91)	4.030 (_2.64_)	.721 (.82)
$\dot{p}(t-1)$	.150 (.71)	.958 (_2.04_)	.171 (.83)	.971 (_2.10_)
$\dot{M}(t-1)$	-.097 (.93)	.005 (.05)	-.051 (.76)	.029 (.36)
$u(t-1)$	-.586 (_2.42_)	-	-.571 (_2.40_)	-
$\dot{W}(t-1)$	-	-.104 (.37)	-	-.118 (.44)
$\dot{r}_w(t-1)$	.004 (.34)	.027 (_2.38_)	.001 (.06)	.028 (_2.42_)
REGIME	3.010 (_2.28_)	-.423 (.64)	2.989 (_2.27_)	-.437 (.67)
RHO1	.880 (_5.72_)	-	.869 (_6.44_)	-
$\bar{R}^2$	.332	.493	.329	.496
DW	2.15	1.68	2.11	1.72
Dh	*	-	*	-
Dm(AR1)	*	1.01	*	.78
Method	HAT	OLS	HAT	OLS
Period	1963-85	1962-85	1963-85	1962-85

Note: The figures in parantheses are absolute values of t-statistics. Significance at the 5% (or higher level) is indicated by **boldface**, at the 10% level by _italics_. The Monetarist hypothesis cannot be rejected if $c_2 > 0$ and $c_3 = 0$; the Keynesian view must be accepted if $c_2 = 0$ and $c_3 < 0$ (with unemployment) or $c_3 > 0$ (with wage inflation). Durbin's m-statistic (Dm) tests the hypothesis of no first-order autocorrelation. In the presence of serial correlation, the equations are re-estimated using Hatanaka's (1974) two-step estimator (HAT); RHO1 is the estimated autocorrelation coefficient. * indicates that Durbin's h-test is not recommended with instrumental variables results. REGIME is a dummy variable for the exchange rate regime break in 1973.

10% level. The coefficients on lagged money growth, on the other hand, are either insignificant or significantly *negative*, with one exception (MB-version for the flexible period with six lags). In the exceptional case, the sum of coefficients is positive and insignificant, but the F-test is significant. Overall, the Monetarist view must be rejected.

The annual regression results (table 5.18, columns 2 and 4) do not favor either view since both money growth and wage inflation coefficients are insignificant. Inflation is explained primarily by its own past and changes in the foreign interest rate.

Additional evidence for equation (R4), where foreign interest rate changes are replaced with foreign inflation, is presented in tables 5.19 (quarterly data) and 5.20 (annual data). The complete quarterly results can be found in tables A5.17b (MB-version) and A5.17d (M1-version) at the end of this chapter.

Our previous conclusions are unchanged by this respecification of the nested inflation equation. For quarterly data (table 5.19, columns 3-4 and 7-8), the German inflationary process follows Keynesian rules since wage inflation affects the overall rate of price inflation significantly. The only exception is the M1-version for the flexible period, where the sum of wage coefficients is insignificant and the coefficient at lag two is significantly *negative* (see table A5.19d in the appendix). Furthermore, foreign inflation matters for all specifications of the inflation equation.

The annual results (table 5.20, columns 2 and 4), however, do not permit any conclusions regarding the Monetarist-Keynesian debate about inflation. None of the regressors, including the lagged dependent variable, is significant, suggesting that this particular equation might suffer from misspecification.

The Role of Foreign Inflation

Estimation of the nested inflation equations (R3) and (R4) indicates that foreign interest rate changes do not affect German inflation significantly and

Table 5.19

Quarterly Nested Inflation Equations:
The Role of Foreign Inflation
Summary of Results

$$\dot{p}(t) = c_0 + \sum_{i=1}^{4} c_{1i}\dot{p}(t-i) + \sum_{i=1}^{4} c_{2i}\dot{M}(t-i) + \sum_{i=1}^{4} c_{3i}X(t-i) + \sum_{i=1}^{4} c_{4i}\dot{p}_w(t-i) + \epsilon(t)$$

| | Monetary Base (MB) | | | | Money Supply (M1) | | | |
| | U-Version | | $\dot{W}$-Version | | U-Version | | $\dot{W}$-Version | |
Variable	Fix	Flex	Fix	Flex	Fix	Flex	Fix	Flex
constant	.040	-.549	-1.785	-1.798	-1.123	.813	-.714	-3.993
(t=)	(.03)	(.20)	(1.53)	(2.17)	(.47)	(.59)	(.36)	(2.42)
$\Sigma\dot{p}(t-i)$	-1.743	-.495	-2.200	-.041	-1.610	-.241	-2.341	-.106
(t=)	(2.83)	(.98)	(2.85)	(.10)	(2.69)	(.47)	(2.93)	(.26)
$\Sigma\dot{M}(t-i)$	.481	-.221	.201	-.019	.322	-.114	.402	.033
(t=)	(.92)	(1.16)	(.45)	(.15)	(.91)	(1.25)	(1.23)	(.44)
F-test	1.17	12.62	1.96	.74	1.60	.47	.96	3.22
$\Sigma u(t-i)$	-1.375	-.202	-	-	-1.381	-.168	-	-
(t=)	(2.15)	(2.26)	-	-	(2.08)	(2.12)	-	-
F-test	2.53	12.78	-	-	2.82	2.16	-	-
$\Sigma\dot{W}(t-i)$	-	-	1.449	.390	-	-	1.303	.108
(t=)	-	-	(2.85)	(1.57)	-	-	(2.22)	(.53)
F-test	-	-	9.15	2.50	-	-	1.95	4.29
$\Sigma\dot{p}_w(t-i)$	2.065	-.039	1.282	.072	1.858	-.002	1.314	.252
(t=)	(2.67)	(.22)	(2.23)	(1.10)	(2.92)	(.03)	(2.40)	(2.18)
F-test	3.45	3.02	8.31	2.73	4.22	3.44	1.68	7.78
RHO1	-	-.674	.017	-	-	-	-	-.629
(t=)	-	(1.50)	(.08)	-	-	-	-	(2.49)
$\bar{R}^2$	.938	.929	.786	.954	.942	.946	.936	.908
DW	2.02	1.81	1.96	2.19	2.10	1.73	1.88	2.10
Dh	-	*	*	-	-	-	-	*
Dm(AR1)	.44	*	*	1.82	.88	1.58	1.26	*
Dm(AR4)	2.94	*	*	2.47	2.00	3.80	3.73	*
CHOW	-		-		2.54		-	
Method	OLS	HAT	HAT	OLS	OLS	OLS	OLS	HAT

Note: See table 5.16.

Table 5.20

Annual Nested Inflation Equations:
The Role of Foreign Inflation
Complete Results

$$\dot{p}(t) = c_0 + c_1\dot{p}(t-1) + c_2\dot{M}(t-1) + c_3X(t-1) + c_4\dot{p}_w(t-1) + c_5REGIME + \epsilon(t)$$

Variable	Monetary Base (MB)		Money Supply (M1)	
	U-Version	$\dot{W}$-Version	U-Version	$\dot{W}$-Version
constant	3.266 (1.58)	.650 (.60)	2.506 (1.44)	1.101 (1.11)
$\dot{p}(t-1)$	.518 (<u>2.24</u>)	.700 (1.36)	.592 (<u>2.38</u>)	.639 (1.24)
$\dot{M}(t-1)$	-.063 (.50)	.092 (.71)	-.025 (.38)	.005 (.06)
$u(t-1)$	-.683 (<u>3.10</u>)	-	-.589 (<u>3.01</u>)	-
$\dot{W}(t-1)$	-	-.053 (.17)	-	.017 (.06)
$\dot{p}_w(t-1)$	-.128 (.77)	.105 (1.07)	-.114 (.81)	.077 (.79)
REGIME	3.940 (<u>2.94</u>)	-.643 (.76)	3.509 (<u>2.90</u>)	-.448 (.55)
RHO1	.418 (<u>3.77</u>)	-	.333 (<u>2.30</u>)	-
$\bar{R}^2$	.400	.373	.381	.356
DW	2.04	1.65	1.89	1.63
Dh	*	-	*	-
Dm(AR1)	*	1.63	*	2.15
Method	HAT	OLS	HAT	OLS
Period	1963-85	1962-85	1963-85	1962-85

Note: See table 5.18.

consistently. To allow for a more direct channel of transmission for foreign factors, we re-estimate both equations with foreign (U.S.) inflation instead of foreign (U.S.) interest rates. A summary of the regression results is presented in tables 5.19 (quarterly data) and 5.20 (annual data). The complete quarterly regressions are given in tables A5.19a-d in the appendix.

The conclusions pertaining to competing views of inflation are basically unchanged. The Monetarist propositions are clearly rejected by the data and the Keynesian hypotheses are supported. In addition, foreign (U.S.) inflation emerges as an additional variable contributing to German inflation, especially in the fixed exchange rate period. For the flexible period, the sum of $\dot{p}_w$-coefficients is insignificant in three of four cases, but the hypothesis that the coefficients are jointly different from zero must be rejected. This result lends support to the argument that the international transmission of inflation is more pronounced under a fixed exchange rate regime where the central bank cannot conduct an independent monetary policy.

The regressions with annual data (table 5.20) over the entire sample period result in insignificant coefficients on foreign rates of inflation. Nevertheless, the earlier findings concering the respective roles of unemployment and money growth are unchanged, that is, the Monetarist hypothesis is clearly rejected while the Keynesian scenario is supported. For the "underlying rate of inflation" equation, however, neither view is supported by the evidence since the coefficients on lagged wage inflation and lagged money growth are insignificant.

The NCE Inflation Equation

The reduced-form inflation equation derived from the structural model under NCE parameter specifications combines elements of both the Monetarist and Keynesian views. A New Classical economist can agreee with the nested inflation equation if contemporaneous anticipated money growth is used instead of lagged actual money growth. Note that the NCE equation also includes lagged real balances.

Table 5.21

Annual NCE Inflation Equations:
Results for Different Models of Anticipated Money Growth

$$\dot{p}(t) = d_0 + d_1\dot{M}^*(t) + d_2u(t-1) + d_3\ln m(t-1) + d_4REGIME + \epsilon(t)$$

| | Univariate Models of $\dot{M}^*$ | | | | Multivariate Models of $\dot{M}^*$ | | | |
| | NSA Data | | SA Data | | NSA Data | | SA Data | |
Variable	MB	M1	MB	M1	MB	M1	MB	M1
constant	5.588	1.054	5.495	.079	4.622	1.542	4.654	1.237
(t=)	(**4.20**)	(.39)	(**3.73**)	(.03)	(**3.85**)	(.60)	(**3.84**)	(.52)
$\dot{M}^*(t)$	-.295	.546	-.193	.899	.317	.250	.300	.402
(t=)	(.42	(1.05)	(.25)	(1.25)	(.63)	(.79)	(.59)	(1.49)
u(t-1)	-.711	-.769	-.722	-.794	-.775	-.773	-.775	-.784
(t=)	(**2.95**)	(**3.18**)	(**3.02**)	(**3.43**)	(**3.25**)	(**3.06**)	(**3.23**)	(**3.36**)
lnm(t-1)	5.555	6.128	5.910	6.687	7.600	6.064	7.641	5.919
(t=)	(1.00)	(1.27)	(1.06)	(1.46)	(1.47)	(1.25)	(1.47)	(1.29)
REGIME	1.038	1.071	.947	1.193	.794	1.235	.775	1.541
(t=)	(.71)	(.83)	(.64)	(.95)	(.60)	(.93)	(.59)	(1.20)
RHO1	.558	.538	.555	.498	.530	.523	.530	.539
(t=)	(**2.75**)	(**2.63**)	(**2.68**)	(**2.15**)	(**2.40**)	(**2.39**)	(**2.41**)	(**2.48**)
$\bar{R}^2$	.564	.571	.561	.586	.571	.560	.569	.601
DW	1.48	1.53	1.49	1.63	1.51	1.53	1.51	1.59
Method	HILU	HILU	HILU	HILU	HILU	HILU	HILU	HILU
Period	63-85	63-85	63-85	63-85	63-85	63-85	63-85	63-85

Note: The variables are: $\dot{p}$ inflation rate; $\dot{M}^*$ anticipated rate of money growth; u unemployment rate; m real balances; REGIME dummy variable for the exchange rate regime break in 1973. The figures in parantheses below the coefficient estimates are absolute values of t-statistics. Significance at the 5% (or higher) level is indicated by **boldface**, at the 10% level by *italics*. The Hildreth-Lu (HILU) method is used to correct for first-order serial correlation; RHO1 is the estimated autocorrelation coefficient. The NCE hypothesis implies $d_1 > 0$ for given (lagged) unemployment and real balances.

Table 5.21 presents the results from estimating the NCE equation with annual data over the entire sample period. To check the robustness of our findings, four alternative models of anticipated money growth are considered for each of the money definitions - the monetary base (MB) and the narrow money supply (M1). To correct for significant first-order serial correlation, the NCE equations are estimated with the Hildreth-Lu (HILU) search procedure.

The NCE proposition that inflation depends contemporaneously on anticipated money growth must be rejected for all eight specifications since the relevant coefficient is statistically insignificant. On the other hand, the coefficient on lagged unemployment, which represents the current anticipated unemployment rate in the NCE model, is significantly negative. This lends further support to the Keynesian belief in the Phillips curve.

Let us conclude this section by summarizing the wealth of empirical information provided on the various theories of inflation. Overall, the evidence strongly supports the Keynesian propositions while rejecting both the Monetarist and NCE scenarios. This result is fairly robust across different specifications of the inflation equation, including lag length, money definitions, models of anticipated money growth, sample period, and data frequency. Our findings differ from those of earlier studies where the Monetarist explanation of German inflation is generally declared the winner. However, these studies use goodness of fit considerations instead of *direct* tests of opposing theories. Our approach employs such direct statistical tests to let the data "speak," and the data have "spoken" in favor of the Keynesian interpretation of inflation.

5. A "CORRECT" MODEL OF THE GERMAN ECONOMY? CONCLUSIONS AND OUTLOOK

This study is motivated by the controversy among Monetarist, Keynesian, and New Classical economists about the short-run determinants of output, unemployment, and inflation. The unsettled state of macroeconomics points toward the need for continued research which focuses on the *substantial* differences between the opposing schools of thought and provides *direct* evidence on the explanatory power of alternative statistical hypotheses. Our study presents such a synthesis theoretical and empirical approach and applies it to the German economy from 1960-85.

In this chapter, we specify a general macrodynamic model of the German economy which incorporates the evidence on the dynamic structure and the causal orderings of macrovariables from chapter IV. The general framework implies the opposing schools of thought as special cases. Monetarist, Keynesian, and New Classical reduced-form equations for unemployment, output, and inflation are derived from the structural model under certain parameter specifications, reflecting each school's crucial propositions. The controversy among macroeconomists about the dynamics between steady states is thus reduced to tests of alternative statistical hypotheses in nested regression equations.

Focusing on *substantial* rather than minor and/or stylistic differences among the three schools of thought, the nested regression equations reflect the views of unemployment, output, and inflation of the *two* schools which are directly opposed to each other. The third school can either accept one of the polar views or combines elements of both polar views.

As far as the "real sector" is concerned, the Monetarist (M) and New Classical (NCE) explanations of unemployment and real output are directly opposed due to each school's assumption about the formation of inflationary expectations. Keynesians (K) can agree, in principle, with the proposed Monetarist regression equations even though they would add a fiscal variable to the list of regressors. The nested regression equations for unemployment and output include the "crucial" variables reflecting the two extreme views: changes in real balances (M) and unanticipated money growth (NCE).

With respect to the short-term determinants of inflation, we focus on the Monetarist-Keynesian debate by considering nested regression equations which include the rate of money growth (M) as well as the unemployment rate or the "underlying rate of inflation" in nominal wages (K). In addition, the role of foreign influences on German inflation is assessed. The New Classical propositions, which combine elements of the polar Monetarist and Keynesian views, are also tested in a non-nested equation.

All tests of competing macroeconomic theories are conducted in the form of *nested* regression equations to avoid the observational equivalence problem present in all three reduced-form equations. The New Classical unemployment and output equations are observationally equivalent to Monetarist equations, if there exists a monetary policy reaction function which includes lagged money growth and lagged inflation. Similarly, if monetary policy responds to lagged inflation and unemployment, the Monetarist inflation equation is observationally equivalent to the Keynesian specification. The multivariate Granger causality tests, performed to specify a money growth forecasting equation, indicate that the observational equivalence problem is an empirical reality in the German case. The problem is avoided by nesting the alternative macroeconomic hypotheses in *single* reduced-form regression equations.

To answer the question posed at the outset of this section, no single model can explain the past twenty-five years of unemployment, real output, and inflation in Germany. However, the evidence clearly rejects the New Classical hypotheses.

Our "real sector" results indicate that unanticipated money growth does not consistently affect unemployment or real output at conventional significance levels, so that the New Classical propositions are inconsistent with the data. Changes in real balances, on the other hand, exhibit significant coefficients in the nested and preferred equations, thus supporting the Monetarist view (which can also be accepted by Keynesians). These findings are fairly robust across different specifications of the unemployment and output equations which consider alternative money definitions, models of unanticipated money growth, and data frequencies.

The evidence for the inflation equation overwhelmingly supports the Keynesian model and confirms the existence of a downward sloping Phillips curve. In addition, the Monetarist and New Classical propositions are strongly rejected by the German data since neither actual (lagged) nor anticipated (contemporaneous) money growth affect inflation significantly. Furthermore, the German rate of inflation is also influenced by foreign variables, most importantly, foreign inflation. These results are robust for different specifications of the inflation equation, using alternative money definitions, proxies for the state of the labor market, measures of foreign impulses, models of anticipated money growth, lag lengths, data frequencies, and subperiods.

It should be stressed that our regression results for the "real sector" are not necessarily stable across different exchange rate regimes. The nested unemployment and output equations uniformly fail the structural stability tests. For the Bretton Woods era of fixed exchange rates, neither Monetarist nor New Classical theories explain the evidence consistently. In some specifications, the NCE propositions are weakly supported since unanticipated money growth matters at marginal significance levels. Under flexible exchange rates, changes in real balances are the only significant and systematic influence on German unemployment and output.

Taken together, the results for the fixed and flexible exchange rate periods are not inconsistent with our prior knowledge of German economic realities. Monetary policy was not used actively as a demand management tool in the 1960's, so that the money supply did not systematically affect the real sector. Instead, the money supply expanded to accommodate the continued (albeit slower) growth of the maturing "Wirtschaftschaftswunder." The influence of unanticipated monetary changes, possibly caused by unanticipated international reserve flows at times of currency crises, reflects the degree of monetary interdependence under fixed exchange rates and the inability of the Bundesbank to sterilize reserve flows completely. With the breakdown of the Bretton Woods system in 1973, Germany gained greater monetary independence allowing the use of monetary policy for domestic stabilization purposes. This fact is reflected by the significant coefficient estimates for real balances in the unemployment and output equations.

For the inflation rate, the transition from monetary interdependence under fixed exchange rates to greater independence under the current system of managed floating does not matter as much. No relationship between money growth and inflation is detected for either subperiod, so that the Keynesian model is always consistent with the data. However, the inverse relationship between unemployment and inflation is not stable across the two exchange rate regimes, indicating that the Phillips curve has shifted and changed its slope over time. Given the transition from fixed to flexible exchange rates and the concurrent increase in the variability of money growth, this finding can be interpreted as indirectly consistent with the New Classical view. However, *direct* tests of the NCE inflation hypothesis reject that school of thought since anticipated contemporaneous money growth is never significant.

The general macrodynamic framework, upon which our empirical analysis is based, is deliberately simple in its structure and, thus, easily subject to criticism. However, the purpose of this exercise is to emphasize *substantial* rather than stylistic differences between the competing schools of macroeconomic thought. Our simple small-scale model is capable of generating reduced-form equations for output, unemployment, and inflation which are consistent with each school's key propositions about the short-term determinants of these macrovariables. In addition, the specification of our model is guided by the major findings from chapter IV about the causal orderings and the dynamic structure of the German economy over the 1960-85 sample period. The inclusion or exclusion of relevant variables on an ad-hoc basis is thus avoided. Several possibilities for extending and generalizing our approach exist.

First, and foremost, the empirical analysis can be extended to explicitly acknowledge and test differences between all *three* competing theories of output, unemployment, and inflation. Our study contrasts the Monetarist and New Classical hypotheses about unemployment and output, but does not incorporate Keynesian considerations explicitely. Similarly, the analysis of inflation is conducted primarily in terms of the Monetarist-Keynesian debate, even though some evidence on the New Classical point of view is also presented.

Second, the inflation equation of the structural model assumes that the overall rate of inflation in Germany can be explained by domestic factors alone. Import prices are not given an explicit role, even though they enter indirectly by affecting the demand for imports and, thus, the excess demand for domestic output. An extended model would express the overall rate of inflation as a weighted average of inflation in home goods and imported goods. Previous findings suggest that import prices do not matter for the German inflationary experience over similar sample periods, but our results support the existence of an international transmission mechanism for inflation.

Third, our model abstracts almost completely from physical capital accumulation since the stock of capital and the growth of productive capacity over time are held constant in the model's production function. The demand side of net investment is captured, to some extent, by including the real interest rate as a determinant of the aggregate demand function. Incorporating physical capital accumulation will make the model more realistic for the analysis of a *growing* economy.

Finally, the structural model and the implied reduced-form equations for unemployment, output, and inflation can be tested further by applying them to other economies. In particular, we would hope for *uniform* results for unemployment/output and inflation, given a constant exchange rate regime and longer sample periods. Evidence from cross-country comparisons - considering, for example, other European economies or the Japanese economy - can only enhance and contribute to the ongoing macroeconomic debate.

Table A5.6

Nested Annual Unemployment Equations
Using Stationary First Differences of the Unemployment Rate:
Results for Different Models of Unanticipated Money Growth

$$Du(t) = a_0 + a_1 Du(t-1) + a_2 \dot{m}(t-1) + a_3 U\dot{M}(t-1) + a_4 REGIME + \epsilon(t)$$

| Variable | Univariate Models of UM | | | | Multivariate Models of UM | | | |
| | NSA Data | | SA Data | | NSA Data | | SA Data | |
	MB	M1	MB	M1	MB	M1	MB	M1
constant	.468	.628	.711	.625	.535	.685	.629	.662
(t=)	(1.03)	(3.06)	(1.91)	(3.01)	(1.16)	(3.48)	(1.53)	(3.37)
Du(t-1)	-.157	.157	-.483	.179	-.187	.128	-.300	.125
(t=)	(.61)	(1.12)	(1.32)	(1.20)	(.71)	(.92)	(.93)	(.92)
$\dot{m}$(t-1)	-.210	-.166	-.239	-.165	-.227	-.183	-.225	-.178
(t=)	(3.35)	(4.34)	(3.31)	(4.23)	(3.58)	(5.55)	(3.50)	(5.41)
U$\dot{M}$(t-1)	-.296	-.128	-.209	-.149	-.095	-.032	-.005	-.216
(t=)	(1.42)	(.84)	(.82)	(.81)	(.30)	(.16)	(.01)	(.75)
REGIME	.930	.381	.885	.361	.936	.387	.856	.399
(t=)	(1.78)	(1.69)	(2.05)	(1.58)	(1.74)	(1.68)	(1.74)	(1.76)
RHO1	.453	-	.873	-	.400	-	.553	-
(t=)	(1.53)	-	(2.01)	-	(1.35)	-	(1.45)	-
$\bar{R}^2$	.393	.660	.418	.659	.318	.647	.299	.657
DW	1.47	1.84	1.50	1.93	1.49	1.88	1.48	1.80
Dh	*	.53	*	.26	*	.40	*	.63
Dm(AR1)	*	.001	*	.06	*	.04	*	.000
Method	HAT	OLS	HAT	OLS	HAT	OLS	HAT	OLS
Period	64-85	63-85	64-85	63-85	64-85	63-85	64-85	63-85

Note: See table 5.6 in the text.

Table A5.7a

Nested Quarterly Unemployment Equations
Using Stationary First Differences of the Unemployment Rate:
Monetary Base (MB)
Summary of Results for Different Models of Unanticipated Money Growth

$$Du(t) = a_0 + \sum_{i=1}^{4} a_{1i}Du(t-i) + \sum_{i=1}^{4} a_{2i}\dot{m}(t-i) + \sum_{i=1}^{4} a_{3i}U\dot{M}(t-i) + \sum_{j=1}^{3} s_j SEAS(j) + \epsilon(t)$$

| | Univariate Models of UṀ | | | | Multivariate Models of UṀ | | | |
| | NSA Data | | SA Data | | NSA Data | | SA Data | |
Variable	Fix	Flex	Fix	Flex	Fix	Flex	Fix	Flex
constant	.846	.554	.868	.612	.843	.516	.809	.268
(t=)	(3.38)	(1.11)	(3.40)	(1.11)	(3.44)	(1.10)	(3.31)	(.55)
ΣDu(t-i)	.287	.076	.322	.084	.267	.307	.260	.301
(t=)	(.84)	(.32)	(.99)	(.36)	(.80)	(1.84)	(.78)	(1.80)
Σṁ(t-i)	.003	-.379	-.007	-.410	.007	-.260	.002	-.261
(t=)	(.04)	(2.87)	(.09)	(2.93)	(.10)	(3.55)	(.02)	(3.64)
F-test	.171	4.719	.051	3.460	.073	5.726	.063	5.711
ΣUṀ(t-i)	-.012	.229	.054	.271	-.031	-.049	-.039	-.076
(t=)	(.16)	(1.11)	(.47)	(1.25)	(.21)	(.28)	(.26)	(.42)
F-test	.180	1.446	.100	.967	.250	1.319	.169	1.121
$\bar{R}^2$	.756	.940	.758	.939	.736	.941	.761	.940
DW	2.05	2.13	1.94	2.13	1.93	2.21	1.95	2.29
Dh	-	-	-	-	-	-	-	-
Dm(AR1)	.43	.63	.05	1.42	.01	1.19	.000	2.71
Dm(AR4)	1.00	.48	.38	.000	.16	.13	.14	.02
CHOW	2.42		2.31		2.33		2.18	
Method	OLS	OLS	OLS	OLS	OLS	OLS	OLS	OLS

Note: The F-statistics test the hypothesis that the four lagged coefficients are jointly equal to zero. The Monetarist view cannot be rejected if $\Sigma a_{2i} < 0$ and $\Sigma a_{3i} = 0$; the NCE hypothesis must be accepted if $\Sigma a_{2i} = 0$ and $\Sigma a_{3i} < 0$. Significance at the 5% (or higher) level is indicated by **boldface**, at the 10% level by *italics*. The figures in parantheses are absolute values of t-statistics. Durbin's m-statistic (Dm) tests the hypothesis of no first (AR1) or fourth-order (AR4) autocorrelation. Due to space limitations, estimates for the seasonal dummies SEAS(j) are not reported here.

Table A5.7b

Nested Quarterly Unemployment Equations
Using Stationary First Differences of the Unemployment Rate:
Money Supply (M1)
Summary of Results for Different Models of Unanticipated Money Growth

$$Du(t) = a_0 + \sum_{i=1}^{4} a_{1i}Du(t-i) + \sum_{i=1}^{4} a_{2i}\dot{m}(t-i) + \sum_{i=1}^{4} a_{3i}U\dot{M}(t-i) + \sum_{j=1}^{3} s_j SEAS(j) + \epsilon(t)$$

| | Univariate Models of UṀ | | | | Multivariate Models of UṀ | | | |
| | NSA Data | | SA Data | | NSA Data | | SA Data | |
Variable	Fix	Flex	Fix	Flex	Fix	Flex	Fix	Flex
constant	.802	.533	.469	.389	.658	.311	.687	.298
(t=)	(2.66)	(1.45)	(1.52)	(.90)	(2.42)	(.89)	(3.13)	(.84)
ΣDu(t-i)	.242	.507	.302	.383	.178	.577	.287	.599
(t=)	(.73)	(3.10)	(.97)	(2.01)	(.53)	(3.89)	(.86)	(4.07)
Σṁ(t-i)	-.055	-.285	-.065	-.316	-.085	-.184	-.071	-.174
(t=)	(.61)	(3.94)	(.80)	(2.89)	(1.25)	(3.87)	(1.25)	(3.78)
F-test	.458	3.907	.497	3.348	.608	3.881	.785	4.003
ΣUṀ(t-i)	-.067	.177	-.070	.267	-.071	.106	-.114	.124
(t=)	(.62)	(1.87)	(.54)	(1.67)	(.58)	(1.28)	(.57)	(.94)
F-test	.159	1.135	.935	1.735	.536	.612	3.064	.692
$\bar{R}^2$	.776	.933	.801	.938	.790	.929	.844	.929
DW	1.90	1.91	1.96	2.11	1.99	2.05	2.02	2.09
Dh	-	-	-	-	-	-	-	-
Dm(AR1)	.54	3.71	.01	.23	.64	1.16	.44	.02
Dm(AR4)	.52	1.70	.004	.11	.19	3.46	.29	2.73
CHOW	1.35		1.62		1.50		2.37	
Method	OLS	OLS	OLS	OLS	OLS	OLS	OLS	OLS

Note: See table A5.7a.

Table A5.8a

Nested Quarterly Unemployment Equation
Using Stationary First Differences of the Unemployment Rate:
Monetary Base (MB)
Complete Results for the Multivariate NSA Model
of Unanticipated Money Growth

$$Du(t) = a_0 + \sum_{i=1}^{4} a_{1i}Du(t-i) + \sum_{i=1}^{4} a_{2i}\dot{m}(t-i) + \sum_{i=1}^{4} a_{3i}U\dot{M}(t-i) + \sum_{j=1}^{3} s_j SEAS(j) + \epsilon(t)$$

Method	Lag	constant	$Du(t-i)$	$\dot{m}(t-i)$	$U\dot{M}(t-i)$	$SEAS(j)$
Fixed Exchange Rates (1962.2-1972.4)						
OLS	1	.843 (<u>3.44</u>)	.267 (1.35)	-.005 (.21)	.040 (.60)	-1.776 (<u>4.40</u>)
	2		-.182 (.91)	-.003 (.11)	-.007 (.10)	-.737 (*1.99*)
	3		.256 (1.27)	.009 (.37)	-.023 (.34)	-.840 (<u>2.10</u>)
	4		-.074 (.37)	.006 (.25)	-.041 (.58)	
	Sum		.267 (.80)	.007 (.10)	-.031 (.21)	
	F-test		.753	.073	.250	
		$\bar{R}^2 = .763$	DW = 1.93	Dm(AR1) = .01		
			Dh = -	Dm(AR4) = .16		
Flexible Exchange Rates (1975.1-1985.4)						
OLS	1	.516 (1.10)	.249 (1.46)	-.121 (<u>2.80</u>)	.020 (.18)	-1.473 (*1.85*)
	2		.236 (1.32)	-.028 (.58)	.022 (.18)	.029 (.05)
	3		-.442 (<u>2.35</u>)	.017 (.34)	-.221 (*1.98*)	.422 (.51)
	4		.263 (1.64)	-.128 (<u>3.24</u>)	.130 (1.25)	
	Sum		.307 (*1.84*)	-.260 (<u>3.55</u>)	-.049 (.28)	
	F-test		*2.438*	<u>5.762</u>	1.319	
		$\bar{R}^2 = .941$	DW = 2.21	Dm(AR1) = 1.19		
			Dh = -	Dm(AR4) = .13		

Note: The figures in parantheses are absolute values of t-statistics. **Boldface** denotes significance at the 5% (or higher) level, *italics* at the 10% level. The F-statistics test the hypothesis that the four lagged coefficients are jointly equal to zero. The Monetarist view cannot be rejected if $\Sigma a_{2i} < 0$ and $\Sigma a_{3i} = 0$; the NCE hypothesis must be accepted if $\Sigma a_{2i} = 0$ and $\Sigma a_{3i} < 0$.

Table A5.8b

Nested Quarterly Unemployment Equation
Using Stationary First Differences of the Unemployment Rate:
Money Supply (M1)
Complete Results for the Multivariate NSA Model
of Unanticipated Money Growth

$$Du(t) = a_0 + \sum_{i=1}^{4} a_{1i} Du(t-i) + \sum_{i=1}^{4} a_{2i} \dot{m}(t-i) + \sum_{i=1}^{4} a_{3i} U\dot{M}(t-i) + \sum_{j=1}^{3} s_j SEAS(j) + \epsilon(t)$$

Method	Lag	constant	Du(t-i)	$\dot{m}$(t-i)	U$\dot{M}$(t-i)	SEAS(j)
Fixed Exchange Rates (1962.2-1972.4)						
OLS	1	.658 (<u>2.42</u>)	.178 (.94)	-.031 (1.44)	-.077 (1.17)	-1.343 (<u>3.04</u>)
	2		-.228 (1.15)	-.014 (.67)	-.041 (.66)	-.428 (.97)
	3		.123 (.62)	-.011 (.46)	.030 (.49)	-.498 (1.15)
	4		.105 (.54)	-.029 (1.19)	.017 (.30)	
	Sum		.178 (.53)	-.085 (1.25)	-.071 (.58)	
	F-test		.722	.608	.536	
	$\bar{R}^2$ = .790		DW = 1.99	Dm(AR1) = .64		
			Dh = -	Dm(AR4) = .19		
Flexible Exchange Rates (1975.1-1985.4)						
OLS	1	.311 (.89)	.247 (1.60)	-.049 (1.63)	.052 (1.10)	-1.055 (<i>1.99</i>)
	2		.100 (.54)	-.043 (1.28)	-.006 (.14)	.141 (.22)
	3		-.256 (1.46)	-.038 (1.06)	.034 (.83)	.398 (.85)
	4		.485 (<u>2.72</u>)	-.054 (1.63)	.025 (.63)	
	Sum		.577 (<u>3.89</u>)	-.184 (<u>3.87</u>)	.106 (1.28)	
	F-test		<u>5.212</u>	<u>3.881</u>	.612	
	$\bar{R}^2$ = .929		DW = 2.05	Dm(AR1) = 1.16		
			Dh = -	Dm(AR4) = 3.46		

Note: See table A5.8a.

Table A5.9a

Preferred Quarterly Unemployment Equation
Using Stationary First Differences of the Unemployment Rate:
Monetary Base (MB)

$$Du(t) = a_0 + \sum_{i=1}^{4} a_{1i}Du(t-i) + \sum_{i=1}^{4} a_{2i}\dot{m}(t-i) + \sum_{j=1}^{3} s_j SEAS(j) + \epsilon(t)$$

Method	Lag	constant	Du(t-i)	$\dot{m}$(t-i)	SEAS(j)
Fixed Exchange Rates (1961.2-1972.4)					
OLS	1	.807 (*3.86*)	.235 (1.39)	-.008 (.43)	-1.676 (**4.90**)
	2		-.154 (.90)	-.002 (.11)	-.721 (**2.27**)
	3		.251 (1.46)	.006 (.31)	-.794 (**2.28**)
	4		-.018 (.11)	.002 (.11)	
	Sum		.314 (1.15)	-.002 (.03)	
	F-test		.996	.105	
		$\overline{R}^2$ = .800	DW = 2.01	Dm(AR1) = .002	
			Dh = -	Dm(AR4) = .06	
Flexible Exchange Rates (1974.1-1985.4)					
OLS	1	.313 (.91)	.156 (1.12)	-.119 (**3.92**)	-1.071 (**2.00**)
	2		.352 (**2.34**)	-.024 (.77)	-.148 (.35)
	3		-.488 (**3.38**)	-.031 (1.02)	1.032 (*1.72*)
	4		.288 (**2.29**)	-.088 (**3.20**)	
	Sum		.308 (*1.93*)	-.262 (**4.55**)	
	F-test		**4.286**	**7.273**	
		$\overline{R}^2$ = .939	DW = 2.08	Dm(AR1) = 2.35	
			Dh = -1.15	Dm(AR4) = .000	

Note: The figures in parantheses are absolute values of t-statistics. Significance at the 5% (or higher) level is indicated by **boldface**, at the 10% level by *italics*. The F-statistics test the hypothesis that the four lagged coefficients are jointly equal to zero.

Table A5.9b

Preferred Quarterly Unemployment Equation
Using Stationary First Differences of the Unemployment Rate:
Money Supply (M1)

$$Du(t) = a_0 + \sum_{i=1}^{4} a_{1i} Du(t-i) + \sum_{i=1}^{4} a_{2i} \dot{m}(t-i) + \sum_{j=1}^{3} s_j SEAS(j) + \epsilon(t)$$

Method	Lag	constant	Du(t-i)	$\dot{m}$(t-i)	SEAS(j)
\multicolumn{6}{c}{**Fixed Exchange Rates (1961.2-1972.4)**}					
OLS	1	.839 (<u>3.90</u>)	.182 (1.07)	-.033 (*1.84*)	-1.597 (<u>4.43</u>)
	2		-.174 (1.04)	-.024 (1.36)	-.717 (<u>2.08</u>)
	3		.198 (1.18)	-.009 (.49)	-.692 (*1.94*)
	4		.036 (.23)	-.015 (.87)	
	Sum		.242 (.89)	-.082 (1.39)	
	F-test		.860	.926	
		$\bar{R}^2 = .817$	DW = 1.98	Dm(AR1) = .02	
			Dh = -	Dm(AR4) = .05	
\multicolumn{6}{c}{**Flexible Exchange Rates (1974.1-1985.4)**}					
OLS	1	.239 (.91)	.279 (*1.98*)	-.037 (1.39)	-1.148 (<u>3.06</u>)
	2		.216 (1.32)	-.044 (1.58)	.076 (.15)
	3		-.314 (<u>2.14</u>)	-.015 (.51)	.736 (*1.85*)
	4		.426 (<u>3.24</u>)	-.051 (<u>2.04</u>)	
	Sum		.608 (<u>4.23</u>)	-.147 (<u>4.24</u>)	
	F-test		<u>6.915</u>	<u>4.917</u>	
		$\bar{R}^2 = .929$	DW = 2.04	Dm(AR1) = .16	
			Dh = -.64	Dm(AR4) = .02	

Note: See table A5.9a.

Table A5.10

Preferred Annual Unemployment Equations
Using Stationary First Differences of the Unemployment Rate

$$Du(t) = a_0 + a_1 Du(t-1) + a_2 \dot{m}(t-1) + a_4 REGIME + \epsilon(t)$$

Variable	Monetary Base (MB)	Money Supply (M1)
constant	.533 (1.11)	.684 (<u>3.77</u>)
Du(t-1)	-.233 (1.26)	.130 (.99)
$\dot{m}$(t-1)	-.233 (<u>4.11</u>)	-.183 (<u>5.92</u>)
REGIME	1.027 (*1.84*)	.390 (*1.82*)
RHO1	.450 (<u>2.98</u>)	-
$\bar{R}^2$	.397	.673
DW	1.65	2.01
Dh	*	-.04
Dm(AR1)	*	.04
Method	HAT	OLS
Period	1963-85	1962-85

Note: The figures in parantheses are absolute values of t-statistics. Significance at the 5% (or higher level) is indicated by **boldface**, at the 10% level by *italics*. REGIME is a dummy variable for the exchange rate regime break in 1973. In the presence of serial correlation, the equations are re-estimated using Hatanaka's (1974) two-step estimator (HAT); RHO1 is the estimated serial correlation coefficient. * indicates that the Durbin's h-test, based on instrumental variables results, is not recommended as a test for autocorrelation.

Table A5.16a

Quarterly Nested Inflation Equation:
Complete Results for the Original Version (R3)
Monetary Base (MB) - 4 Lags

$$\dot{p}(t) = c_0 + \sum_{i=1}^{4} c_{1i}\dot{p}(t-i) + \sum_{i=1}^{4} c_{2i}\dot{M}(t-i) + \sum_{i=1}^{4} c_{3i}u(t-i) + \sum_{i=1}^{4} c_{4i}\dot{r}_w(t-i) + \epsilon(t)$$

Method	Lag	constant	$\dot{p}(t-i)$	$\dot{M}(t-i)$	$u(t-i)$	$\dot{r}_w(t-i)$

Fixed Exchange Rates (1961.2-1972.4)

Method	Lag	constant	$\dot{p}(t-i)$	$\dot{M}(t-i)$	$u(t-i)$	$\dot{r}_w(t-i)$
OLS	1	2.297 (1.16)	-.496 (_2.94_)	.138 (.50)	-1.684 (1.66)	-.020 (.69)
	2		-.294 (_1.81_)	-.004 (.02)	.324 (.22)	-.016 (.48)
	3		-.313 (_2.06_)	-.348 (1.15)	-1.008 (.68)	-.014 (.44)
	4		.416 (_2.86_)	-.463 (1.61)	1.012 (.93)	-.033 (1.10)
	Sum		-.685 (1.23)	-.676 (1.34)	-1.356 (_1.84_)	-.084 (1.46)
	F-test			.77	1.70	.66

$\bar{R}^2 = .915$ DW = 2.15   Dm(AR1) = .94
Dh = -   Dm(AR4) = .32

Flexible Exchange Rates (1975.1-1985.4)

Method	Lag	constant	$\dot{p}(t-i)$	$\dot{M}(t-i)$	$u(t-i)$	$\dot{r}_w(t-i)$
HAT	1	1.560 (.93)	-.548 (_2.09_)	-.204 (1.34)	-.836 (_2.02_)	-.015 (_2.26_)
	2		-.266 (1.66)	-.011 (.05)	1.467 (1.64)	.012 (1.67)
	3		.015 (.10)	.455 (_2.45_)	-.375 (.38)	.001 (.07)
	4		-.224 (1.50)	-.403 (_2.87_)	-.490 (1.01)	.011 (1.51)
	Sum		-1.022 (_2.52_)	-.163 (1.23)	-.234 (_3.97_)	.009 (.86)
	χ^2-test			_15.77_	_23.50_	7.98

$\bar{R}^2 = .942$ DW = 1.77   Dm(AR1) = *   RHO1 = -.24
Dh = *   Dm(AR4) = *   (1.03)

Note: The F-statistics (χ^2 with HAT-method) test the hypothesis that the four lagged coefficients are jointly equal to zero. The Monetarist view cannot be rejected if $\Sigma c_{2i} > 0$ and $\Sigma c_{3i} = 0$; the Keynesian propositions are $\Sigma c_{2i} = 0$ and $\Sigma c_{3i} < 0$. Significance at the 5% (or higher) level is indicated by **boldface**, at the 10% level by _italics_. Durbin's m-statistic (Dm) tests the hypothesis of no first (AR1) or fourth-order (AR4) autocorrelation. In the presence of serial correlation, the equations are re-estimated using Hatanaka's (1974) two-step estimator (HAT); RHO1 is the estimated autocorrelation coefficient. * indicates that Durbin's h-test is not recommended as a test for autocorrelation with instrumental variables results. The regressions also include three seasonal dummies, but the coefficient estimates are not reported due to space limitations.

Table A5.16b

Quarterly Nested Inflation Equation:
Complete Results for the Original Version (R3)
Monetary Base (MB) - 6 Lags

$$\dot{p}(t) - c_0 + \sum_{i=1}^{4} c_{1i}\dot{p}(t-i) + \sum_{i=1}^{6} c_{2i}\dot{M}(t-i) + \sum_{i=1}^{4} c_{3i}u(t-i) + \sum_{i=1}^{4} c_{4i}\dot{r}_w(t-i) + \epsilon(t)$$

Method	Lag	constant	$\dot{p}(t-i)$	$\dot{M}(t-i)$	$u(t-i)$	$\dot{r}_w(t-i)$
Fixed Exchange Rates (1961.4-1972.4)						
OLS	1	2.423 (1.00)	-.528 (_2.76_)	.103 (.33)	-1.728 (1.54)	-.026 (.77)
	2		-.342 (_1.70_)	.044 (.13)	.274 (.17)	-.018 (.46)
	3		-.330 (_1.78_)	-.287 (.74)	-1.118 (.68)	-.016 (.45)
	4		.409 (_2.50_)	-.522 (1.36)	1.121 (.87)	-.036 (.97)
	5		-	-.121 (.33)	-	-
	6		-	.035 (.12)	-	-
	Sum		-.792 (1.20)	-.748 (1.24)	-1.451 (_1.70_)	-.095 (1.29)
	F-test			.43	1.49	.50
		$\bar{R}^2 - .894$	DW - 2.11	Dm(AR1) - .36		
			Dh - -	Dm(AR4) - .45		
Flexible Exchange Rates (1974.3-1985.4)						
OLS	1	.209 (.14)	-.532 (_3.24_)	-.459 (_2.60_)	-.273 (.57)	-.006 (.80)
	2		.093 (.52)	.479 (_2.77_)	.671 (.99)	.005 (.71)
	3		-.013 (.08)	.073 (.56)	-.063 (.09)	-.000 (.02)
	4		-.054 (.39)	-.052 (.38)	-.490 (1.16)	.010 (1.29)
	5		-	-.410 (_3.48_)	-	-
	6		-	.412 (_2.95_)	-	-
	Sum		-.505 (1.28)	.044 (.17)	-.154 (_2.11_)	.009 (.66)
	F-test			_5.00_	2.05	.48
		$\bar{R}^2 - .967$	DW - 1.89	Dm(AR1) - 1.02		
			Dh - -	Dm(AR4) - .18		

Note: See table A5.16a.

Table A5.16c

Quarterly Nested Inflation Equation:
Complete Results for the Original Version (R3)
Money Supply (M1) - 4 Lags

$$\dot{p}(t) = c_0 + \sum_{i=1}^{4} c_{1i}\dot{p}(t-i) + \sum_{i=1}^{4} c_{2i}\dot{M}(t-i) + \sum_{i=1}^{4} c_{3i}u(t-i) + \sum_{i=1}^{4} c_{4i}\dot{r}_w(t-i) + \epsilon(t)$$

Method	Lag	constant	$\dot{p}(t-i)$	$\dot{M}(t-i)$	$u(t-i)$	$\dot{r}_w(t-i)$
			Fixed Exchange Rates (1961.2-1972.4)			
OLS	1	-1.402 (.44)	-.513 (_3.03_)	-.393 (1.16)	-.375 (.32)	-.044 (1.54)
	2		-.345 (_1.99_)	.329 (.95)	-1.739 (.99)	-.036 (1.16)
	3		-.293 (_1.78_)	.325 (.89)	-.261 (.16)	-.028 (.94)
	4		.466 (_3.07_)	-.344 (1.03)	1.789 (1.51)	-.009 (.32)
	Sum		-.685 (1.17)	-.083 (.22)	-.587 (.89)	-.118 (_1.84_)
	F-test			1.07	1.79	1.11
		$\overline{R}^2 = .918$	DW = 2.13	Dm(AR1) = .37		
			Dh = -	Dm(AR4) = .34		
			Flexible Exchange Rates (1974.1-1985.4)			
OLS	1	.938 (.55)	-.481 (_1.98_)	.075 (.72)	-.705 (1.31)	-.009 (.87)
	2		-.078 (.32)	-.095 (.84)	1.337 (1.47)	.011 (1.14)
	3		-.071 (.32)	-.020 (.21)	-.445 (.47)	.012 (1.09)
	4		.048 (.26)	-.016 (.18)	-.375 (.69)	.002 (.14)
	Sum		-.582 (.96)	-.055 (.51)	-.188 (_2.11_)	.016 (.78)
	F-test			.32	1.74	.95
		$\overline{R}^2 = .929$	DW = 1.82	Dm(AR1) = 2.61		
			Dh = -	Dm(AR4) = _3.65_		

Note: See table A5.16a.

Table A5.16d

Quarterly Nested Inflation Equation:
Complete Results for the Original Version (R3)
Money Supply (M1) - 6 Lags

$$\dot{p}(t) = c_0 + \sum_{i=1}^{4} c_{1i}\dot{p}(t-i) + \sum_{i=1}^{6} c_{2i}\dot{M}(t-i) + \sum_{i=1}^{4} c_{3i}u(t-i) + \sum_{i=1}^{4} c_{4i}\dot{r}_w(t-i) + \epsilon(t)$$

Method	Lag	constant	$\dot{p}(t-i)$	$\dot{M}(t-i)$	$u(t-i)$	$\dot{r}_w(t-i)$

Fixed Exchange Rates (1963.2-1972.4)

Method	Lag	constant	$\dot{p}(t-i)$	$\dot{M}(t-i)$	$u(t-i)$	$\dot{r}_w(t-i)$
HAT	1	-3.271 (.71)	-.367 (*2.01*)	-.552 (1.30)	-.699 (.58)	-.051 (1.64)
	2		-.374 (*2.01*)	.384 (.82)	-.743 (.37)	-.020 (.58)
	3		-.128 (.74)	.579 (1.23)	-1.136 (.54)	-.050 (1.40)
	4		.628 (<u>3.84</u>)	-.549 (1.15)	2.035 (1.59)	.026 (.66)
	5		-	.356 (.84)	-	-
	6		-	-.562 (1.66)	-	-
	Sum		-.241 (.41)	-.344 (.85)	-.543 (.91)	-.095 (1.17)
χ^2-test				9.16	6.89	6.76

$\overline{R}^2$ = .754   DW = 1.91   Dm(AR1) = *   RHO1 = .32
Dh = *   Dm(AR4) = *   (1.42)

Flexible Exchange Rates (1974.3-1985.4)

Method	Lag	constant	$\dot{p}(t-i)$	$\dot{M}(t-i)$	$u(t-i)$	$\dot{r}_w(t-i)$
OLS	1	2.458 (1.47)	-.385 (1.67)	.043 (.46)	-.948 (*1.83*)	-.011 (1.21)
	2		-.132 (.59)	-.088 (.87)	1.397 (*1.75*)	.011 (1.34)
	3		-.134 (.68)	.012 (.13)	-.251 (.28)	.005 (.52)
	4		.046 (.26)	.043 (.51)	-.415 (.76)	.008 (.72)
	5		-	-.174 (<u>2.20</u>)	-	-
	6		-	-.040 (.49)	-	-
	Sum		-.605 (1.14)	-.205 (1.65)	-.217 (<u>2.65</u>)	.014 (.80)
	F-test			1.39	*2.56*	.94

$\overline{R}^2$ = .945   DW = 2.05   Dm(AR1) = .10
Dh = -   Dm(AR4) = .55

Note: See table A5.16a.

Table A5.17a

Quarterly Nested Inflation Equation:
Complete Results for the "Underlying Rate of Inflation" Version (R4)
Monetary Base (MB) - 4 Lags

$$\dot{p}(t) = c_0 + \sum_{i=1}^{4} c_{1i}\dot{p}(t-i) + \sum_{i=1}^{4} c_{2i}\dot{M}(t-i) + \sum_{i=1}^{4} c_{3i}\dot{W}(t-i) + \sum_{i=1}^{4} c_{4i}\dot{r}_w(t-i) + \epsilon(t)$$

Method	Lag	constant	$\dot{p}(t-i)$	$\dot{M}(t-i)$	$\dot{W}(t-i)$	$\dot{r}_w(t-i)$
			Fixed Exchange Rates (1961.2-1972.4)			
OLS	1	-.563 (.48)	-.858 (<u>4.01</u>)	.182 (.69)	.706 (<u>2.32</u>)	.031 (1.10)
	2		-.721 (<u>3.24</u>)	.037 (.16)	.636 (<u>2.14</u>)	.009 (.30)
	3		-.693 (<u>3.29</u>)	-.339 (1.23)	.400 (1.32)	.030 (.99)
	4		.104 (.54)	-.460 (*1.77*)	.424 (1.56)	-.022 (.76)
	Sum		-2.169 (<u>2.75</u>)	-.580 (1.34)	2.166 (<u>3.38</u>)	.048 (.96)
	F-test			.92	<u>3.06</u>	.70

$\overline{R}^2 = .927$ DW = 1.99   Dm(AR1) = .25
Dh = -   Dm(AR4) = *3.55*

Method	Lag	constant	$\dot{p}(t-i)$	$\dot{M}(t-i)$	$\dot{W}(t-i)$	$\dot{r}_w(t-i)$
			Flexible Exchange Rates (1975.1-1985.4)			
HAT	1	-1.458 (1.09)	-.378 (1.03)	-.147 (.79)	.517 (<u>2.28</u>)	.005 (.54)
	2		.153 (.77)	.324 (1.44)	-.192 (.59)	.006 (.60)
	3		.113 (.57)	.045 (.17)	-.082 (.31)	.002 (.16)
	4		.073 (.46)	-.255 (1.23)	.022 (.11)	.013 (1.44)
	Sum		-.039 (.09)	-.032 (.27)	.266 (1.05)	.026 (<u>2.04</u>)
	χ^2-test			3.91	7.14	4.68

$\overline{R}^2 = .926$ DW = 1.70   Dm(AR1) = *   RHO1 = -.10
Dh = *   Dm(AR4) = *   (.27)

Note: See table A5.16a.

Table A5.17b

Quarterly Nested Inflation Equation:
Complete Results for the "Underlying Rate of Inflation" Version (R4)
Monetary Base (MB) - 6 Lags

$$\dot{p}(t) = c_0 + \sum_{i=1}^{4} c_{1i}\dot{p}(t-i) + \sum_{i=1}^{6} c_{2i}\dot{M}(t-i) + \sum_{i=1}^{4} c_{3i}\dot{W}(t-i) + \sum_{i=1}^{4} c_{4i}\dot{r}_w(t-i) + \epsilon(t)$$

Method	Lag	constant	$\dot{p}(t-i)$	$\dot{M}(t-i)$	$\dot{W}(t-i)$	$\dot{r}_w(t-i)$

Fixed Exchange Rates (1961.4-1972.4)

Method	Lag	constant	$\dot{p}(t-i)$	$\dot{M}(t-i)$	$\dot{W}(t-i)$	$\dot{r}_w(t-i)$
OLS	1	-1.175 (.82)	-.883 (<u>3.87</u>)	.245 (.85)	.680 (<u>2.10</u>)	.035 (1.10)
	2		-.708 (<u>2.94</u>)	.189 (.63)	.640 (<u>2.04</u>)	.016 (.48)
	3		-.694 (<u>3.03</u>)	-.361 (1.01)	.411 (1.29)	.043 (1.26)
	4		.076 (.37)	-.682 (*1.96*)	.565 (*1.74*)	-.013 (.36)
	5		-	-.167 (.54)	-	-
	6		-	.074 (.28)	-	-
	Sum		-2.208 (<u>2.62</u>)	-.701 (1.43)	2.295 (<u>3.35</u>)	.082 (1.33)
	F-test			.76	<u>2.99</u>	.82

$\overline{R}^2 = .912$ DW = 1.98   Dm(AR1) = .01
Dh = -   Dm(AR4) = 2.40

Flexible Exchange Rates (1974.3-1985.4)

Method	Lag	constant	$\dot{p}(t-i)$	$\dot{M}(t-i)$	$\dot{W}(t-i)$	$\dot{r}_w(t-i)$
OLS	1	-2.008 (2.27)	-.378 (<u>2.29</u>)	-.397 (<u>2.18</u>)	.358 (*1.82*)	.004 (.53)
	2		.254 (1.32)	.503 (<u>2.83</u>)	-.102 (.65)	.005 (.66)
	3		.274 (1.48)	.056 (.30)	.102 (.69)	-.000 (.03)
	4		.074 (.52)	-.098 (.74)	-.165 (1.16)	.006 (.77)
	5		-	-.388 (<u>2.90</u>)	-	-
	6		-	.329 (<u>2.77</u>)	-	-
	Sum		.224 (.55)	.004 (.03)	.193 (.74)	.015 (1.11)
	F-test			<u>3.38</u>	1.16	.43

$\overline{R}^2 = .963$ DW = 1.43   Dm(AR1) = *3.62*
Dh = -   Dm(AR4) = .84

Note: See table A5.16a.

Table A5.17c

Quarterly Nested Inflation Equation:
Complete Results for the "Underlying Rate of Inflation" Version (R4)
Money Supply (M1) - 4 Lags

$$\dot{p}(t) = c_0 + \sum_{i=1}^{4} c_{1i}\dot{p}(t-i) + \sum_{i=1}^{4} c_{2i}\dot{M}(t-i) + \sum_{i=1}^{4} c_{3i}\dot{W}(t-i) + \sum_{i=1}^{4} c_{4i}\dot{r}_w(t-i) + \epsilon(t)$$

Method	Lag	constant	$\dot{p}(t-i)$	$\dot{M}(t-i)$	$\dot{W}(t-i)$	$\dot{r}_w(t-i)$

Fixed Exchange Rates (1961.2-1972.4)

Method	Lag	constant	$\dot{p}(t-i)$	$\dot{M}(t-i)$	$\dot{W}(t-i)$	$\dot{r}_w(t-i)$
OLS	1	-.232 (.08)	-.798 (<u>3.44</u>)	-.232 (.74)	.651 (*1.86*)	.013 (.44)
	2		-.699 (<u>2.90</u>)	.285 (.90)	.664 (<u>2.14</u>)	-.002 (.08)
	3		-.659 (<u>2.88</u>)	.002 (.01)	.258 (.81)	.012 (.40)
	4		.152 (.72)	-.074 (.22)	.223 (.80)	-.014 (.46)
	Sum		-2.004 (<u>2.32</u>)	-.019 (.05)	1.795 (<u>2.62</u>)	.009 (.15)
	F-test			.33	2.05	.10

$\overline{R}^2 = .921$ DW = 1.87   Dm(AR1) = 2.59
Dh = -   Dm(AR4) = .04

Flexible Exchange Rates (1974.1-1985.4)

Method	Lag	constant	$\dot{p}(t-i)$	$\dot{M}(t-i)$	$\dot{W}(t-i)$	$\dot{r}_w(t-i)$
OLS	1	-1.224 (1.32)	-.357 (*1.81*)	-.027 (.26)	.525 (<u>3.51</u>)	-.002 (.29)
	2		-.206 (.98)	-.006 (.06)	-.113 (.69)	.012 (1.44)
	3		.076 (.40)	.028 (.31)	.336 (<u>2.09</u>)	.005 (.47)
	4		.196 (1.25)	-.015 (.19)	-.174 (1.11)	.008 (.72)
	Sum		-.291 (.60)	-.021 (.23)	.574 (<u>2.12</u>)	.022 (1.40)
	F-test			.04	<u>3.73</u>	.75

$\overline{R}^2 = .942$ DW = 1.90   Dm(AR1) = .05
Dh = -   Dm(AR4) = .78

Note: See table A5.16a.

Table A5.17d

Quarterly Nested Inflation Equation:
Complete Results for the "Underlying Rate of Inflation" Version (R4)
Money Supply (M1) - 6 Lags

$$\dot{p}(t) = c_0 + \sum_{i=1}^{4} c_{1i}\dot{p}(t-i) + \sum_{i=1}^{6} c_{2i}\dot{M}(t-i) + \sum_{i=1}^{4} c_{3i}\dot{W}(t-i) + \sum_{i=1}^{4} c_{4i}\dot{r}_w(t-i) + \epsilon(t)$$

Method	Lag	constant	$\dot{p}(t-i)$	$\dot{M}(t-i)$	$\dot{W}(t-i)$	$\dot{r}_w(t-i)$
			Fixed Exchange Rates (1961.4-1972.4)			
OLS	1	-1.253 (.34)	-.792 (<u>3.15</u>)	-.197 (.56)	.644 (1.65)	.014 (.40)
	2		-.670 (<u>2.50</u>)	.257 (.70)	.675 (*2.01*)	-.001 (.02)
	3		-.654 (<u>2.59</u>)	.079 (.21)	.217 (.61)	.015 (.43)
	4		.164 (.72)	-.170 (.42)	.252 (.77)	-.008 (.19)
	5		-	.121 (.32)	-	-
	6		-	-.124 (.40)	-	-
	Sum		-1.953 (<u>2.08</u>)	-.034 (.07)	1.788 (<u>2.37</u>)	.020 (.26)
	F-test			.24	1.76	.07

$\overline{R}^2 = .901$ DW = 1.87   Dm(AR1) = 2.96
Dh = -   Dm(AR4) = 1.45

			Flexible Exchange Rates (1974.3-1985.4)			
OLS	1	-.436 (.44)	-.344 (1.60)	-.002 (.02)	.504 (<u>2.18</u>)	.001 (.09)
	2		-.151 (.72)	-.029 (.25)	-.106 (.61)	.013 (1.60)
	3		.042 (.22)	.017 (.17)	.342 (<u>2.19</u>)	.006 (.60)
	4		.108 (.63)	.068 (.81)	-.142 (.85)	.008 (.73)
	5		-	-.146 (*1.80*)	-	-
	6		-	-.011 (.14)	-	-
	Sum		-.345 (.71)	-.102 (1.01)	.597 (<u>2.07</u>)	.028 (*1.77*)
	F-test			.82	*2.30*	1.06

$\overline{R}^2 = .943$ DW = 1.93   Dm(AR1) = .33
Dh = -   Dm(AR4) = .21

Note: See table A5.16a.

Table A5.19a

Quarterly Nested Inflation Equation:
Complete Results Considering the Role of Foreign Inflation
Monetary Base (MB) with Unemployment Rate

$$\dot{p}(t) = c_0 + \sum_{i=1}^{4} c_{1i}\dot{p}(t-i) + \sum_{i=1}^{4} c_{2i}\dot{M}(t-i) + \sum_{i=1}^{4} c_{3i}u(t-i) + \sum_{i=1}^{4} c_{4i}\dot{p}_w(t-i) + \epsilon(t)$$

Method	Lag	constant	$\dot{p}(t-i)$	$\dot{M}(t-i)$	$u(t-i)$	$\dot{p}_w(t-i)$

Fixed Exchange Rates (1961.2-1972.4)

Method	Lag	constant	$\dot{p}(t-i)$	$\dot{M}(t-i)$	$u(t-i)$	$\dot{p}_w(t-i)$
OLS	1	.040 (.03)	-.799 (4.60)	.342 (1.70)	-1.133 (1.31)	-1.027 (1.02)
	2		-.600 (3.49)	.367 (1.63)	-.534 (.39)	-.825 (.77)
	3		-.538 (3.28)	.017 (.07)	-.354 (.24)	1.708 (1.83)
	4		.194 (1.23)	-.245 (1.01)	.646 (.60)	2.209 (2.23)
	Sum		-1.743 (2.83)	.481 (.92)	-1.375 (2.15)	2.065 (2.67)
	F-test			1.17	2.53	3.45

$\bar{R}^2 = .938$ DW = 2.02 Dm(AR1) = .44
Dh = - Dm(AR4) = 2.94

Flexible Exchange Rates (1975.1-1985.4)

Method	Lag	constant	$\dot{p}(t-i)$	$\dot{M}(t-i)$	$u(t-i)$	$\dot{p}_w(t-i)$
HAT	1	-.549 (.20)	-.134 (.32)	-.310 (1.85)	-.755 (1.70)	.203 (1.22)
	2		-.246 (1.41)	.131 (.53)	1.818 (1.77)	-.009 (.04)
	3		.033 (.21)	.270 (1.08)	-1.244 (1.00)	-.091 (.34)
	4		-.149 (.88)	-.312 (1.51)	-.021 (.03)	-.143 (.52)
	Sum		-.495 (.98)	-.221 (1.16)	-.202 (2.26)	-.039 (.22)
χ^2-test				12.62	12.78	3.02

$\bar{R}^2 = .929$ DW = 1.81 Dm(AR1) = * RHO1 = -.67
Dh = * Dm(AR4) = * (1.50)

Note: See table A5.16a.

Table A5.19b

Quarterly Nested Inflation Equation:
Complete Results Considering the Role of Foreign Inflation
Monetary Base (MB) with Wage Inflation

$$\dot{p}(t) = c_0 + \sum_{i=1}^{4} c_{1i}\dot{p}(t-i) + \sum_{i=1}^{4} c_{2i}\dot{M}(t-i) + \sum_{i=1}^{4} c_{3i}\dot{W}(t-i) + \sum_{i=1}^{4} c_{4i}\dot{p}_w(t-i) + \epsilon(t)$$

Method	Lag	constant	$\dot{p}(t-i)$	$\dot{M}(t-i)$	$\dot{W}(t-i)$	$\dot{p}_w(t-i)$
			Fixed Exchange Rates (1962.2-1972.4)			
HAT	1	-1.785 (1.53)	-.913 (<u>3.98</u>)	.295 (1.23)	.504 (1.56)	-.475 (.40)
	2		-.601 (<u>2.87</u>)	.174 (.71)	.459 (1.21)	.266 (.16)
	3		-.732 (<u>3.62</u>)	-.108 (.39)	.161 (.42)	2.468 (1.44)
	4		.047 (.23)	-.160 (.58)	.324 (.98)	-.977 (.73)
	Sum		-2.200 (<u>2.85</u>)	.201 (.45)	1.449 (<u>2.85</u>)	1.282 (<u>2.23</u>)
χ^2-test				1.96	9.15	8.31
		$\bar{R}^2 = .786$	DW = 1.96	Dm(AR1) = *	RHO1 = .02	
			Dh = *	Dm(AR4) = *	(.08)	
			Flexible Exchange Rates (1974.1-1985.4)			
OLS	1	-1.798 (<u>2.17</u>)	-.086 (.46)	-.015 (.10)	.408 (<u>3.07</u>)	-.004 (.13)
	2		-.021 (.11)	.133 (.97)	-.075 (.46)	.088 (<u>2.75</u>)
	3		-.164 (.92)	-.038 (.26)	.168 (1.11)	-.069 (<u>2.02</u>)
	4		.230 (*1.71*)	-.099 (1.19)	-.111 (.80)	.057 (*1.68*)
	Sum		-.041 (.10)	-.019 (.15)	.390 (1.57)	.072 (1.10)
F-test				.74	2.50	<u>2.73</u>
		$\bar{R}^2 = .954$	DW = 2.19	Dm(AR1) = 1.82		
			Dh = -	Dm(AR4) = 2.47		

Note: See table A5.16a.

Table A5.19c

Quarterly Nested Inflation Equation:
Complete Results Considering the Role of Foreign Inflation
Money Supply (M1) with Unemployment Rate

$$\dot{p}(t) = c_0 + \sum_{i=1}^{4} c_{1i}\dot{p}(t-i) + \sum_{i=1}^{4} c_{2i}\dot{M}(t-i) + \sum_{i=1}^{4} c_{3i}u(t-i) + \sum_{i=1}^{4} c_{4i}\dot{p}_w(t-i) + \epsilon(t)$$

Method	Lag	constant	$\dot{p}(t-i)$	$\dot{M}(t-i)$	$u(t-i)$	$\dot{p}_w(t-i)$

Fixed Exchange Rates (1961.2-1972.4)

Method	Lag	constant	$\dot{p}(t-i)$	$\dot{M}(t-i)$	$u(t-i)$	$\dot{p}_w(t-i)$
OLS	1	-1.123 (.47)	-.790 (<u>4.75</u>)	.084 (.32)	-.637 (.66)	-.975 (.99)
	2		-.579 (<u>3.44</u>)	.415 (1.40)	-1.464 (.97)	-1.142 (1.13)
	3		-.481 (<u>2.88</u>)	.095 (.33)	-.114 (.08)	1.220 (1.30)
	4		.240 (1.55)	-.272 (1.03)	.833 (.76)	2.755 (<u>2.87</u>)
	Sum		-1.610 (<u>2.69</u>)	.322 (.91)	-1.381 (<u>2.08</u>)	1.858 (<u>2.92</u>)
	F-test			1.60	<u>2.82</u>	<u>4.22</u>

$\bar{R}^2 = .942$ DW = 2.10 Dm(AR1) = .88
Dh = - Dm(AR4) = 2.00

Flexible Exchange Rates (1974.1-1985.4)

Method	Lag	constant	$\dot{p}(t-i)$	$\dot{M}(t-i)$	$u(t-i)$	$\dot{p}_w(t-i)$
OLS	1	.813 (.59)	-.186 (.85)	-.037 (.48)	-.669 (1.45)	-.023 (.58)
	2		.128 (.64)	.008 (.09)	.894 (1.07)	.105 (<u>2.83</u>)
	3		-.267 (1.45)	-.060 (.70)	.128 (.15)	-.098 (<u>2.62</u>)
	4		.084 (.53)	-.025 (.31)	-.521 (1.17)	.013 (.33)
	Sum		-.241 (.47)	-.114 (1.25)	-.168 (<u>2.12</u>)	-.002 (.03)
	F-test			.47	2.16	<u>3.44</u>

$\bar{R}^2 = .946$ DW = 1.73 Dm(AR1) = 1.58
Dh = - Dm(AR4) = 3.80

Note: See table A5.16a.

Table A5.19d

Quarterly Nested Inflation Equation:
Complete Results Considering the Role of Foreign Inflation
Money Supply (M1) with Wage Inflation

$$\dot{p}(t) = c_0 + \sum_{i=1}^{4} c_{1i}\dot{p}(t-i) + \sum_{i=1}^{4} c_{2i}\dot{M}(t-i) + \sum_{i=1}^{4} c_{3i}\dot{W}(t-i) + \sum_{i=1}^{4} c_{4i}\dot{p}_w(t-i) + \epsilon(t)$$

Method	Lag	constant	$\dot{p}(t-i)$	$\dot{M}(t-i)$	$\dot{W}(t-i)$	$\dot{p}_w(t-i)$
			Fixed Exchange Rates (1961.2-1972.4)			
OLS	1	-.714 (.36)	-.886 (<u>4.22</u>)	-.136 (.53)	.343 (1.08)	-.597 (.60)
	2		-.797 (<u>3.63</u>)	.431 (1.42)	.644 (<u>2.27</u>)	-.537 (.50)
	3		-.739 (<u>3.45</u>)	.118 (.41)	.249 (.85)	.916 (.92)
	4		.080 (.41)	-.011 (.04)	.068 (.26)	1.532 (1.38)
	Sum		-2.341 (<u>2.93</u>)	.402 (1.23)	1.303 (<u>2.22</u>)	1.314 (<u>2.40</u>)
	F-test			.96	1.95	1.68
		$\bar{R}^2 = .936$	DW = 1.88	Dm(AR1) = 1.26		
			Dh = -	Dm(AR4) = 3.73		
			Flexible Exchange Rates (1975.1-1985.4)			
HAT	1	-3.993 (<u>2.42</u>)	.095 (.39)	.075 (.80)	.406 (1.58)	.212 (1.08)
	2		-.094 (.43)	-.183 (1.37)	-.435 (1.31)	-.289 (1.03)
	3		-.084 (.45)	.205 (1.66)	.147 (.58)	.239 (.74)
	4		-.024 (.14)	-.064 (.80)	-.010 (.05)	.090 (.34)
	Sum		-.106 (.26)	.033 (.44)	.108 (.53)	.252 (<u>2.18</u>)
	χ^2-test			3.22	4.29	7.78
		$\bar{R}^2 = .908$	DW = 2.10	Dm(AR1) = *	RHO1 = -.63	
			Dh = *	Dm(AR4) = *	(<u>2.49</u>)	

Note: See table A5.16a.

DATA SOURCES

The German and U.S. time series data used in this study were obtained from the
following sources:

(1) Databank, Institut für Weltwirtschaft (IWW), Kiel.

(2) *Jahresgutachten*, Sachverständigenrat (SVR), Wiesbaden.

(3) Databank and *Monatsberichte*, Deutsche Bundesbank (DBB), Frankfurt.

(4) *Preise und Preisindizes*, Statistisches Bundesamt (SBA), Wiesbaden.

(5) *Main Economic Indicators*, OECD, Paris.

(6) *International Financial Statistics*, IMF, Washington, D.C.

(7) Databank, Federal Reserve Banks (FED), St.Louis and Kansas City.

Complete references are given in the bibliography. The regressions in chapters
IV and V use seasonally unadjusted quarterly data or annual averages of quarterly
data. The stylized facts presented in chapter II are based on annual data or annual
averages of quarterly data. The sample period is 1960-85 for annual data and
1960.1-85.4 for quarterly data.

The following list identifies the raw time series, the data frequency, and the
source (by abbreviation). Time series for implicit deflators and certain real
variables as well as growth rates and shares are based on own computations.

German Data

Unemployment Rate: % p.a.; quarterly (NSA); IWW.

Total Employment (incl. self-employed): domestic residents; annual; SVR.

Wage Employment (excl. self-employed): domestic residents; annual; SVR.

Foreign Wage Employment ("guest workers"): annual; SVR.

Hourly Wage Index (all sectors): 1980=100; quarterly (NSA); IWW.

Productivity Index (real GDP per employed worker): 1980=100; quarterly (NSA); IWW.

International Reserves (excl. gold): Bio. $; end of period; quarterly (NSA); IFS.

Central Bank Money Stock: Bio. DM; period average; quarterly (SA); DBB.

Monetary Base: Bio. DM; period average; quarterly (NSA); IWW/DBB.

Money Supply M1/M2: Bio. DM; period average; quarterly (NSA); IWW.

Nominal Interest Rates (short/long-term): % p.a.; quarterly (NSA); IWW.

Industrial Production Index (all sectors): 1980=100; quarterly (NSA); OECD.

Nominal/Real Potential GNP: (1980) Bio. DM; annual; SVR.

Nominal/Real GNP: (1980) Bio. DM; quarterly (NSA); IWW.

Nominal/Real Gross National Expenditure: (1980) Bio. DM; quarterly (NSA); IWW.

Real Net Investment: 1980 Bio. DM; quarterly (NSA); IWW.

Nominal/Real Exports of Goods & Services: (1980) Bio. DM; quarterly (NSA); DBB.

Nominal/Real Imports of Goods & Services: (1980) Bio. DM; quarterly (NSA); DBB.

Exports/Imports of Goods & Services (by country): Mio. DM; annual; SVR.

Current Account Balance: Bio. DM; quarterly (NSA); DBB.

Capital Account Balance: Bio. DM; quarterly (NSA); DBB.

Exchange Rate Index (trade-weighted): end of 1972=100; quarterly (NSA); DBB.

Bilateral Exchange Rate (DM/$): market rate; period average; quarterly (NSA); IFS.

Consumer Price Index: 1980=100; quarterly (NSA); IWW/OECD.

Import Price Index: 1980=100; quarterly (NSA); IWW.

Price Index for Imported Crude Oil: 1980=100; quarterly (NSA); SBA.

Federal Government Revenue (budgetary operations): Bio. DM; quarterly (NSA); IFS.

Federal Government Expenditure (budgetary operations): Bio. DM; quarterly (NSA); IFS.

Total Government Revenue (incl. social security system): Bio. DM; annual; SVR.

Total Government Outlays (incl. social security system): Bio. DM; annual; SVR.

Total Government Spending (incl. social security system): Bio. DM; annual; SVR.

Government Revenue (federal, state, local): Bio. DM; annual; SVR.

Government Outlays (federal, state, local): Bio. DM; annual; SVR.

Government Spending (federal, state, local): Bio. DM; annual; SVR.

U.S. and other Foreign Data

U.S. Industrial Production Index (all sectors): 1980=100; quarterly (NSA); OECD.

U.S. Consumer Price Index: 1980=100; quarterly (NSA); OECD.

U.S. Implicit GNP-Deflator: 1982=100; quarterly (SA); FED.

U.S. Adjusted Monetary Base: Bio. $; quarterly (NSA); FED.

U.S. Money Supply (M1): Bio. $; quarterly (NSA); FED.

U.S. Nominal Interest Rates (short/long-term): % p.a.; quarterly (NSA); FED.

Eurodollar Deposit Rate (3-month, London): % p.a.; quarterly (NSA); FED.

BIBLIOGRAPHY

Aghevli, B. and C. Rodriguez (1979), Trade, Prices and Output in Japan: A Simple Monetary Model, _IMF Staff Papers_, Vol. 26, No. 1, 38-54.

Andersen, L.C. and J.L. Jordan (1968), Monetary and Fiscal Actions: A Test of Their Relative Importance in Economic Stabilization, _Review_, Federal Reserve Bank of St.Louis, November, 11-24.

Andersen, L.C. and K.M. Carlson (1970), A Monetarist Model for Economic Stabilization, _Review_, Federal Reserve Bank of St.Louis, April, 7-25.

Argy, V. and P. Kouri (1974), Sterilization Policies and the Volatility in International Reserves, in: R.Z. Aliber (ed.), _National Monetary Policies and the International Financial System_, Chicago, London: University of Chicago Press, 209-230.

Argy, V. and E. Spitäller (1980), The Joint Determination of Changes in Output and Prices in the Seven Main Industrial Countries, _Weltwirtschaftliches Archiv_, Bd. 116, Heft 1, 87-113.

Artus, J.R. (1976), Exchange Rate Stability and Managed Floating: The Experience of the Federal Republic of Germany, _IMF Staff Papers_, Vol. 23, No. 2, 312-333.

Barro, R.J. (1977), Unanticipated Money Growth and Unemployment in the United States, in: R.E. Lucas, Jr. and T.J. Sargent (eds.), _Rational Expectations and Econometric Practice_, Vol. 2, Minneapolis: University of Minnesota Press, 563-584.

Barro, R.J. (1978), Unanticipated Money Growth, Output, and the Price Level in the United States, in: R.E. Lucas, Jr. and T.J. Sargent (eds.), _Rational Expectations and Econometric Practice_, Vol. 2, Minneapolis: University of Minnesota Press, 585-616.

Batchelor, R.A. (1982), Expectations, Output and Inflation: The European Experience, _European Economic Review_, Vol. 17, 1-25.

Batten, D.S. and R.W. Hafer (1982), Short-Run Money Growth Fluctuations and Real Economic Activity: Some Implications for Monetary Targeting, _Review_, Federal Reserve Bank of St.Louis, May, 15-20.

Batten, D.S. and R.W. Hafer (1983), The Relative Impact of Monetary and Fiscal Actions on Economic Activity: A Cross-Country Comparison, _Review_, Federal Reserve Bank of St.Louis, January, 5-12.

Benderly, J. and B. Zwick (1985), Money, Employment and Inflation, _Review of Economics and Statistics_, Vol. 67, 139-143.

Black, S.W. (1983), The Use of Monetary Policy for Internal and External Balance in Ten Industrial Countries, in: J.A. Frenkel (ed.), _Exchange Rates and International Macroeconomics_, NBER Conference Report, Chicago, London: University of Chicago Press, 189-225.

Blejer. M.I. (1979), On Causality and the Monetary Approach to the Balance of Payments: The European Experience, European Economic Review, Vol. 12, 289-296.

Bombach, G. (1988), Beschäftigung und Arbeitsproduktivität im Konjunkturverlauf - 25 Jahre Okun'sches Gesetz, in: W. Franz, W. Gaab, and J. Wolters (eds.), Theoretische und angewandte Wirtschaftsforschung: Heinz König zum 60. Geburtstag, Berlin, Heidelberg, New York, London, Paris, Tokyo: Springer-Verlag, 3-18.

Borts, G.H. and J.A. Hanson (1979), The Monetary Approach to the Balance of Payments with an Empirical Application to the Case of Panama, in: J. Behrman and J.A. Hanson (eds.), Short-Term Macroeconomic Policy in Latin America, Cambridge, Mass.: Ballinger, 257-288.

Buscher, H.S. (1984), Zur Stabilität der Geldnachfrage: Eine empirische Betrachtung, Kredit und Kapital, No. 4, 507-539.

Cassese, A. and J.R. Lothian (1982), The Timing of Monetary and Price Changes and the International Transmission of Inflation, Journal of Monetary Economics, Vol. 10, 1-23.

Chatfield, C. (1980), The Analysis of Time Series: An Introduction, 2nd edition, London, New York: Chapman and Hall.

Darby, M.R. and A.C. Stockman (1983), The Mark III International Transmission Model: Estimates, in: M.R. Darby and J.F. Lothian (eds.), The International Transmission of Inflation, NBER Research Monograph, Chicago, London: University of Chicago Press, 113-161.

Darrat, A.F. (1985), Anticipated versus Unanticipated Monetary Policy and Real Output in Germany, The American Economist, Vol. 29, No. 1, 73-77.

Desai, M. (1981), Testing Monetarism: An Econometric Analysis of Professor Stein's Model of Monetarism, Journal of Economic Dynamics and Control, Vol. 3, 141-156.

Desai, M. and D. Blake (1982), Monetarism and the U.S. Economy: A Re-Evaluation of Stein's Model 1960-1973, Journal of Monetary Economics, Vol. 10, 111-125.

Deutsche Bundesbank (1982), The Deutsche Bundesbank: Its Monetary Policy Instruments and Functions, Deutsche Bundesbank Special Series No. 7.

Deutsche Bundesbank, Monatsberichte der Deutschen Bundesbank, various issues.

Dewald, W.G. and W.T. Gavin (1981), Money and Inflation in a Small Model of the German Economy, Empirical Economics, Vol. 6, 173-185.

Dewald, W.G. and M.N. Marchon (1978), A Modified Federal Reserve of St.Louis Spending Equation for Canada, France, Germany, Italy, the United Kingdom, and the United States, Kredit und Kapital, Vol. 11, No. 2, 194-212.

Dewald, W.G. and M.N. Marchon (1979), A Common Specification of Price, Output, and Unemployment Rate Responses to Demand Pressure and Import Prices in Six Industrial Countries, Weltwirtschaftliches Archiv, Bd. 115, Heft 1, 1-19.

Dornbusch, R. (1980), Open Economy Macroeconomics, New York: Basic Book.

Dutton, D.S. (1978), The Economics of Inflation and Output Fluctuations in the United States: 1952-1974, in: K. Brunner and A.M. Meltzer (eds.), The Problem of Inflation, Carnegie-Rochester Conference Series, Vol. 8., Amsterdam, New York, Oxford: North-Holland, 203-231.

Dyreyes, F.R. et al. (1980), Tests of the Direction of Causality between Money and Income in Six Countries, Southern Journal of Economics, Vol. 47, No. 2, 477-487.

Emminger, O. (1976), Deutsche Geld- und Währungspolitik im Spannungsfeld zwischen innerm und äußerem Gleichgewicht: 1948-1975, in: Deutsche Bundesbank, Währung und Wirtschaft in Deutschland 1876-1975, Frankfurt: Verlag Fritz Knapp GmbH, 485-554.

Feige, E.L. and J.M. Johannes (1981), Testing the Causal Relationship between Domestic Credit and Reserve Components of a Country's Monetary Base, Journal of Macroeconomics, Vol. 3, No. 1, 55-76.

Fels, G. (1977), Inflation in Germany, in: L.B. Krause and W.S. Salant (eds.), Worldwide Inflation, Washington, D.C.: The Brookings Institution, 590-622.

Fischer, S. (1977), Long-Term Contracts, Rational Expectations, and the Optimal Money Supply Rule, in: R.E. Lucas, Jr. and T.J. Sargent (eds.), Rational Expectations and Econometric Practice, Vol. 1, Minneapolis: University of Minnesota Press, 261-276.

Fitzgerald, M.D. and G. Pollio (1983), Money, Activity and Prices: Some Inter-Country Evidence, European Economic Review, Vol. 23, 299-314.

Fourcans, A. (1978), Inflation and Output Growth: The French Experience: 1960-1975, in: K. Brunner and A.M. Meltzer (eds.), The Problem of Inflation, Carnegie-Rochester Conference Series, Vol. 8, Amsterdam, New York, Oxford: North-Holland, 81-140.

Franz, W. (1983), The Past Decade's Natural Rate and the Dynamics of German Unemployment: A Case against Demand Policy?, European Economic Review, Vol. 21, 51-76.

Fratianni, M. (1978), Inflation and Unanticipated Changes in Output in Italy, in: K. Brunner and A.M. Meltzer (eds.), The Problem of Inflation, Carnegie-Rochester Conference Series, Vol. 8, Amsterdam, New York, Oxford: North-Holland, 141-180.

Geweke, J. (1981), The Approximate Slopes of Econometric Tests, Econometrica, Vol. 49, No. 6, 1427-1442.

Giersch, H. (1977), Konjunktur- und Wachstumspolitik in der offenen Wirtschaft, Allgemeine Wirtschaftspolitik (2. Bd.), Wiesbaden: Dr. Th. Gabler.

Gisser, M. and T.H. Goodwin (1985), Crude Oil and the Macroeconomy: Tests of Some Popular Notions, Journal of Money, Credit, and Banking, Vol. 18, No. 1, 95-103.

Granger, C.W.J. (1969), Investigating Causal Relations by Econometric Models and Cross-Spectral Methods, Econometrica, Vol. 37, No. 3, 424-438.

Granger, C.W.J. (1988), Some Recent Developments in a Concept of Causality, Journal of Econometrics, Vol. 39, 199-211.

Gschwendtner, H. (1977), Wirkungen von Konjunktur und Wachstum auf die Inflation in der BRD: 1953-1974, Jahrbücher für Nationalökonomie und Statistik, Bd. 199, Heft 2, 114-126.

Gutierrez-Camara, J.L. and R. Vaubel (1981), International Shifts in the Demand for Money in a Small Monetarist Model: Some Further Evidence, Kieler Arbeitspapiere, No. 121.

Hagen, J. von (1984), The Causal Role of Money in West Germany - Some Contradicting Comments and Evidence, Weltwirtschaftliches Archiv, Bd. 120, Heft 3, 558-571.

Hamburger, M.J. (1977), The Demand for Money in an Open Economy: Germany and the U.K., Journal of Monetary Economics, Vol. 3, 25-40.

Hansen, G. (1986), Der konjunkturelle Einfluß der Geld- und Fiskalpolitik in der Bundesrepublik 1972-1982: Eine ökonometrische Analyse unter rationalen Erwartungen, Kyklos, Vol. 39, Facs. 2, 180-208.

Hatanaka, M. (1974), An Efficient Two-Step Estimator for the Dynamic Adjustment Model with Autoregressive Errors, Journal of Econometrics, Vol. 2, 199-220.

Heilemann, U. (1981), Zur Prognosegenauigkeit ökonometrischer Konjunkturmodelle für die Bundesrepublik Deutschland, Allgemeines Statistisches Archiv, 65. Bd, No. 3, 242-272.

Herring, R.J. and R.C. Marston (1977), Sterilization Policy: The Trade-off between Monetary Autonomy and Control over Foreign Exchange Reserves, European Economic Review, Vol. 10, 325-343.

Hsiao, C. (1981), Autoregressive Modelling and Money-Income Causality Detection, Journal of Monetary Economics, Vol. 7, 85-106.

International Monetary Fund (IMF), International Financial Statistics, various issues.

Jäger, W. and A. Ocker (1978), Makroökonomische Funktionalzusammenhänge in simultanen deutschen Prognosemodellen: Darstellung und Probleme, Jahrbücher für Nationalökonomie und Statistik, Bd. 192, Heft 5, 385-413.

Johnson, H.G. (1972), The Monetary Approach to Balance-of-Payments Theory, in: H.G. Johnson, Further Essays in Monetary Economics, London: George Allen & Unwin Ltd., 229-249.

Joint Economic Committe of the Congress of the United States (1981), Monetary Stability and Industrial Adaption in West Germany, in: Monetary Policy, Selective Credit Policy, and Industrial Policy in France, Britain, West Germany, and Sweden, Staff Study, June 26, 92-135.

Judge, G.G. et.al. (1985), The Theory and Practice of Econometrics, 2nd edition, New York: John Wiley and Sons.

Kmenta, J. (1986), Elements of Econometrics, 2nd edition, New York: Macmillan.

Knöbl, A. (1974), Price Expectations and Actual Price Behavior in Germany, IMF Staff Papers, Vol. 21, 83-100.

Kohli, U. and G. Rich (1986), Monetary Control: The Swiss Experience, The Cato Journal, Vol. 5, No. 3, 911-926.

König, H. (1978), Ein monetaristisches Modell zur Erklärung von Arbeitslosigkeit und Inflation: Modellprobleme und -implikationen für die BRD, Zeitschrift für Nationalökonomie, Vol. 38, No. 1-2, 85-104.

Korteweg, P. (1978), The Economics of Inflation and Output Fluctuations in the Netherlands, 1954-1975: A Test of Some Implications of the Dominant-Impulse-cum-Rational-Expectations Hypothesis, in: K. Brunner and A.M. Meltzer (eds.), The Problem of Inflation, Carnegie-Rochester Conference Series, Vol. 8, Amsterdam, New York, Oxford: North-Holland, 17-68 and 77-79.

Laidler, D. and P. O'Shea (1980), An Empirical Macro-Model of an Open Economy under Fixed Exchange Rates: The U.K.: 1954-1970, Economica, Vol. 47, No. 186, 141-158.

Läufer, N.K.A. (1975), Fiskalpolitik versus Geldpolitik: Zur Frage ihrer relativen Bedeutung: Eine empirirsche Untersuchung für die BRD, Kredit und Kapital, Vol. 8, 346-378.

Läufer, N.K.A. (1977), Further Evidence on the Relative Importance of Fiscal and Monetary Actions in the Federal Republic of Germany, in: S.F. Frowen et al. (eds.), Monetary Policy & Economic Activity in West Germany, New York: Halsted Press, 195-206.

Leiderman, L. (1980a), Output Supply in the Open Economy: Some International Evidence, Review of Economics and Statistics, May, 180-189.

Leiderman, L. (1980b), Relationships Between Macroeconomic Time Series in a Fixed-Exchange-Rate Economy: The Case of Italy, European Economic Review, Vol. 14, 61-77.

McCallum, B.T. (1980), Rational Expectations and Macroeconomic Stabilization Policy, Journal of Money, Credit, and Banking, Vol. 12, No. 4, 716-746.

McKenna, E.J. and D.C. Zannoni (1984), Comment on Stein and Weintraub: "The Acceleration of Inflation," Journal of Post Keynesian Economics, Vol. 6, No. 3, 470-478.

Minford, P. (1980), A Rational Expectations Model of the United Kingdom under Fixed and Floating Exchange Rates, in: K. Brunner and A.H. Meltzer (eds.), On the State of Macro-Economics, Carnegie-Rochester Conference Series, Vol. 12, Amsterdam, New York, Oxford: North-Holland, 293-355.

Mishkin, F.S. (1982a), Does Anticipated Monetary Policy Matter? An Econometric Investigation, Journal of Political Economy, Vol. 90, No. 1, 22-51.

Mishkin, F.S. (1982b), Does Anticipated Aggregate Demand Policy Matter? Further Econometric Results, American Economic Review, Vol. 72, No. 4, 788-802.

Mishkin, F.S. (1983), A Rational Expectations Approach to Macroeconomics: Testing Policy Ineffectiveness and Efficient-Markets Models, NBER Research Monograph, Chicago, London: University of Chicago Press.

Myhrman, J. (1979), The Determination of Inflation and Economic Activity in Sweden, in: A. Lindbeck (ed.), Inflation and Employment in Open Economies, Amsterdam, New York, Oxford: North-Holland, 307-335.

Neumann, M.J.M. (1978), The Impulse-Theoretic Explanation of Changing Inflation and Output Growth: Evidence from Germany, in: K. Brunner and A.M. Meltzer (eds.), The Problem of Inflation, Carnegie-Rochester Conference Series, Vol. 8, Amsterdam, New York, Oxford: North-Holland, 233-269.

Obstfeld, M. (1983), Exchange Rates, Inflation, and the Sterilization Problem: Germany: 1975-1981, European Economic Review, Vol. 21, 161-189.

Ohr, R. and P. Lang (1982), Währungssystem, Inflation und Beschäftigung: Eine ökonometrische Analyse für die BRD, Wirtschaftsdienst, Bd. 10, 515-520.

Okun, A.M. (1970), The Political Economy of Prosperity, New York: W.W. Norton.

Organization for Economic Co-operation and Development (OECD), Main Economic Indicators, various issues.

Parkin, M. (1984), Discriminating between Keynesian and Classical Theories of the Business Cycle: Japan 1967-1982, Monetary and Economic Studies, Bank of Japan, Vol. 2, No. 2, 23-59.

Pearce, D.W. (1983), ed., _The Dictionary of Modern Economics_, revised edition, Cambridge, Mass.: MIT Press.

Pierce, D.A. and L.D. Haugh (1977), Causality in Temporal Systems: Characterizations and a Survey, _Journal of Econometrics_, Vol. 5, 265-293.

Rea, J.D. (1983), The Explanatory Power of Alternative Theories of Inflation and Unemployment: 1895-1979, _Review of Economics and Statistics_, Vol. 65, No. 2, 183-195.

Reineke, U. (1986), _Segmentationstheorien des Arbeitsmarktes und Beschäftigungsniveau: Eine Auseinandersetzung mit der theoretischen und empirischen Relevanz der Entkopplungshypothese_, Europäische Hochschulschriften, Bd. 743, Reihe V, Frankfurt, Bern, New York: Peter Lang.

Risch, B. (1980), Arbeitslosigkeit und Inflation - Anmerkungen zu unliebsamen Schleifen, _Konjunkturpolitik_, 26. Jahrg., Heft 6, 321-341.

Sachverständigenrat zur Begutachtung der gesamtwirtschaftlichen Entwicklung, _Jahresgutachten_, various issues.

Sargent, T.J. (1976), The Observational Equivalence of Natural and Unnatural Rate Theories of Macroeconomics, in: R.E. Lucas, Jr. and T.J. Sargent (eds.), _Rational Expectations and Econometric Practice_, Vol. 2, Minneapolis: University of Minnesota Press, 553-562.

Scheide, J. (1982), Geldpolitik, Einkommen und Preisniveau: Kausalitätstests für die Bundesrepublik Deutschland, Kieler Arbeitspapiere, No. 135.

Scheide, J. (1984), _Geldpolitik, Konjunktur und rationale Erwartungen_, Kieler Studien 188, Tübingen: J.C.B. Mohr (Paul Siebeck).

Sims, C.A. (1972), Money, Income, and Causality, _American Economic Review_, Vol. 62, 540-552.

Sims, C.A. (1977), Comment, _Journal of the American Statistical Association_, March, 23-24.

Sims, C.A. (1980), Macroeconomics and Reality, _Econometrica_, Vol. 48, No. 1, 1-48.

Small, D.H. (1979), Unanticipated Money Growth and Unemployment in the United States: Comment, _American Economic Review_, Vol. 69, 996-1003.

Spitäller, E. (1978), A Model of Inflation and Its Performance in the Seven Main Industrial Countries: 1958-76, _IMF Staff Papers_, Vol. 25, No. 2, 254-277.

Statistisches Bundesamt, _Preise und Preisindizes für die Ein- und Ausfuhr_, Fachserie 17 (Preise), Reihe 8, various issues.

Stein, J.L. (1974), Unemployment, Inflation, and Monetarism, _American Economic Review_, Vol. 64, No. 6, 867-887.

Stein, J.L. (1978), Inflation, Employment, and Stagflation, _Journal of Monetary Economics_, Vol. 4, 193-228.

Stein, J.L. (1982a), The Realism and Relevance of the Consensus Model of the Balance of Payments, _Economies et Societés_, Cahiers de l'Institut de Sciences Matématiques et Economiques Appliquées, Série MO, No. 3.

Stein, J.L. (1982b), _Monetarist, Keynesian and New Classical Economics_, New York: New York University Press.

Stein, J.L. (1985), Asymptotically Rational Expectations and Monetarism or Muth Rational Expectations and New Classical Economics: The Use of Futures Markets Analysis to Elucidate Macro-Economics, Working Paper, No. 85-36, Brown University.

Trapp, P. (1976), Geldmenge, Ausgaben und Preisanstieg in der BRD, Kieler Studien 138, Tübingen: J.C.B. Mohr (Paul Siebeck).

Tsay, R.S. (1984), Detecting Linear Relationships Between Variables: A Direct Multiple Time Series Approach, Working Paper, Department of Statistics, Carnegie-Mellon University.

Turnovsky, S.J. and M.E. Wohar (1984), Monetarism and the Aggregate Economy: Some Longer-Run Evidence, Review of Economics and Statistics, Vol. 66, 619-629.

Uebe, G. (1981), Eine Übersicht zu den gesamtwirtschaftlichen ökonometrischen Modellen für die Bundesrepublik Deutschland, DIW Vierteljahresheft, Vol. 2/3, 134-146.

Van Hoa, T. (1981), Causality and Wage Price Inflation in West Germany: 1964-1979, Weltwirtschaftliches Archiv, Bd. 117, Heft 1, 110-123.

Vaubel, R. (1980), International Shifts in the Demand for Money, their Effects on Exchange Rates and the Price Level, and their Implications for the Preannouncement of Monetary Expansions, Weltwirtschaftliches Archiv, Bd. 116, Heft 1, 1-44.

Weissenberger, E. and J.J. Thomas (1983), The Causal Role of Money in West Germany, Weltwirtschaftliches Archiv, Bd. 119, Heft 1, 64-83.

Willms, M. (1971), Controlling Money in an Open Economy: The German Case, Review, Federal Reserve Bank of St.Louis, Vol. 53 (April), 10-27.

Vol. 236: G. Gandolfo, P.C. Padoan, A Disequilibrium Model of Real and Financial Accumulation in an Open Economy. VI, 172 pages. 1984.

Vol. 237: Misspecification Analysis. Proceedings, 1983. Edited by T. K. Dijkstra. V, 129 pages. 1984.

Vol. 238: W. Domschke, A. Drexl, Location and Layout Planning. IV, 134 pages. 1985.

Vol. 239: Microeconomic Models of Housing Markets. Edited by K. Stahl. VII, 197 pages. 1985.

Vol. 240: Contributions to Operations Research. Proceedings, 1984. Edited by K. Neumann and D. Pallaschke. V, 190 pages. 1985.

Vol. 241: U. Wittmann, Das Konzept rationaler Preiserwartungen. XI, 310 Seiten. 1985.

Vol. 242: Decision Making with Multiple Objectives. Proceedings, 1984. Edited by Y. Y. Haimes and V. Chankong. XI, 571 pages. 1985.

Vol. 243: Integer Programming and Related Areas. A Classified Bibliography 1981–1984. Edited by R. von Randow. XX, 386 pages. 1985.

Vol. 244: Advances in Equilibrium Theory. Proceedings, 1984. Edited by C.D. Aliprantis, O. Burkinshaw and N. J. Rothman. II, 235 pages. 1985.

Vol. 245: J. E.M. Wilhelm, Arbitrage Theory. VII, 114 pages. 1985.

Vol. 246: P. W. Otter, Dynamic Feature Space Modelling, Filtering and Self-Tuning Control of Stochastic Systems. XIV, 177 pages. 1985.

Vol. 247: Optimization and Discrete Choice in Urban Systems. Proceedings, 1983. Edited by B.G. Hutchinson, P. Nijkamp and M. Batty. VI, 371 pages. 1985.

Vol. 248: Plural Rationality and Interactive Decision Processes. Proceedings, 1984. Edited by M. Grauer, M. Thompson and A.P. Wierzbicki. VI, 354 pages. 1985.

Vol. 249: Spatial Price Equilibrium: Advances in Theory, Computation and Application. Proceedings, 1984. Edited by P. T. Harker. VII, 277 pages. 1985.

Vol. 250: M. Roubens, Ph. Vincke, Preference Modelling. VIII, 94 pages. 1985.

Vol. 251: Input-Output Modeling. Proceedings, 1984. Edited by A. Smyshlyaev. VI, 261 pages. 1985.

Vol. 252: A. Birolini, On the Use of Stochastic Processes in Modeling Reliability Problems. VI, 105 pages. 1985.

Vol. 253: C. Withagen, Economic Theory and International Trade in Natural Exhaustible Resources. VI, 172 pages. 1985.

Vol. 254: S. Müller, Arbitrage Pricing of Contingent Claims. VIII, 151 pages. 1985.

Vol. 255: Nondifferentiable Optimization: Motivations and Applications. Proceedings, 1984. Edited by V. F. Demyanov and D. Pallaschke. VI, 350 pages. 1985.

Vol. 256: Convexity and Duality in Optimization. Proceedings, 1984. Edited by J. Ponstein. V, 142 pages. 1985.

Vol. 257: Dynamics of Macrosystems. Proceedings, 1984. Edited by J.-P. Aubin, D. Saari and K. Sigmund. VI, 280 pages. 1985.

Vol. 258: H. Funke, Eine allgemeine Theorie der Polypol- und Oligopolpreisbildung. III, 237 pages. 1985.

Vol. 259: Infinite Programming. Proceedings, 1984. Edited by E. J. Anderson and A.B. Philpott. XIV, 244 pages. 1985.

Vol. 260: H.-J. Kruse, Degeneracy Graphs and the Neighbourhood Problem. VIII, 128 pages. 1986.

Vol. 261: Th. R. Gulledge, Jr., N. K. Womer, The Economics of Made-to-Order Production. VI, 134 pages. 1986.

Vol. 262: H. U. Buhl, A Neo-Classical Theory of Distribution and Wealth. V, 146 pages. 1986.

Vol. 263: M. Schäfer, Resource Extraction and Market Structure. XI, 154 pages. 1986.

Vol. 264: Models of Economic Dynamics. Proceedings, 1983. Edited by H.F. Sonnenschein. VII, 212 pages. 1986.

Vol. 265: Dynamic Games and Applications in Economics. Edited by T. Başar. IX, 288 pages. 1986.

Vol. 266: Multi-Stage Production Planning and Inventory Control. Edited by S. Axsäter, Ch. Schneeweiss and E. Silver. V, 264 pages. 1986.

Vol. 267: R. Bemelmans, The Capacity Aspect of Inventories. IX, 165 pages. 1986.

Vol. 268: V. Firchau, Information Evaluation in Capital Markets. VII, 103 pages. 1986.

Vol. 269: A. Borglin, H. Keiding, Optimality in Infinite Horizon Economies. VI, 180 pages. 1986.

Vol. 270: Technological Change, Employment and Spatial Dynamics. Proceedings 1985. Edited by P. Nijkamp. VII, 466 pages. 1986.

Vol. 271: C. Hildreth, The Cowles Commission in Chicago, 1939–1955. V, 176 pages. 1986.

Vol. 272: G. Clemenz, Credit Markets with Asymmetric Information. VIII, 212 pages. 1986.

Vol. 273: Large-Scale Modelling and Interactive Decision Analysis. Proceedings, 1985. Edited by G. Fandel, M. Grauer, A. Kurzhanski and A.P. Wierzbicki. VII, 363 pages. 1986.

Vol. 274: W.K. Klein Haneveld, Duality in Stochastic Linear and Dynamic Programming. VII, 295 pages. 1986.

Vol. 275: Competition, Instability, and Nonlinear Cycles. Proceedings, 1985. Edited by W. Semmler. XII, 340 pages. 1986.

Vol. 276: M.R. Baye, D.A. Black, Consumer Behavior, Cost of Living Measures, and the Income Tax. VII, 119 pages. 1986.

Vol. 277: Studies in Austrian Capital Theory, Investment and Time. Edited by M. Faber. VI, 317 pages. 1986.

Vol. 278: W.E. Diewert, The Measurement of the Economic Benefits of Infrastructure Services. V, 202 pages. 1986.

Vol. 279: H.-J. Büttler, G. Frei and B. Schips, Estimation of Disequilibrium Models. VI, 114 pages. 1986.

Vol. 280: H.T. Lau, Combinatorial Heuristic Algorithms with FORTRAN. VII, 126 pages. 1986.

Vol. 281: Ch.-L. Hwang, M.-J. Lin, Group Decision Making under Multiple Criteria. XI, 400 pages. 1987.

Vol. 282: K. Schittkowski, More Test Examples for Nonlinear Programming Codes. V, 261 pages. 1987.

Vol. 283: G. Gabisch, H.-W. Lorenz, Business Cycle Theory. VII, 229 pages. 1987.

Vol. 284: H. Lütkepohl, Forecasting Aggregated Vector ARMA Processes. X, 323 pages. 1987.

Vol. 285: Toward Interactive and Intelligent Decision Support Systems. Volume 1. Proceedings, 1986. Edited by Y. Sawaragi, K. Inoue and H. Nakayama. XII, 445 pages. 1987.

Vol. 286: Toward Interactive and Intelligent Decision Support Systems. Volume 2. Proceedings, 1986. Edited by Y. Sawaragi, K. Inoue and H. Nakayama. XII, 450 pages. 1987.

Vol. 287: Dynamical Systems. Proceedings, 1985. Edited by A.B. Kurzhanski and K. Sigmund. VI, 215 pages. 1987.

Vol. 288: G.D. Rudebusch, The Estimation of Macroeconomic Disequilibrium Models with Regime Classification Information. VII, 128 pages. 1987.

Vol. 289: B.R. Meijboom, Planning in Decentralized Firms. X, 168 pages. 1987.

Vol. 290: D.A. Carlson, A. Haurie, Infinite Horizon Optimal Control. XI, 254 pages. 1987.

Vol. 291: N. Takahashi, Design of Adaptive Organizations. VI, 140 pages. 1987.

Vol. 292: I. Tchijov, L. Tomaszewicz (Eds.), Input-Output Modeling. Proceedings, 1985. VI, 195 pages. 1987.

Vol. 293: D. Batten, J. Casti, B. Johansson (Eds.), Economic Evolution and Structural Adjustment. Proceedings, 1985. VI, 382 pages. 1987.

Vol. 294: J. Jahn, W. Krabs (Eds.), Recent Advances and Historical Development of Vector Optimization. VII, 405 pages. 1987.

Vol. 295: H. Meister, The Purification Problem for Constrained Games with Incomplete Information. X, 127 pages. 1987.

Vol. 296: A. Börsch-Supan, Econometric Analysis of Discrete Choice. VIII, 211 pages. 1987.

Vol. 297: V. Fedorov, H. Läuter (Eds.), Model-Oriented Data Analysis. Proceedings, 1987. VI, 239 pages. 1988.

Vol. 298: S.H. Chew, Q. Zheng, Integral Global Optimization. VII, 179 pages. 1988.

Vol. 299: K. Marti, Descent Directions and Efficient Solutions in Discretely Distributed Stochastic Programs. XIV, 178 pages. 1988.

Vol. 300: U. Derigs, Programming in Networks and Graphs. XI, 315 pages. 1988.

Vol. 301: J. Kacprzyk, M. Roubens (Eds.), Non-Conventional Preference Relations in Decision Making. VII, 155 pages. 1988.

Vol. 302: H.A. Eiselt, G. Pederzoli (Eds.), Advances in Optimization and Control. Proceedings, 1986. VIII, 372 pages. 1988.

Vol. 303: F.X. Diebold, Empirical Modeling of Exchange Rate Dynamics. VII, 143 pages. 1988.

Vol. 304: A. Kurzhanski, K. Neumann, D. Pallaschke (Eds.), Optimization, Parallel Processing and Applications. Proceedings, 1987. VI, 292 pages. 1988.

Vol. 305: G.-J.C.Th. van Schijndel, Dynamic Firm and Investor Behaviour under Progressive Personal Taxation. X, 215 pages. 1988.

Vol. 306: Ch. Klein, A Static Microeconomic Model of Pure Competition. VIII, 139 pages. 1988.

Vol. 307: T.K. Dijkstra (Ed.), On Model Uncertainty and its Statistical Implications. VII, 138 pages. 1988.

Vol. 308: J.R. Daduna, A. Wren (Eds.), Computer-Aided Transit Scheduling. VIII, 339 pages. 1988.

Vol. 309: G. Ricci, K. Velupillai (Eds.), Growth Cycles and Multisectoral Economics: the Goodwin Tradition. III, 126 pages. 1988.

Vol. 310: J. Kacprzyk, M. Fedrizzi (Eds.), Combining Fuzzy Imprecision with Probabilistic Uncertainty in Decision Making. IX, 399 pages. 1988.

Vol. 311: R. Färe, Fundamentals of Production Theory. IX, 163 pages. 1988.

Vol. 312: J. Krishnakumar, Estimation of Simultaneous Equation Models with Error Components Structure. X, 357 pages. 1988.

Vol. 313: W. Jammernegg, Sequential Binary Investment Decisions. VI, 156 pages. 1988.

Vol. 314: R. Tietz, W. Albers, R. Selten (Eds.), Bounded Rational Behavior in Experimental Games and Markets. VI, 368 pages. 1988.

Vol. 315: I. Orishimo, G.J.D. Hewings, P. Nijkamp (Eds.), Information Technology: Social and Spatial Perspectives. Proceedings, 1986. VI, 268 pages. 1988.

Vol. 316: R.L. Basmann, D.J. Slottje, K. Hayes, J.D. Johnson, D.J. Molina, The Generalized Fechner-Thurstone Direct Utility Function and Some of its Uses. VIII, 159 pages. 1988.

Vol. 317: L. Bianco, A. La Bella (Eds.), Freight Transport Planning and Logistics. Proceedings, 1987. X, 568 pages. 1988.

Vol. 318: T. Doup, Simplicial Algorithms on the Simplotope. VIII, 262 pages. 1988.

Vol. 319: D.T. Luc, Theory of Vector Optimization. VIII, 173 pages. 1989.

Vol. 320: D. van der Wijst, Financial Structure in Small Business. VII, 181 pages. 1989.

Vol. 321: M. Di Matteo, R.M. Goodwin, A. Vercelli (Eds.), Technological and Social Factors in Long Term Fluctuations. Proceedings. IX, 442 pages. 1989.

Vol. 322: T. Kollintzas (Ed.), The Rational Expectations Equilibrium Inventory Model. XI, 269 pages. 1989.

Vol. 323: M.B.M. de Koster, Capacity Oriented Analysis and Design of Production Systems. XII, 245 pages. 1989.

Vol. 324: I.M. Bomze, B.M. Pötscher, Game Theoretical Foundations of Evolutionary Stability. VI, 145 pages. 1989.

Vol. 325: P. Ferri, E. Greenberg, The Labor Market and Business Cycle Theories. X, 183 pages. 1989.

Vol. 326: Ch. Sauer, Alternative Theories of Output, Unemployment, and Inflation in Germany: 1960–1985. XIII, 206 pages. 1989.